GARDENING IN THE SOUTH AND WEST

GARDENING IN THE SOUTH AND WEST

Edited by MRS. GROSS R. SCRUGGS
and MARGARET ANN SCRUGGS

Illustrated by
MARGARET ANN SCRUGGS

GARDEN CITY BOOKS
Garden City, New York

Sponsored by
TEXAS
FEDERATION
of
GARDEN CLUBS

SB453.4
.S382

9561

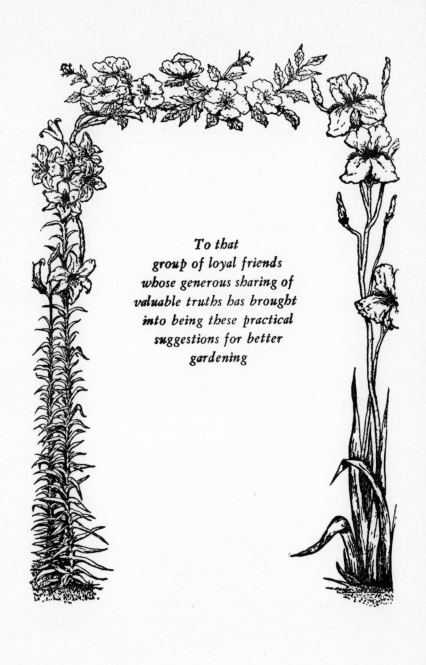

*To that
group of loyal friends
whose generous sharing of
valuable truths has brought
into being these practical
suggestions for better
gardening*

Acknowledgments

IT IS SURPRISING how few books or articles are available for reference and study on the propagation and cultivation of *native,* or foreign, plants in the Southwest. Recognizing this fact, a questionnaire was sent to a large number of Garden Club members, and other experienced gardeners, who, by living with and learning the needs of their plants, were peculiarly qualified to share their knowledge. Because of the quantity of material received through their generous response, it was found impossible to note and give credit for each specific bit of information, yet all have been incorporated into the composite whole. Each chapter contains a contribution from an experienced grower together with many additional notes by the Editors.

Special thanks are extended Hon. Hatton Sumner for enlisting the coöperation of the United States Department of Agriculture, from whom was received a quantity of valuable scientific data.

The coöperation and assistance given, also, by the staff of the Texas Agricultural and Mechanical College; S. H. Yarnell, Chief of Division of Horticulture; A. B. Conner, Director of Texas Agricultural Experimental Station; N. M. McGinnis; C. E. Seicke, Director; R. F. Balthis, Assistant Texas Forestry Service; F. M. Hensel, Head of Landscape Department; J. J. Taubenhaus, Chief, Division of Plant Pathology; R. H. Stansel, Angleton; John J. Bayless, Balmorhea; H. F. Morris, Nacogdoches; D. L. Jones, Lubbock; E. Mortensen, Winterhaven; and those connected with the Oklahoma Agricultural and Mechanical College: Dr. H. J. Harper, Department of Soils; Frank B. Cross, Department of Horticulture;

H. I. Featherly, Department of Botany; George Merrill, Department of Horticulture; Sam Smith; Franklin J. Reudel, Superintendent of Greenhouses; Harry Coke; Mrs. L. A. Cleverdon; and to Prof. Adlai Feather of New Mexico State College (Mesilla Valley), Mrs. Gertrude Howells, Mrs. W. H. Benners, Mr. R. A. Gilliam, Mr. W. A. Bridwell, Mrs. R. A. Hightower and Mrs. Thos. Rives—has been invaluable. They have not only given of their personal knowledge and encouragement, but have granted us the privilege of quoting from their publications.

The articles contributed by Mr. John C. Wister and Mrs. Wm. Crocker will be of special interest because of their accurate knowledge of all that is new in the plant world through affiliations with experimental research. Also data on pests from Mr. and Mrs. W. L. Jonson, is appreciated.

Thanks are extended to the following who so promptly answered the questionnaire:

AMARILLO—Mrs. Tabor, Mrs. L. A. Wells, Lahay White, Mr. T. M. Robertson.
ARLINGTON—Mrs. J. D. Faulkner, Mrs. C. B. Snyder.
AUSTIN—Mrs. O. O. Norwood, Mrs. M. S. Dickerson, Mrs. J. Frank Dobie, Mr. J. M. Ramsey, Mr. C. B. Tharp, Mrs. S. F. Smith.
BEAUMONT—Mr. W. Gunter.
BRADY—Brady Garden Club Members, Mrs. S. W. Hughes, *President*.
BROWNWOOD—Mrs. H. H. Negus, Mrs. R. M. Ramsey.
BRYAN—C. N. Wyatt, J. W. Westbrook.
CARTHAGE—Carthage Circulating Book Club, sent in by Mrs. V. D. Hooker, Mrs. W. W. Hester.
CHILDRESS—Mrs. W. E. Davis, Mrs. O. S. Barnett, Mrs. John Czewski.
CISCO—Cisco Garden Club.
COMANCHE—Mrs. J. B. Chilton.
COMMERCE—Mrs. W. B. DeJarnett, Mrs. B. P. Bingham, Mr. Rixhead, *Agricultural Department, East Texas State Teachers' College*.
DALLAS—Mrs. J. H. Simpson, Mr. Joe S. Lambert, Mrs. Eugene McDermott.
DENISON—Mrs. George O. Morgan.
DENTON—Mr. Thos. B. Foster.

EL PASO—Mr. H. H. Reeves, T. J. Vinson.
FORT WORTH—Mrs. Kitty Barry Crawford, Mrs. B. C. Rhome, Jr., Mrs. Roy Vaughan, Mrs. James T. Taylor, Mrs. Willard Burton, Mrs. E. P. Van Zandt.
GARLAND—Mrs. B. N. Freeman.
LONGVIEW—Miss Dollie Northcutt, Mrs. J. T. Stickey.
LUBBOCK—Mrs. A. B. Cunningham, Mr. Chas. S. Mahoney, *Chief, Department of Horticulture, Texas Technological College;* Mr. Cyrus E. Russell.
McKINNEY—Mrs. J. L. Lovejoy, Mrs. Joe W. Largent.
PARIS—Mrs. J. C. Wooten, Mrs. Joe Gillespie, Mrs. Yost, Mrs. J. T. Simmons, Mrs. H. C. Armstrong, Mrs. Floyd, Mrs. Boyd, Mrs. Scott Galbreath, Mrs. Golden Alexander, Mrs. F. D. Mallory, Mrs. E. B. Lowery.
STEPHENVILLE—Mr. H. M. Brundus, *Professor of Horticulture, Tarleton College.*
TEMPLE—Mrs. S. E. Roddy, Mrs. L. B. Leake, Mrs. J. E. Jackson, Mrs. J. E. Robertson, Mrs. W. E. Hume, Mrs. C. Cox, Mrs. George W. Owens, Mrs. Spencer.
TYLER—Mrs. Walter Connally, Mrs. Elizabeth Potter, Mrs. W. S. Hanley, Mrs. A. L. Thompson.
WACO—Mrs. W. M. Kelley, Mrs. E. B. Richie, Mrs. Lee Davis.
WICHITA FALLS—Mrs. Orville Bullington, Mrs. S. P. Timberlake, Mrs. Horace Robbins, Mrs. E. B. Hayne, Mrs. T. O. Shappell, Mrs. Curtis Atkison, Mrs. Guy Rogers, Mrs. B. L. Fain, Mrs. C. J. Bardard, Mr. N. H. Downing, Mr. Edwin C. Bebb.

Attention is called to the unusual feature—distinctly unique, not found elsewhere—contributed by Mrs. Lee Newbury, that of discriminatingly selecting and describing those *NATIVE* plants of definite garden value, that are listed by Commercial growers.

Gardening in the South and West is most fortunate, also, to include in its pages the graphic account of the cultivation of Lilies by Mrs. George M. Stuart, as her untimely death occurred soon after her notes were written. Her experience is of special value because her deep love of flowers engendered an intimate, intelligent observation of their individual requirements.

Because no one individual could possibly in one lifetime gather through experience and experimentation such a wealth of accurate, widespread, and exhaustive information of *every* type of plant life, specific information has been sought and secured; and certain chapters in this book (as listed) were based on information furnished by the following people:

Shrubs—Mrs. E. A. Belsterling and F. K. McGinnis.
Perennials—Mrs. Garrett O. Moore.
Soil—Mrs. Robert Hughes.
Chrysanthemums—Mrs. Herbert Marcus.
Propagation—Mrs. H. M. Doolittle.
Bulbs—Mrs. T. T. Price.
Roses—Mrs. John Loomis.
Herbs—Mrs. Will Lake.
Pests—Mrs. Dorothy Doran Walker.
Bloom—Mrs. Lewis Dabney.

The unique value of this book, therefore, lies in its being a record of the combined experience of many individuals.

MARIAN PRICE SCRUGGS,
MARGARET SCRUGGS,
Editors, 1939.

Contents

xi

CONTENTS

GARDENING IN THE SOUTH AND WEST

The Conflict of the Winds

OUR GREAT Southwest—that section of this vast country that extends down to the Gulf and to the very borders of Old Mexico—possesses greater variety of climate and vegetation than has any similar area of this United States. From the lowlands of the semi-tropics to the foothills of the Rockies is little more than a day's journey. The trail passes quickly from the land of the Oleander and the Orange trees —across the flower-studded prairies—through the dry plains, covered with strange plants, and stunted trees—on to the mountainous districts where cacti and Alpine plants all but mingle together.

Here the winds play an important part! The soft moist breezes from the Gulf are counterbalanced by the icy blizzards from the Rockies, intermingled with the fierce heat-blasts from the arid desert regions. Each controls a special section, yet wields its influence over all.

The extremes of heat and cold, however, are *not* the controlling factors in estimating the great difference between planting conditions. It lies, rather, in prolonged summer, when there are so many *more* long days than are reckoned in other localities, which cause a halt, or cessation, of *all* activities both in the plant world as well as with human beings. In other parts of the country, plants take a long winter nap, while in the Southwest their rest period is a summer *siesta*.

Charts, tables or deductions, based primarily on the range of the thermometer from extremes of heat to cold, cannot be accepted in the Southwest as an accredited basis for estimating plants' adaptability to the locality; nor can it be said to be determined entirely by the content of the soil, for a third factor plays an almost equally important part in plants' survival of development. This is a certain "hardening process" to which all must be subjected where climatic conditions are governed by cruel winds and lack of moisture.

Extending northward from the Gulf and the Rio Grande, where semi-tropic plants predominate, *every hundred miles* a *marked* change in climate and vegetation is encountered. Noticeably distinct groups of plants grow in each well-defined belt. In addition to climatic variabilities, definite characteristics have been developed by the effect of soil, altitude, and general topography of the land. Specific families are to be found, also, in the various altitudes, for some demand mountain peaks or rocky hillsides, while still others will grow only in woods or partial shade, in swamps or on the banks of streams.

However, the great majority of garden plants, given proper protection in location and exposure, will thrive in any soil that has been brought to the desired garden texture, the predominant type of soil being usually non-acid (toward neutral).

HOW TO DETERMINE TIME FOR PLANTING

The general observation that for every one hundred miles northward, or southward, there seems to be from one to two weeks' *difference* in plant development, taken as a guide, enables one safely and easily to reckon or estimate dates for garden activities.

Travelling eastward from the Mississippi River to the Atlantic Coast, there is a perceptible change in the character of the soil, although in the main it is pale yellow and light brown to reddish in color, mostly residual soil of medium-textured, mineral types resting generally on heavy clay subsoils. The heavy black limestone soils of central Texas, resting on calcareous bases, shift from alkalinity to neutral to acid as one nears the Mississippi, so that plants that can be grown in Louisiana practically coincide with those advised for east Texas, where the temperature is the same.

The entire group of Southern states—familiarly known as the Old South—in general may be classified as congenial to acid-loving plants, although the soil is calcareous in some sections (lime) and neutral in others. As the vast majority of plants prefer neutral to acid soil rather than alkalinity, a much greater range of plant-life may be enjoyed in this area, the temperature-belt being the same and the part the wind plays less definite, than can be had in the western section of the belt.

On the northern portion of the temperature-belt, the soil in Oklahoma and Arkansas being on the whole not as acid as Louisiana—more nearly neutral—in general neither plants that are tender or semi-tropical, nor extreme acid-loving can be recommended for general use.

"A very simple statement in regard to soil conditions in Oklahoma would be that in the east half of the state the major portion of the soils are deficient in phosphorus and this should be added to all soils in order to make conditions more favorable for the growth of plants. About thirty per cent of the soils in the eastern half of Oklahoma are very acid and if the plants which are being grown are lime-loving plants, success cannot be secured without the addition of lime to these acid soils."—*Horace J. Harper.*

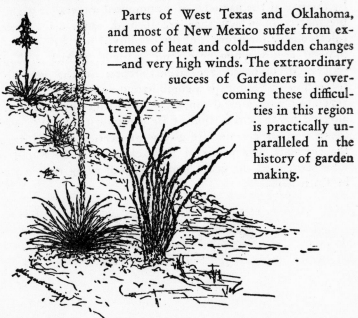

Parts of West Texas and Oklahoma, and most of New Mexico suffer from extremes of heat and cold—sudden changes —and very high winds. The extraordinary success of Gardeners in overcoming these difficulties in this region is practically unparalleled in the history of garden making.

Consider the Soil

Ideal Soil

THE SECRET of success in a garden lies in the soil. It must be loose enough not to crowd the small rootlets and to allow free circulation of water and air, yet firm enough to hold sufficient moisture for their nourishment—not soggy, but well-drained and containing in correct proportion those chemical ingredients required for plant growth—nitrogen, potash and phosphorus.

Texture and Structure of Soil

Classes

Geologists have divided soil into several classes identified by the size of the particles of decomposed mineral or vegetable matter of which they are formed, sand, clay, adobe, calcareous or limestone and silt or alluvial soil, being of the Mineral group, while peat- and leafmold (which embody strictly decomposed vegetation) represent the vegetable formation and humus is a combination of both decomposed vegetation and minerals, in which the former predominates, affected by the circulation of air through it, together with absorption of certain life-giving properties derived from the elements. Every one of these classes may be found in some section of the great Southwest—all being represented in Texas alone.

SAND

What Is Sand? Coast-Line Mostly

Sand, which is generally disintegrated quartz, is the coarsest of all soils. The looseness of its particles allows water to pass through them readily so that most of its plant food is thus carried away. It should be mixed with clay to bind its particles together and leafmold or humus to hold moisture and supply in soluble form the food qualities inherent in it, needing sometimes also a complete chemical fertilizer that is a well-balanced food ration. The finer the grains of the sand, the better is the garden loam that is formed from it.

Value

The chief value of sand is that its large particles hold that warmth so necessary both to plant germination and growth and enables the fertilizers to give up readily those ingredients required for plant food. Care should be taken to add fertilizer and manures to sand only at the time they will be needed by the plant, otherwise much of their valuable contents may be lost.

CLAY

East Texas, La., Ark., and Eastern Oklahoma Characteristics of Clay

Clay, whose particles are fine and smooth to the touch and form a compact mass (sticky when wet) too close to admit free circulation of water and air, must have sufficient sand to separate its particles and humus to bring it to that texture needed for an ideal garden loam.

In preparing a garden in clay soil, two points should be noted: first, that it should not be disturbed while wet, and second, that good underdrainage adds remarkably to its productivity, for clay contains a high degree of plant food, notably potash. When fertilizers are added to it, use those in which nitrogen and phosphorus predominate.

SILT

Along Streams

Silt is coarser in texture than clay and finer than sand. It is exceedingly rich in plant food and mixes well with humus. It is also useful as a binder for sand and clay. Often it is what is also termed "Alluvial Soil." Alluvial soil is that finely-ground deposit, or residue, which is transported by rivers and streams, many times to great distances. The widest belt in the Southwest is located along the Rio Grande Basin, while the Mississippi River delta and banks as well as the overflow sides of all streams, great and small, contain silt in varying depths, and degrees of fertility-character.

ADOBE

Character West Texas, Western Oklahoma, and Eastern New Mexico

Adobe soil, being composed largely of alluvial, or "playa," clay (accumulations by deposit on broad level spots in arid or desert regions) and silt with some sand, the requirements for clay soil apply to this type also with the additional caution that though high in potential productivity, it needs careful handling. Irrigation has been found to be the best method of supplying moisture where sufficient quantities of humus and sand have been added to release the fertility within this very fine-textured type of soil. *(See p. 17.)*

The extreme compactness of its particles renders it very sticky when wet and hard enough when dry to be used as material for constructing buildings.

Demands

Sifted coal ashes or wood ashes, together with straw and manure—sand, humus and sawdust—will render an adobe soil perfect in texture for garden loam, which texture may be maintained largely by deep tillage, good drainage and adequate moisture.

ADOBE TYPES

(A) *Desert Soil* is extremely rich in plantfood and is more or less alkaline (generally lying on clay subsoils). It demands humus and irrigation to release its valuable content. By tillage or deep mulches the necessary moisture is conserved to make this vast semi-arid plains country yield its wealth in productivity.

(B) *Rolling Plains Soil* is similar to the desert soil in character, yet differs in that its fine sandy or clay loams are more friable and are deeper and darker in color. Both respond to tillage and the addition of humus and sufficient moisture during the plant's growing season. A distinct group of plants thrive in these regions.

(c) *The Edwards Plateau* contains little tillable soil because it is shallow, stony land, yet the soil, where of sufficient depth to sustain vegetation is mostly dark and calcareous, resting on limestone.

(d) *Western New Mexico* contains soil similar in character to eastern Arizona—largely alkaline, adobe sands, while the mountainous regions differ but slightly in soil-texture, differentiation being mostly in the shifting extremes in temperature every twenty-four hours.

CALCAREOUS

Derivation The calcareous, or disintegrated limestone, soils of the central section of the Southwest, have had very little written about them. They are extremely rich, having supported a series of crops year after year for many years, without the need of fertilization nor any reduction in productiveness.

Being "derived through the disintegration of the underlying beds of highly calcareous rocks, these strata contain much lime carbonate [*P. 1323*].[1] The accumulation of decayed vegetable-matter under the prevailing humid conditions and in the presence of lime carbonate has caused the surface soil of the greater part of these prairie lands to have a decidedly dark or black color. This type is locally called 'black waxy land' [*P. 1227*]."[1]

Identification Often "large [*P. 1227*][1] deep cracks form in this soil in very dry weather." Another "characteristic is, this soil will crumble down on drying to a mass of small aggregates. . . . Even clods turned up when wet crumble at the first rain and assume a desirable tilth. Extending [*P. 1231*][1] back from the stream valleys the depth of the soil increases and

[1]*Soil Survey*—Texas A. & M.—William Carter—1924.

the quantity of rock fragments on the surface decreases. The surface soil of many acres is strewn with fragments of the parent rock." These "weather rapidly into soil. This soil varies in productivity according to the depth of material over the basic chalk or limestone rock."[1] Being more or less clayey in texture, the addition of humus, leaf-mold and sand is necessary to render it more friable under all conditions. It will then grow any type of plant except those demanding a high degree of acidity.

Central Oklahoma contains black, heavy soil, calcareous in the main and yet not as rich nor as deep as the "black-waxy" lands.

Deficiencies   The chief deficiency of this soil is phosphorus. Sudden variations in temperature in winter, coupled with the hot winds of summer, are the chief problems to be met to secure successful gardening. Choice of plants therefore, that are adapted to these conditions obviates this difficulty.

ROCK SPLITTING OR SHALED BY FROST   LICHENS

COMBINATIONS OF SOILS

Where one does not find soil pure in type, it is usually intermingled in varying proportions, the name given to a specific mixture being designated by the name of the predominating class or type—clayey sand, sandy-clay, etc. For example, surrounding the "black, waxy belt" to the east, north and west is a sandy-clay belt, part of which rests in a limestone or other heavy subsoil, the other part on a clay subsoil.

[1]*Soil Survey*—Texas A. & M.—William Carter—1924.

SUBSOIL VS. TOPSOIL

Because of its lack of decomposed vegetation, the subsoil has only potential value for plant growth. It is, therefore, not as advisable to use as topsoil. Topsoil is usually much darker in color than the subsoil that lies in varying depths beneath it. This coloring is caused by the accumulation of decayed vegetable matter (humus, which is more readily available to plants for food, being mostly decomposed leaves, roots and stalks). The darker the soil the richer it is in plant-food, and because of this richness (being an ideal basis for a productive garden loam) in preparing a bed for a flower garden, the topsoil should be carefully separated from the paler subsoil and piled to one side that none of it may be lost. After a portion of the subsoil has been removed and the remainder well pulverized and brought to productive consistency (by mixing manures, sandy-loam or whatever other ingredient it lacks) then the topsoil may be added and forked well into the bed.

CHEMICAL ANALYSIS

No type of soil contains sufficient nourishment to continue to sustain a large group of plants. Therefore, additional nutriment must be supplied, for plants demand quantities of nitrogen, phosphorus and potash for perfection of development.

NITROGEN

Nitrogen is needed to produce color and brilliance in fruit and flowers, as well as aid in developing leaf and stem-growth, being taken up by the plant in its early stages of growth. Cottonseed meal, dried blood, nitrate of soda and sulphate of ammonia help to supply sufficient nitrogen to plants.

PHOSPHORUS

Phosphorus (or phosphoric acid) supplies those qualities that assist in the maturing of seed, in the development of root-growth and in perfection of flower, giving to the plants power to counteract that weakening tendency toward contracting disease which is caused by nitrogen, and being absorbed by the plants about uniformly during the period of their active growth. Its natural source is to be found in bonemeal and the other mineral phosphates.

POTASH

Potash helps phosphoric acid in making plants disease-resistant and supplies that which brings them to normal maturity, producing larger, more vigorous plants. It can be supplied by *hardwood* ashes, or from various potassium salts, obtainable through commercial fertilizers.

SOURCES

The chief sources of nitrogen, phosphorus and potash for plantfood are to be found in the various kinds of manures and especially prepared chemical or commercial fertilizers.

pH:

Through the facilities of comparatively inexpensive soil-testing equipments, greater interest is being aroused in the scientific analysis of soils to determine the ratio of the available plantfood elements therein.

The symbol *pH* indicates the degree of concentration of hydrogen ion in any soil—expressing the degree of acidity or alkalinity—the figure 7 being the numeral used to indicate neutrality. All numerals above 7 indicate the alkaline content, while those below express the degree of acidity.

Tables have been arranged on this *pH* basis, giving the soil-requirements of many specific plants. For example, Azaleas require about 4.5 *pH* (most intolerant of lime). Sweet peas want a neutral to alkaline soil, about 7.5 *pH*. Roses prefer 6.5 *pH*.

It must be noted, however, that a great many plants can adapt themselves to any soil.

THE THREE CHIEF CHEMICAL ELEMENTS NECESSARY TO PROMOTE PLANT GROWTH

Elements	*Add Whenever*	*Affects Primarily, or Controls*
NITROGEN (Ammonia) *Sources: nitrate or sulphur, ammonium sulphate, ammonium nitrate, calcium nitrate, etc. Manure*	Foliage and stems are lacking in color, pale. General growth stunted. *Oversupply: Weakens and increases susceptibility to disease, etc.*	Leaf-growth. Rapidity of growth. Increases size of bloom when applied to plants in bud. Healthy green color of leaf and stem.
POTASH (Potassium) *Sources: Woodashes Manure Muriate of Potash Sulphate of potash, etc.*	Foliage and stems poor. Fruit undeveloped. *Oversupply: Delays ripening, sometimes causes burns.* To be available must be soluble.	Fruition. Texture of plant. Is the disease-resistant element. Contributes to brilliance of color. Importance for root-growth.
PHOSPHORUS (Phosphoric Acid) *Sources: Superphosphate* (Apply in Spring) *Bonemeal* (Apply in Fall) *Manure*	Flowers scarce, or poor. Insufficient roots. In dry seasons add to soil. *Oversupply: No ill effects.*	Root-growth. Flowers. Seed development and maturity. Hastens maturity. Improves quality, durability. Stiffens stems, produces hardiness.

SOIL FOR HOUSE PLANTS

The general proportion of required ingredients for rich, well-balanced soil for pot-plants is a mixture of:

¼ garden soil ¼ humus, or leaf-mold ¼ peat moss
¼ sand and complete fertilizer mixed in equal parts, except when the garden soil is of a markedly sandy nature

Some plants—acid-lovers—thrive in peat-moss, alone.
Information regarding the culture of house plants may be secured from books dealing with indoor gardening.

THE THREE TYPES OF SOIL

Neutral Soil

All soils have been grouped under three large general classes, determined by whether the specific base is lime or its antithesis, acid; or a balance of the two. This latter is termed neutral soil and is best for most flowers and vegetables. The intensity of acidity or alkalinity (lime) depends on the character of the soil, what kind of rock it is derived from, as well as its subsoil and its degree of friability. Any soil may be made neutral by adding five pounds of lime to a bale of peat-moss and working this into the soil. Epsom Salts, also, has a neutralizing effect. Instead of peat-moss, certain products made from sugar cane are most effective and satisfactory.

SOIL ANALYSIS

Soil Analysis

In order to determine exactly what is lacking, chemically, to insure productivity, a soil analysis by the litmus-paper test is often of great value. However, generally speaking, this is not necessary, except when one desires to grow a lime-loving plant in acid or neutral soil or vice versa (for in the classification of plant-life, there are many that demand a certain soil or will flourish only in one or the other of the three specific types).

Acid Localities

Acid soil is usually sandy loam, light colored, usually shades of yellow to reds, although the highest degree of acidity is to be found in those low lands that are often inundated. One of the chief agencies for overcoming this condition is the use of lime, the hydrated or burnt forms, obtainable at the building supply dealers, being the most convenient to use.

Where lime is needed, apply *before* cultivating. *If* applied at the same time as manure it counteracts the desired results. Lime acts, also, as a "tonic"—often releasing other needed elements that remain dormant without its agency. In many instances it acts as an insecticide and fungicide, too. *Value of Lime*

Where drainage is poor and the soil soured, or on small areas where plants have been grown in profusion and the soil made acid by the decomposed vegetation, lime can be used sparingly to correct this condition.

Attention must be called to the fact that lime should *never* be used *at the same time* that intensive fertilizers or manures are employed.

In the major part of the Southwest and certain specific areas of the South and Southeast, there is little occasion to use lime where the structural composition of the soil is largely decomposed limestone. These, the brown, certain greys, and black soils, are known as "sweet" or alkaline, the degrees or shade of dark color being dependent on the amount of certain specific salts that are predominant. *Alkaline Soils*

All these salts (sodium chloride, s. carbonate, s. sulphate, s. nitrate, calcium sulphate, calcium chloride, calcium bicarbonate, magnesium sulphate) are white, yet where there is a predominance of sodium carbonate the soil is rich, black, greasy in appearance. A predominance of the nitrates produces brown (color) alkali soil, while the predominance of sulphates and chlorides is indicated in the white alkaline soils.

It is readily understood, therefore, why products of calcium (lime) and sodium (soda, especially sodium nitrate) tend to reduce acidity.

Chemical sulphates generate acidity while the muriates create or increase alkalinity tendencies.

PREPARATION OF ACID SOIL BED

In heavily impregnated lime soil those plants that object to lime must have an area especially prepared for them. Consult landscape authorities for specific needs.

Acid Bed

To prepare the ground and to prevent the seepage of water carrying lime from the surrounding earth into the acid-bed, line the bottom of the two-foot excavation with at least three inches of gravel and cinders, and the wall with cement or bricks. Place over the cinders alternate layers of six inches of oak leaves and four inches of sand, leaving a layer of sand at the top. Over this scatter one-half pound of aluminum sulphate to each square yard. Keep wet until the leaves have rotted, stirring every two weeks, taking care not to disturb the cinders. After the mixture has remained 21-28 days, test the soil for acidity (by submerging a blue litmus paper in the bed for thirty minutes). If the paper turns red, it is the right degree for acid-loving plants. (See p. 70.)

Another method is to place alternate layers of garden soil and *hardwood* shavings or chip-loam and sand over the cinders, giving the same treatment as above.

Fertilizer for Acid-Soil Bed

The following proportion of fertilizers will be found correct for an acid bed, generally (consult local chemists):

5 parts cottonseed meal	10 pounds
3 parts superphosphate or rock phosphate, finely ground (acid phosphate)	4 pounds
2 parts sulphate of potash	2 pounds
2 parts aluminum sulphate	2 pounds

Mix thoroughly and add lightly to peat moss. Apply ratio one pound to every four square yards. Water to soak it into the soil, taking care *not* to let fertilizer *touch* tips of branches, or stems.

Products of sulphur and sulphates (of ammonia, etc.) increase acidity. Sulphur is slow acting (as bonemeal for lime areas) and is recommended to be applied at ratio of 2 lbs. to every 10 square feet.

ACID WATER FORMULA

Limestone or "sweet" water can be made acid by dissolving one heaping tablespoonful of aluminum sulphate or solution of tannic acid to one gallon of water, applying every two or three weeks, thoroughly saturating the ground.

PREPARATION OF AREAS FOR PLANTING

BEDS

For specific details of how to prepare the soil for:

Perennials (See p. 83)	Annuals (See p. 127)
Delphiniums (See p. 94)	Lilies (See p. 161)
Roses (See p. 206)	Bulbs (See p. 152)

TRENCHING

Many people have found that the preparation of a long border or other large space for planting is most easily accomplished by a method known as "trenching."

Drainage If underdrainage is necessary (as with clay and some of the heavier soils) the depth of the subsoil to be removed will be down to about five feet below the surface level and broken tile, brick, cinders or some such material be put in for drainage. However, if the area is well drained, the subsoil need only be excavated about two feet.

Sections The first step in trenching is to mark off the area to be prepared into sections—the most easily handled being two-foot sections—and remove the topsoil, placing it in a pile apart, because all of it is used in preparing a flower bed.

Treatment of Subsoil If the subsoil thereby exposed is sand, remove some of it (about one-third) and add clay, humus or barnyard manure, forking all well into a loose texture. If it is clay (whether red, brown or black-waxy) it must be thoroughly broken up to a depth of three to five feet (dependent on drainage requirements), part removed and the remaining lightened with sand, sifted coal ashes and humus, forking the barnyard manure well into the mixture. If it is very stony, it must all be removed, and the correct mixture of sand, clay, humus and manure, so necessary to plant growth, be substituted. The amount of ingredients to be added varies with the texture of the subsoil, the desired tilth being comparable to the crumbly condition of a ball of earth, which if squeezed tightly while moist, will fall apart when released.

Subsoil Dormant

The food values in the subsoil being dormant and incapable of assimilation by the plant until released by the action of the elements—sun, light, air, water, etc.—it is most important to spade and separate its particles thoroughly, and then to insure its remaining an available food-source by the recommended addition of sand and humus.

Treatment of Topsoil

When the subsoil has been thoroughly prepared, the next step is carefully to pulverize the topsoil and enrich it by the addition of sufficient manure, sand, clay and humus to bring it to the standard of good garden loam. As with the topsoil, this varies according to its general character and when correct will meet the requirements for an ideal[1] soil.

BARREN SPOTS

Where nothing will grow, try spading up the soil; then pile and burn on the spot a fair-sized quantity of leaves, twigs and rubbish (to sterilize the ground by fire and to fertilize it by the minerals contained in the wood-ash and bits of charcoal thus obtained). Spade again thoroughly; adding barnyard (or commercial) fertilizer. Then plant. Almost everything will *now* grow in the spot!

SUGGESTED TREATMENT TO ENRICH DIFFICULT SOIL

Clay Soil. Spade deep and apply about six inches of manure. Spade it in well. A generous amount of straw in the manure is advised. Add land plaster or gypsum (at the ratio of 15 pounds per 100 square feet) and mix well. Give final top-dressing of air-slaked lime (ratio: 10 pounds per 100 square feet). Stir well every two to three weeks. To pulverize stubborn clay try one sack of lime to 40 by 50 foot

[1] See opening paragraph.

areas. Chopped tobacco stems help to loosen, to supply humus, and act as a fertilizer as well as a preventive fungicide or insecticide.

Sandy Soil. Apply about ten inches of cow manure (*or* green manure, such as peas, vetch, or rye) and turn under well. Work in land plaster or gypsum (ratio: 10 pounds per 100 square feet) and after this is well spaded in mix in lime (ratio: 5 pounds per 100 square feet). Never leave sandy soil bare to the elements. Rye broadcast in the fall will enrich when turned under in the spring when about two inches high.

Manures and Fertilizers

HOW PLANTS EAT

Since only a small percentage of a plant's food is derived from the earth (approximately two per cent only), the major part being assimilated from the elements (water, heat, sun and air) it is very essential that correct soil conditions be maintained. An abundance of strength-giving properties may be present in the soil, yet not available for the plant's use until they have been put into soluble form or released by the chemical action of organic matter. This latter is largely contributed by the use of barnyard manures, leguminous green manures, and commercially prepared fertilizers.

I. ORGANIC FERTILIZERS

GREEN MANURES

Books on soil deal largely with the use of green manures which consist of the growing of certain leguminous crops that, when plowed into the ground, furnish specific qualities to the soil. But the flower gardener has little opportunity of resorting to this means of fertilization, because of the desire to have the garden always beautiful, therefore objects to giving a whole season to replenishing the soil.

BARNYARD MANURES

Apply Manures Before Spading. In building up a soil to a desired condition, barnyard manure is of equal value in the garden as it is over large areas. It is considered of inestimable value because it contributes much more than just the chemicals it so generously supplies. Its decomposed vegetable matter adds all those good qualities desired from humus, making the soil mellow, helping it retain moisture and releasing those life-giving qualities that lie latent.

1. *Hot Manures*. All barnyard manures are not alike in quality. Those that are classed as "hot manures," which will burn the roots of young plants when fresh, must be used sparingly. It is best to allow them to decompose for at least six months before using.

a. POULTRY. Of these, poultry manure is richest in nitrogen, but should be used with greatest care. Containing no straw or decomposed vegetable matter, wood ashes and sand added to it benefit the soil greatly when used judiciously.

b. HORSE. Horse manure is also hot. It is low in phosphorus, therefore commercial phosphates or bonemeal should be added, yet it ranks high in nitrogen.

c. RABBIT. Rabbit manure is extremely high in all three chemicals necessary to plant growth. It is exceedingly hot, therefore demands the greatest care in using.

2. *Cool Manures*.

a. COW AND PIG MANURES. Cow and pig manures are cool and are lower in nitrogen. They are especially desirable to use in sand, because their non-heating qualities are not detrimental to germinating seed.

b. SHEEP MANURE. Sheep manure is one of the best barnyard manures to use because it is cool and yet ranks next to poultry manure in its nitrogen content. It, too, is low in phosphorus, therefore the addition of bonemeal makes it a more balanced plantfood.

3. *Proportion to Use:* Generally the required amount of barnyard manure to be forked into the garden soil may be estimated at one wheelbarrow load to every two square yards, or a three-inch depth forked in for three successive springs, while adding five (5) pounds of superphosphate for each one hundred (100) square feet (or one-quarter of a pound per square foot) being also very beneficial.

LIQUID MANURE

The most effective way of hastening and increasing a plant's development is by the use of that concentrated plantfood known as "liquid manure." This is made by suspending a sack of fresh or dried animal manure in a barrel or keg of water (which preferably has a spigot at the bottom). A fivegallon container, filled one-third with barnyard manure to which is added water to the level of capacity—allowed to soak at least two days, stirring two or more times daily, will be the desired strength to be "watered in." This solution must be diluted to the color of weak tea. Apply near the roots (preferably at least three inches from the stalk) of plants after they have been thoroughly watered, then water again after applying the liquid manure. (See p. 96.)

Liquid manure is of especial value to plants, in every type of soil, applied *just before* the blooming season, *not* during season.

Chemical liquid manure is made by combining the following ingredients:

> 1 level teaspoonful of nitrate of soda
> 1 heaping tablespoonful of superphosphate
> 1 teaspoonful of nitrate of potash
> 2 gallons of water

Apply ration to each plant: 1 pint per plant every two to three weeks.

II. INORGANIC FERTILIZERS

*Amount
to Use*

Many people advocate the use of commercial fertilizer because it does not introduce weeds, undesirable grasses, worms, etc., but in heavier soils it must have ground peat (or some similar loosening element) used in combination with it. However, where the soil has reached a desired tilth, commercial fertilizer can be of great value, although its benefits usually do not last more than a season. Generally speaking, the amount to use is about one pound to every twenty square feet. *Beware* of using *in*organic fertilizer exclusively!

Correctly used, commercial (inorganic) fertilizers are **very** valuable, being plantfood *in highly concentrated form.* There is danger of injury to plants by over-stimulation, which is less apt to be the case with organic food-material. These latter (manures, etc.) have the added value of "conditioning" the soil by their humus content (lacking in inorganic fertilizers) in addition to supplying nutriment Perhaps highest in nutritive value is dried blood, but its odor is most offensive.

Contents

All commercial fertilizers are composed of materials that contain varying proportions of nitrogen, phosphorus and potash. To use them to the best advantage, the specific requirements of the soil to be enriched must be understood, that its deficiencies may be overcome. Treatises on soil give a number of interesting methods of determining what is lacking, called "soil tests," but a general knowledge of the character of the prevailing type of soil makes this rather difficult work usually unnecessary.

Formulas

Commercial fertilizers are sold under many trade names. The best grades state an analysis of the content formula on the outside of the package, usually designated by a set of numerals thus, 6:8:4 means there are six parts of nitrogen, eight parts of phosphorus and four parts of potash (nitrogen, phosphorus and potash always being given in the order named) presenting at a glance the information desired.

Bonemeal

Bonemeal is forty per cent lime, therefore in using it know the type of soil to which it is to be added. Superphosphate is bonemeal in soluble form, with additional plantfood value

Generally speaking, commercial fertilizers should be applied in February or the first part of March to obtain the maximum results. For ordinary needs 4:8:4 or 4:12:4 are the correct ratios, applied at the rate of 100 pounds per 60 x 60 feet for large areas (lawns, etc.), or a dessert-spoonful scattered in a circle three to four inches from a plant and scratched in to the depth of two to three inches—then water. This will protect the rich food from "burning." Large plants, even shrubs and trees, do not require fertilization to a greater depth than an auger hole six to seven inches filled with 4:12:4 and watered in. (See p. 62.)

Cottonseed hulls, or meal, are excellent in food values, but care should be taken never to apply hulls, especially, independent of the correct degree of nitrogen accompanying them.

Tobacco dust, or chopped stems, scattered once or twice a year is recommended.

Plants require loose, well pulverized soil and drainage.

As weeds sap the soil of its phosphoric acid and assist in "packing," their removal loosens the texture, yet requires the addition of phosphorus to recondition the food values in the soil to their correct ratios. This is most readily achieved by the application of commercial fertilizer, and compost. (See p. 10.)

Oklahoma—"If the phosphorus content of the soil is increased by fertilization, if lime is applied where it is needed, and if the organic matter content of the soil is maintained by the use of cottonseed meal or well-rotted farm manures, the probability of plant-food becoming a limiting factor in the growth of plants is very unlikely to occur. A good complete fertilizer for plants in Oklahoma would be 4-8-6, or 4-12-4, which is commonly used on potatoes or truck crops. The rate of application of this material should be about one to two pounds per hundred square feet of soil. In case of shrubs where the area is usually irrigated, a handful for each plant will give very good results."—*Horace J. Harper, Professor of Soils, Oklahoma A. & M. College, Stillwater, Oklahoma.*

III. SOME FEEDING NOTES

Azaleas, Camellias and other acid-loving plants—as well as some which prefer neutral soil (such as Rose)—enjoy a generous feeding—5 parts cottonseed meal to 3 parts *Superphosphate* and 2 parts *Sulphate of Potash* thoroughly mixed. One to eight handfuls around each plant—depending on size of bush—seldom is more than one handful ever needed.

Chrysanthemums. (See p. 95.)

Dahlias and *Cannas* in hot weather appreciate a generous drink of one heaping tablespoonful of *nitrate of soda* dissolved in two gallons of water—soak the ground around each plant thoroughly once a month—as they require a minimum of *nitrogen*, during bloom season every two weeks give a feeding of one ounce per plant of 10 parts *superphosphate* to two parts *muriate of potash* and one part *manganese sulphate*. They will produce huge blossoms if disbranched to joint nearest main stalk on each lateral branch as it appears. (See also p. 170.) They relish bonemeal also.

Gladioli coming into bloom need same enriching as Hydrangeas, but do not *over* water. The *Primulinus* hybrids are best adapted to heat and drought. Bloom appears six weeks after planting.

Hydrangeas. Soil should at all times be kept loose and reasonably moist. When blooming, demand rich food, therefore add fertilizer (well-rotted manure, bonemeal, *nitrate of soda*, etc.).

Peonies that fail to bloom perhaps are set too deep. (P. 170.)

Iris. Fertilize with *superphosphate*.

Roses. (See p. 207.)

Primroses and *Bleeding Heart* require ½ leaf mold. Sow seed from garden three days after gathering.

Do not feed *Wisteria*.

Grass. In the dormant season a generous spreading of fertilizer over the lawn will usually be watered in by the rains and give astonishing results. But if the season is dry, water it in. Burning grass off lawns and lots is a mistake, and is most injurious to the root-system, as well as unsightly. Burning destroys many desirable wild plants, too, for many lovely wild flowers require proximity of other plants, especially grass, to live. Where there are weeds in the lawn, it is an indication of impoverished soil. Aerate (by sticking fork here and there) to loosen compactness.

Bermuda Grass is most dependable for the "blacklands," African Bermuda being the finer-textured variety. Blue Grass is used in the lime areas of the "Old South"; while a mixture of grasses is recommended for other soil conditions. "St. Augustine" will grow in shade, but requires rich soil, much water, constant mowing and is coarse-textured ("Centipede" being its fine-textured variety). These latter will *not* survive *great amounts* of cold, nor drought.

COMPOST

Compost is the commonsense, thrifty utilization of those natural resources that all too often are consumed by fire or carted away.

Small areas seldom admit of extensive use of these "waste products," but always may be planned to convert the leaves that fall in autumn into well-rotted earth by spring *if* three simple rules will be kept in mind and followed: *Vegetable Compost*

1. Either dig a slight pit or simply pile the leaves at a fence corner—the imperative need being that the pile rest on the earth so that living organisms (earthworms, etc.) may freely penetrate. Never use chemicals on the pile, for though they may hasten decomposition they kill or "burn" these desired organisms and vegetable matter.

2. With each half-bushel basket of leaves water them down *thoroughly*—soak them.

3. Turn the pile bottom upward every three weeks to hasten decomposition, and if rains are infrequent wet the mass every ten days or so. By spring all will be turned to garden tilth.

Areas that are large need deeper and wider or more pits or piles, which may accommodate not only fallen leaves but grass cuttings and all vegetation from the garden or kitchen. If the area is large enough even the other kitchen refuse (meat trimmings, *every*thing) placed in alternate layers of vegetation, refuse from kitchen and stable (cattle, etc.), *Animal Compost* and light covering of earth to cut the odors, will also decompose in three to four months if watered and turned.

Compost is Nature's reconversion and conservation of resources. Man is wise when he emulates Nature here.

Moisture

Moisture

The fertility of the soil is controlled to a great extent, also, by the amount of moisture it is capable of retaining, which, in turn, depends greatly on the composition and texture of the soil, itself, for each of its component grain-particles is, under usual circumstances that support growth of vegetation, surrounded by a thin film of moisture. The larger these particles are, the less water they will retain, because the nature of loose soil does not admit of freedom of capillary movement.

Capillary Movement from the Water Table in Soil

Underlying almost all soils at varying depths is an accumulation of water, known as the "water-table." From this reservoir an attraction of the film-water around the grain-particles of soil draws moisture up toward the surface, known as "capillary movement." When the ground is left undisturbed, little tubes or "water-channels" are created, whereby moisture is the more rapidly brought to the surface and exhausted than when the soil is broken up by tillage (or frequent stirrings) which prevent these channels from forming.

Mulches

Chief among the other suggested methods for the conservation of moisture is mulching or surface covering with grass clippings that contain no grass-seed, straw, leaves, peat-moss, paper, sawdust, etc., or in some cases, a surface-layer (from two to five inches) of *very* dry soil will act as a blanket to hold in the moisture. The depth of a mulch varies with the climatic conditions to be met. Yet, since it *must be perfectly dry* to be effective, usually the deeper it is, the greater will be its usefulness. In arid regions, mulching has been found to be most successful, although it is questioned whether mulches other than dry soil are advisable where the pill-bugs or sow-bugs are prevalent as it will afford a harbor for them.

WATERING

Most plants need water frequently, even in winter—especially where there is a scarcity of rainfall. It is best, however, not to use a sprinkler except for refreshing foliage (after a dust storm, etc.) as spraying water is apt to encourage fungus and destroy perfection of blossom.

Whenever the soil is dry to the depth of an inch, water is needed.

Use the hose without nozzle, and moderate pressure, to avoid waste or serious disturbance of soil. Sub-irrigation and trench-watering, also, have proved successful methods, though somewhat expensive to install.

If the water contains too much sulphur, lime, gypsum, or other chemicals injurious to plants—consult a chemist for an analysis and advice how to counteract the conditions. There usually is an inexpensive way that this trouble may be eliminated.

For specific details on watering perennials (see p. 83); annuals (see p. 83); lilies (see p. 162); roses (see p. 208); semi-dry gardening (see p. 249).

Generally it is best not to water a drooping plant while the sun is still high—wait until it is low or sets—then soak (never sprinkle foliage) the earth thoroughly.

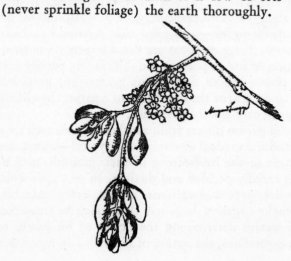

Creating Beautiful Surroundings

JUST AS THE careful selection of the proper design of the setting displays to the fullest the peculiar charm of a gem, so harmonious planting creates ideal coördination between house and grounds. Our homes may be likened to jewels whose value is determined by perfection rather than by size, for some of the smallest are the dearest. There are a few whose outlines need only the simplest of design, while others will admit of more elaboration. Although each architectural style of house demands quite definite surroundings, yet all may be softened into an exquisite picture when blended by greens and toned by splashes of colorful flowers.

Chief Divisions of Landscaping

Design in landscaping, presenting as it does both the simple and elaborate means for color expression, has been developed along two comprehensive, or general, lines—Formality and Informality—with particular reference to racial interpretations. These divisions are based largely on individual adaptation of life to climate and soil; falling readily into two main classes—those that are of geometrical precision, repetition, or design; or the simulation of a natural loveliness, which is apparently wholly unstudied.

Racial Interpretations

Just as each person differs from another, so does each race, or nation, and the gradual evolution of a typical architecture and treatment in the landscaping of their grounds, may be classified as racially decided and distinct. In past ages when law and order were non-existent, or lax, every man was forced to enclose against despoilers that which he treasured. Degrees of wealth determining the extent of his power to protect his possessions, the nature of his walled-in recreation spots varied in relative proportion. These earliest known gardens of Egypt, Persia, China, and the Far East, were, of necessity, small plots of green, with a bit of shade (a fruit or nut tree, or a vine-covered arbor) with a tiny pool or fountain; designed for meditation and relaxation.

Adapting this idea from the Great Moguls of the East, *Latin* Spain, Italy, and France have elaborated on it, producing racial variations of the theme. The Italian characteristic is few blossoms on their triple-terraced vistas which emphasize reflected beauty of many shades, together with diversity of texture and height, in dominant green, mirrored in still pools that are bordered with occasional statues and inviting walks to quiet nooks. France is more architecturally inclined, adding numerous rest, or summer houses, and a variety of arbors. Their plants are clipped and forced into unnatural shapes and their vistas are more studied; while the Spanish interpretation more nearly follows the Oriental, with potted, blooming plants about a pool within their walled enclosures.

The Anglo-Saxon passion for freedom and intense feeling *Anglo-* for color—born, possibly, of their reaction to the dreariness *Saxon* and struggle for brightness during long, cold, grey winters— is clearly demonstrated in their gardens. Theirs was not a need for the coolness of a shaded nook or relief for the eye from the intensity and brilliance of copper-hot sky. So, the inclusion of gay flowers into the garden in quantity was introduced by them. With the gradual awakening of appreciation for the beauties of Nature's garden, in comparatively modern times, the Oriental, conventional, or formal garden is being rivalled today by the naturalistic or informal garden.

The underlying needs of individual temperament are being *America* recognized, studied and met by adapting and combining ideas from East, West, North and South. In America a new type of garden is being evolved. It has been suggested that perhaps our contribution to the theme will be our interpretation of the hillside garden (a development which is distinctly ours) . . . down a gradual slope that has been planted to simulate Nature at her loveliest, one is lured to a pool, a sunken garden, or sometimes to a formal rose garden.

Southwest

In the strong yellow glow of the Southwestern sunlight, pouring over rolling plains and hillsides in intensity for six to eight months of the year, the ideas of both the Orient and Europe must be altered and adapted to meet the specific needs. This climatic range, which includes some of the features that both experience, makes the designs of each peculiarly applicable to their individual requirements. They like the sense of geometric order which is gotten from formal design, yet the temper of the people—that all-pervading cordiality, hospitality and geniality—will not admit of stiffness! They insist on that appropriate arrangement of grounds to house which, like one's clothes, must fit, be becoming and in style!

Physical Requirements

To secure this latter there are several important factors that everyone everywhere must consider carefully. Certain physical conditions must be recognized to insure perfection of detail and successful results. Such vital though general questions as the range of the temperature (heat and cold); the amount of moisture (natural or artificial); the quality of the soil; the exposure of the location; and the contour of the land, must be known and intelligently studied.

Information Needed

Everyone must cope with these essentials, yet each gardener's problem is different, due to the fact that the combination of these five factors is infinitely varied. Therefore, no decided rules can be given, although certain specific directions may be stated, and attention be called to those established lines upon which the landscaping of a well-balanced, well-planned garden and grounds depend.

Stress has too often been placed by landscape and garden experts upon creating the garden itself an example of landscaping perfection, without enough thought having been paid to its specific place as merely a *part* of the whole picture of the buildings in relation to their surroundings. The design to be complete must present a pleasing effect when viewed on approaching the property, yet offer small framed sketches from each of the various windows of the house.

Much of the interrelationship of the building to the

grounds and surroundings depends on the development of the natural lay of the land, and the utilization of whatever native growth there is on it. To this must be added those trees, shrubs and flowers which will satisfy its demands. Most enviable is that property which can boast large established trees, for these lend a charm nothing else can give. And yet even trees can be supplied, where desired, if one chooses wisely and has patience. *Appropriate Interpretation of Buildings to Surroundings*

Since a year lost in gardening can never be regained, it is wisest to follow a very definite plan of planting, taking care that in placing every tree and shrub, neither their shade nor their roots infringe on the flower garden; and choosing them for texture and color tone of leaf, in addition to variabilities in height and spread. *Trees*

Most Oaks, particularly the Live Oaks, demand a great spread and like the graceful Elms and Cedars are slow of growth. The stately Cottonwood (*Populus Balsamifera*) and Poplar-like Sycamore (*Platanus*, or *Ficus Sycamorus*) are both rapid in growth and share that exquisite beauty of the Birches—whiteness of limb emphasized by lovely light-green leaves.

The Pecan (*Carya*) and Black Walnut (*Juglans nigra*) are both ornamental and nut-bearing. Honey Locust (*Gleditsia triancanthus*), Redbud (*Cercis*) Catalpa, and the Flowering Desert Willow (*Chilopsis linearis*) are beautiful all the year round.

Magnolias, though very slow of growth, amply repay with their showy, fragrant white blossoms and dark glossy foliage. Hackberries, though quick-growing and hardy, are disease carriers, and some of the Elms develop root-rot in lime-impregnated soil—the Cedar Elm being most resistant, therefore the most desirable of the Elms.

Second in importance only to the trees are the shrubs. Of these a large increase in number and types has been contributed by the efforts of the late E. H. Wilson, famous horticulturist, keeper of the Arnold Arboretum, who brought into the United States great quantities of valuable plants from foreign lands, many of which have proved especially adapt- *Shrubs* able to the South. The variety and amazing range of choice offered by this large group of plants is most interesting. There are those which all during the spring and summer hold the admiration by their lovely flowers; yet most valuable indeed are those that keep their glossy green leaves during the winter or cheer with their brilliant berries and colorful stems.

Combinations

Shrubs are becoming more generally recognized, also, for the numerous uses to which they may be put. Together with running roses and perennials, they form a practically unchanging background for a wide choice of colorful bedding plants, which may be varied each year in an unlimited number of combinations. Thus a cycle of blossoms paints ever new pictures against the sympathetic green of the background.

Nooks and Vistas

By judicious placing, shrubs may shut in a secluded nook of rare beauty and capture that elusive privacy so treasured, or they may create a vista. Besides being a decorative feature of a landscape plan, a vista, particularly a long vista, is one of the most restful things in nature. It is wise, however, to have some definite point of interest at the end of the view. This focal point is usually a trellised arbor, a gate, a seat, a wall fountain or some structural garden-furnishing, rustic or classic in design, the choice of which depends on whether formality or informality has been chosen to be stressed.

Balance and Good Taste

If one has a Spanish *hacienda,* one's grounds will generally be landscaped with a more or less geometrical precision of balance and counterbalance in accordance with the accepted Spanish method of treatment of grounds and gardens. But if one owns a cottage or bungalow, informality is often much the better taste, although it is not a requisite.

Generally speaking, the plan or pattern of the flower garden should definitely conform to the architecture of the house, or be so screened from the buildings by plantings of hedges, as to present a complete picture within its own boundaries. The latter is especially true of an all-rose garden, which practically demands formal design, irrespective of the treatment given the rest of the property.

The fundamental principles of the art of landscaping emphatically state that to achieve the maximum results one *must* employ the secrets of good design coupled with correct planting, and choice of materials. The one is as essential as the other. The pattern will be glorified or ruined by the skill or ignorance used in handling the materials.

All successful gardens—formal or informal—are built on a main or central axis, which usually centers with an exit (door or window) from the home or building, its actual length being immaterial, although its width is always a trifle greater than all other paths or vistas. At its terminus, there is usually some specific detail featured. On either side of this main axis the distribution of masses, open spaces or plantings, whether regular or irregular, must be so handled that there is a sense of effective proportioning of free and planted areas.

Areas of less than a quarter of an acre do not often afford space for naturalistic treatment unless very irregular in outline, or treated extremely cleverly. Large places, ideally, give the effect of a clearing in the midst of the wilderness.

Whether large or very tiny, a home may present the height of artistic expression. The garden and grounds can be as exquisite as a miniature on ivory, or as breath-takingly beautiful as Versailles or Hampton Court, for accomplishment of perfection depends largely on the skillful use of available materials, blended to a nicety of proportion, balance and symmetry.

The Green Frame of the Garden

HEN THE home grounds have been plotted, the next step is the arrangement for skeleton planting, which should provide a balanced, properly-proportioned framework around which the remaining planting may be grouped for form, symmetry, color and accent. This skeleton or framework is essentially composed of shrubs and trees. As this planting is more or less permanent, it should be most carefully considered.

Gardeners learn from experience, but much loss of time and material may be saved by first making a plan on paper.

General Plan

Learn the soil requirements (whether lime, acid, neutral, sandy, moist or dry—whether in open sun or in semi-shade) —that the garden project will not end in disappointment and the plants in premature death, for should Azaleas and Rhododendrons be planted with Cacti and Yaupon sickness and death are inevitable!

Outlook

Those who build on a new or vacant lot should study the future position of the house, garage, and any auxiliary buildings that they may be grouped for most convenient service, using the minimum of ground, and above all to occupy the least and less desirable space for future planting. Also, take into consideration the outlook from the living and dining rooms, that the growing garden may be a picture from these windows during the greater part of the year. Some have suffered from a north exposure with the south garden a part of the kitchen outlook; or a driveway that fills a south and east side, when a north would have been more direct and released the better growing space to the south and east.

Where massed arrangement is desired, the broad and nar- *Evergreens*
row-leaved evergreens and conifers are essential, but beware
of overdoing this branch of the scheme! Pause and consider
the size, spread, and height of each *type of plant* when per-
mitted to attain perfection in mature growth and avoid
crowding by *over*planting!

However, their infinite variety in texture, form, color,
and manner of growth adds definite interest and contributes
a special beauty to the garden during the winter months,
rendering evergreens indispensable.

A portion of the garden should always be devoted to flow- *Flowering*
ering shrubs of various kinds. Those of striking color, or tex- *Shrubs*
ture of leaf or blossom, however, should be used sparingly,
being especially valuable as accents in the general scheme
of planting. All show to better advantage against green
backgrounds.

It is advisable, also, to consider carefully combinations and *Harmony in*
accents for harmonious grouping, for even in plants and *Grouping*
blossoms many colors clash rather than harmonize. Flowering
Willow* tipped with exquisite, orchid-like blooms is good
for cutting and its finely divided leaves change the outline
and massing of the more commonly used shrubs. Red-leafed
Maple, and the maiden-hair-fern-like foliage of the Gingko-
tree, well placed, make splendid accents.

In May, the Tamarix* resplendent with long waving *As Accents*
plumes of deep or pale pink, whose foliage is like sparse pine-
needles, grows loosely and to some size. Crape Myrtle of various hues may be used with great success, is a splendid
accent as well as useful as a single lawn specimen. (If sharply
pruned, the flowers will attain great size, otherwise the bush
will increase in proportion and be a veritable bouquet of
smaller panicles.) *Robinia hispida* (Rose Acacia) with its
pink, pea-like clusters, is a fine specimen or accent plant.

Try accenting the garden with evergreens—lowgrowing
where needed, or tall erect Italian Cypress for the background.

A Nandina placed near an Arbor Vitae or Arizona Cypress
displays its magnificent color of leaf and berry!

Some other combinations and accents for harmonious planting are: Pink-flowering Peach, Lilac, and *Kerria japonica* —a charming early spring grouping. *Deutzia gracilis* and "Bridal Wreath" (*Spirea*), with early blue Iris and Narcissi, is a delight to the eye! Visualize *Rosa Hugonis,* the early-blooming, yellow shrub-rose, with blue Larkspur and deep purple Tulips! or Scotch Broom surrounded by Poppies! or Dwarf Iris under Forsythia bells!

Later in the summer, *Cassia floribundia** (Senna), easily grown from seed, forms a compact shrub covered with clusters of gorgeous yellow blooms that combine or contrast charmingly with various Altheas. *Anisacanthus,** another native, summer-blooming shrub bearing small orange trumpet-flowers among shiny foliage, harmonizes delightfully with Buddleia (Summer Lilac), whose lovely lavender tone is prized in the late garden.

The bush Honeysuckle (*Lonicera*) is a joy forever—laden with coral blooms! *Parkinsonia** growing almost to tree proportions, makes a splendid corner-accent, with its plumy foliage and yellow flowers. Mimosa* (*Acacia* or *Albizzia*) with its dainty pink tufts and *Poinciana** ("Bird-of-Para-dise") with its handsome scarlet and yellow flowers have similar, feathery, willow-like foliage.

Pomegranates, both tall and dwarf, make stunning spots in the garden, but must be planted where their very vivid blooms and fruits will not clash with surrounding colors.

Citrus trifoliata (*poncirus trifoliata*),* making an impenetrable barrier when used as a hedge, is beautiful in spring with its fragrant shower of white blossoms, followed in autumn with small, decorative, yellow, orange-like fruits; and in winter its bare green branches and stems are not devoid of beauty.

It is amazing how many of the most valued garden plants —including shrubs and trees—are native to Southwestern United States, the vast majority of these coming from Texas. Many of these have not yet reached to commercial nurseries, but wherever possible to secure them they prove much more adaptable (especially to those localities that have a limited supply of water) to climatic conditions than plants from other lands, for generally they prefer the minimum of acidity in the soil in which they thrive, for the major part of the soil of the Southwest is non-acid.

The following groupings—including those native plants that have proved desirable for cultivation—have been assembled according to height, soil and moisture requirements, and a general description of each plant's individual characteristics is given.

I. VARYING HEIGHTS: SHRUBS OR TREES

All native plants are starred in this book.

Among the shrubs whose different varieties or species vary widely in height and character of growth, for a specific need one may choose:

EVERGREEN

*Agave or Aloe (*Amaryllidaceae*)—Rosettes of sword-like leaves, tall fl. stalks bearing bell-like cream or white blossoms. Desert, semi-arid regions. Increase by suckers, shoots from main root.

Arbor Vitae (*Thuja—Bioto—Pinaceae*)—Narrow pyramid habit of growth. Prefers moist, loamy soil. Hardy. Transplant easily. *Thuja orientalis Bakeri*, green, best for lime soils. *T . . aurea conspicua; globosa;* and *orientalis compacta* also are recommended, height 6–8 ft.; *T . . Ramsey* and *T . . Golden pyramidal* 20–30 ft. The Chinese var. is said to be drought-resistant to a remarkable degree. This and *T . . Ramsey* have proved the most resistant to sudden climatic changes.

Azalea—(See RHODODENDRON.)

Cacti—Adapts self to poorest conditions, though relishes rich loam. Many var. with widely different habits, hues of blossoms (white, yellow, orange red, etc.). Native to Texas and Southwest. Prop. readily from div., seed, and cuttings.

Euonymus—Hardy almost everywhere. *E . . patens* (climbing, spreading) turns yellow in fall; red berries. E . . *atropurpurea* (Spindle tree) has blue berries. E . . *coloratos* leaves turn bronze.

Ficus—Widely different types of foliage, and fruit delicious. Fig. Banyan tree, and Rubber plant are perhaps the best known species of this large family. Prop. readily from suckers or cuttings. Prefer moist, sheltered positions. Deciduous, sometimes winter-kill in northern sections.

Holly (*Ilex*)—Many var. are evergreen, requiring moisture and neutral to acid soil. A few are deciduous, tolerating lime. All are valued for their red berries, prefer rich well-drained positions and prop. readily from cuttings or seed. Blooms are small white or yellow fls. *I* . . *vomitoria* (Yaupon), *I* . . *decidua* ('Possum Haw) and *I* . . *opaca* are native as far west as N. M. *I* . . *verticillata* (Black Alder), *I* . . *glabra* (Inkberry) and *I* . . *Amelanchier* are deciduous. *I* . . *laevigata* (Winterberry), *I* . . *Cassine* (Dahoon), *I* . . *monticola* becomes a tree. *I* . . *myrtifolia* ("Dahoon") are all native American hollies. When young or newly transplanted all holly requires a great deal of water. Best to plant in Spring. (For Texas "Desert Holly" see AGARITA— *Berberis trifolata,* not an *Ilex.*) *I* . . *cornuta* and *I* . . *Burfordii* (smooth lvs.; very large berries) are both excellent. Secure all *Ilex* cutting-grown.

Juniperus (Cedar—Junipers)—Perhaps the largest family having the widest range of types, hues and tones of foliage, ranging from low, wide-spreading shrubs to tall trees. Most of these thrive in all types of soil except adobe. *J* . . *communis depressa* is recommended for rock gardens. *J* . . *Chinensis Neaboriensis* has been acclimated in some sections of the adobe soil areas. *J* . . *conferta* is the Shore Juniper. *J* . . *glauca* is the Silver Cedar. *J* . . *virginiana* is the native Red Cedar, and of these there are many types of growth, color of foliage, berries and heights. *J* . . *Repens,* *J* . . *prostrata* or *horizontalis,* *J* . . *pfitzeriana* (creeping varieties). *J* . . *Cannarti* and *J* . . *Dundee* (Upright, similar to Arbor Vitae) are excellent—also *J* . . *Columnaris* (green and grey var.)

Ligustrum (Privet)—Perhaps our most satisfactory hedge material. Many types. Majority have dark green, shiny foliage and blue-black berries. There are both evergreen and deciduous varieties. Grow both in shade and full sun, in any soil. *L* . . *vulgare* and *L* . . *lucidum* (Wax), *L* . . *recurvifolia* (Crinkleleaf), *L* . . *nanum compactum* (Lodense), *L* . . *japonicum,* *L* . . *Reevesiana* (Dwarf), *L* . . *siniense* (Chinese), *L* . . *ovalifolium* (California), and *L* . . *amurense* (Amoor River) are especially recommended. All grow readily from cuttings. *L* . . *lucidum erectum* (Upright) withstands cold.

Magnolia—Both evergreen and deciduous types. Dark green, waxy foliage. Handsome large fls., white and a number of shades of red and purple. Require rich soil and much water when newly transplanted or young plants. Plant in the Spring. Two native varieties, M . . *grandiflora* and M . . *glauca* (evergreen), very fragrant fls. (Sweet Bay). Prop. by grafting or seed. There are many deciduous trees, some tall, some dwarf. M . . *Soulangeans* (Tulip tree) has many showy hybrid varieties. M . . *Michelia fuscuta* (Banana shrub), evergreen in the south, prefers sandy soil with quantities of humus.

Mahonia (Oregon Grape) (*Berberis*)—Prefers humid soil. Foliage brilliant in fall. Yellow fls. in conspicuous panicles in late spring. Requires shelter from sun. Mahonia *Dealli* will grow in dense shade.

Palm (*Palmetto*)—Generally tropical in habit, though a few will withstand 18° to 20°F. Nearly all must be prop. by seed, though a few by suckers. Some semi-hardy as far north as Arkansas.

Ulex (Gorse—Furze—Whin)—Closely allied to *Cytisus* (Broom). Few leaves, handsome fls. yellow. Shiny dark green branches. Valuable binders for dry, sandy banks. Resent transplanting. Grow readily from seed sown in Spring.

Yucca (*Bracenaceae*)—Sharp-pointed, stiff leaves in radiating rosettes. Handsome fl. stalk bearing white or creamy, bell-like blossoms. Inhabitant of the dry, hot, desert regions. "Spanish Dagger", "Don Quixote's Lance", "Bear Grass", "Adam's Needles", and "Saw-tooth Yucca", or "Sotol" are among the most widely known varieties.

DECIDUOUS

Acacia (Mimosa)—Quick-growing, short-lived. Prefer even temperature, not too hot, and moderately rich leaf mold. Winterkill in northern part of zone. A few will tolerate lime. Leaves feathery, fls. very fragrant white, pink, creamy or yellow balls in clusters. Attract bees, honey-source. Require water. Nine (9) native Texas varieties. A . . *amentacea* very tall and thorny. A . . *berlandieri* and A . . *filicina* (*timbe*) both thornless, ash-grey, with white fls. A . . *Calliandra eriophylla* has pink, reddish or purplish fls. A . . *acuan Belutanum* has white fls. A . . *Farnesiana* (Huisache) has yellow fls. and is also identified as A . . *leptophylla*, especially used as perfume essence. A . . *Greggi* (Mimosa tree, Devil's Claw) has pink fls. and prefers semi-arid region. A . . *roemeriana* (Round-flowered Catsclaw) has yellow fls. and is very thorny. A . . *arabica* or *Drummondii* (Gum Arabic tree) is sometimes classed as a var. of A . . *Farnesiana*, source of gum Arabic and other products of the perfume industry. A . . *acapulcensis*, extremely fast-growing with yellow fls. is the Lower Valley of Texas var., and tender.

Almond, Flowering (*Prunus communis japonica*)—Grows rapidly nearly everywhere. Pink and white fls. very decorative. *P . . triloba* secure cuttings grown.

Black Haw—See VIBURNUM.

Broom (*Cytisus scoparius*)—Scotch Broom for seashore planting. Prefers moisture and acidity. Fine, slender stem-foliage dark or bright green. Handsome yellow fl. clusters. Bean-like seed pods. (*Genista*)—Spiny, needle-like foliage, green stems. Rapid growth. Yellow pea-like fls. in spring. Very attractive.

Cherry, Flowering (*Prunus serrulata*, etc.)—Prefers neutral, rich soil. Foliage varies from pale to rich green. Lovely pale pink and white fls.

Cotoneaster—Dense in growth. Showy bright red fruit. White fls. Requires fairly sheltered position. Rather slow-growing. Evergreen in south.

Crabapple, Flowering (*Malus floribunda*)—Hardy. Fls. rose or rose-red in abundance. Showy rather small leaves.

Deutzia—Fls. fragrant, white or rose-pink. Some varieties require semi-shelter.

Eleagnus (Russian Olive) (*Oleaster*)—Hardy, Widespread. Attractive fruit. Handsome wooly foliage. Fragrant yellow flowers.

Forsythia (*Golden Bell*)—Bell-like, yellow flowers in early spring. Deep green foliage on graceful, showering sprays. *F . . viridissima* is more bush-form than the other weeping forms.

Honeysuckle (*Lonicera*)—Grows everywhere. Medium-sized, light green leaves. Blossoms very fragrant, cream-white or yellow, pinkish and coral. Of the several bush forms the early spring *L . . fragrantissima* and *L . . Maacki* (valued for its scarlet fruit) are recommended; the lovely coral *L . . sempervirens* (Scarlet Trumpet) is native to Texas and *L . . periclymenum Belgica* is very fragrant and showy red and yellow fls. The variegated gold and green leaves of the *L . . japonica aureo reticulata* are handsome, though slow of growth.

Jasmine (*Jessamine*)—Erect or semi-climbing shrubs. Fragrant fls. cream-white and yellow. Readily grown from cuttings. *J . . nudiflorum* produces waxy yellow fls. on bare branches. *J . . humile* (Italian) has dark green foliage and is a free bloomer. *J . . Sambac* ("Grand Duke") is very double-flowered, white, intensely fragrant fls. *J . . primulinum* (Primrose) drooping foliage and golden-yellow fls. The "Carolina Jasmine" is not a Jasmine but is *Gelsemium Loganiaceae. . .* The True Jasmine is *J . . officinale*, the jasmine of poetry. The "Nightblooming Jasmine" is not a Jasmine but is *Cestrum nocturnum*, and the Day-blooming is *C . . diurnum*. The "Cape Jasmine" is a *Gardenia*, the dwarf var. of it being *G . . radicans*. The "Confederate Jasmine" is a *Trachelospermum jasminoides*, also known as the "Star Jasmine."

Lilac (Syringa or Philadelphus)—About thirty species from Europe and Asia, having fls. of many shades of violet, red, and white. Prefer moderately rich moist soil. Usually prop. by cuttings or shoots. Flower-panicles all fragrant.

Lonicera—See HONEYSUCKLE.

Malvaviscus (Red Mallow, "Turk's Cap")—Brilliant crimson fls. Large, broad lvs. velvety. Tubular fls. similar to hibiscus. Tender. Prefers rich, slightly acid soil. Fr. red apple-like and edible. *M . . Drummondii* native to Texas and *M . . arboreus domestica* may be trained as a specimen-plant. Make good flowering informal hedges on the Gulf Coastal regions.

Mock Orange—(See Below).

Philadelphus (Mock Orange) (Sweet Syringa)—Extremely hardy. Prefers deep rich, moist loam and semi-protection from sun. White single, rose-like fls. very fragrant, similar to orange blossoms. *P . . serpyllifolius* is native as far west as New Mexico. Prop. by hardwood cuttings or suckers. Significant fact they generally begin blooming in June, remarkable for this characteristic. The Mock Orange of the South (native) much prized evergreen with black fruit is the *Prunus caroliniana*. The *Pittisporum undulatum* is another Mock Orange valued for hedges; while the *Citrus trifoliata* (Otaheite Orange) has a mawkish taste and has lemon-like fls. and fruit. The Osage Orange (Bois D'Arc, *Ma-*) *chura*) is sometimes called Mock Orange, too. All are excellent hedge or screen material.

Poinciana (*Caesalpina*) ("Bird-of-Paradise")—Prefers rich, though acid loam. Prop. readily from seed. Thrives on gulf coast. Will live in poor soil. Foliage lacy. Fls. scarlet and yellow. Rapid growth. Blooms from spring to fall. Called aso "Mexican Spider Flower" from resemblance to spider lilies.

Pomegranate (*Punica*)—Ornamental, bright red fruit among bright green lvs. Orange-red fls. Prop. from cuttings. Desirable for hedges. Hardy. Many shoots.

Pyracantha (Firethorn) (*Cotoneaster*)—Bright red fruit, or orange-red. Upright and spreading var. *P . . yunnanensis* (Dwarf), *P . . coccinea Lalandii* (Bush) and *P . . coccinea* (Red berries). All have white flowers.

Rhus (Sumac)—Handsome foliage, brilliant in fall. Fruit-spikes purple, red or reddish brown in fall. Prop. by seed or cuttings. Many varieties, a few are semi-evergreen. Most var. grow well in dry, poor soil. Poison Ivy, Poison Oak, Poison Elder (Sumac) are of this family. The Staghorn Sumac is most ornamental. *R . . vivens* relieves asthma when smoked with tobacco. *R . . verniciflua* produces lacquer and is very poisonous. *R . . cotinoides* appears to be grey smoke when seen at a distance, its grey plumelike bunches of fruit giving it the name of Smoke Tree, or Smoke Bush. It is the Chittim-Wood of the Bible. *R . . lanceolata* yields a black dye especially used for coloring wool, and *R . . trilobata* yields the yellow dye, also was used for arrowshafts by the Indians. All these except the lacquer var. are native to Texas, including many others, giving a wide choice within this single family.

Sophora—The name is Arabic for tree with pea-like flowers. *S . . affinis** (Eve's Necklace) a small, round-headed tree-shrub has white fls. tinged with rose. *S . . japonica* (Pagoda Tree) fls. are yellowish white, also in long racemes; while *S . . secundiflora** has violet-blue, very fragrant clusters. *S . . affinis* has seed pods that are black beaded. *S . . Japonica* has quite long pods and both fls. and fr. yield a yellow dye. *S . . secundiflora* has white pods with scarlet beans which contain a poisonous alkaloid, sophorine. All are handsome, tree-like with dark green foliage and branches; thrive in well drained, sandy, rather dry loam.

Spirea—Prefers moderately moist, neutral to acid (peaty) soil. Some var. will tolerate lime. All have graceful habit of growth, profuse bloom of white, rose-pink or carmine fls., in corymbs or panicles. Rather small, delicate foliage. Prop. by cuttings, shoots or seed. The early blooming are *S . . Thunbergii* and *S . . prunifolia* (Bridal Wreath), followed by *S . . Van Houttei.* The best known, summer-blooming pink var. is *S . . Anthony Waterer. S . . reevesiana* (double and single) is preferable to *S . . Vanhouttei.*

Syringa—See LILAC, or PHILADELPHUS.

*Tamarix (Salt Cedar)—Adapted to dry land conditions and alkaline soils, also thrive near seashore. Prop. by seed or cuttings. Showy panicles or racemes of plume-like rose-pink or whitish fls. Fine, graceful foliage, light-green. Slender branches. *T . . gallica,* exceedingly drought-resistant, is native in Texas and N. M. Along the gulf coast is planted as windbreaks. *T . . odessena* fls. are deeper rose than most of the other varieties. Root system largely surface-feeding, shallow.

Viburnum—Popular names for the very distinct var. include Snowball, Bush Cranberry, Guelder Rose, Arrow-wood, Nannyberry, Wayfaring Tree, Dockmackie, and the Black Haw native of Texas (*V . . prunifolium*). Some var. are evergreen. All are upright, rather large compact shrubs or small trees. Foliage shiny, brilliant in fall. Fruit berry-like or oblong red, dark blue or black. Habitat of most is along water courses in edge of thickets. Fls. fragrant clusters of white or pinkish color. *V . . rhytidophyllum* is one of the hardiest, with crinkly lvs. *V . . odoratissimum* is particularly recommended for the Valley, Tex.) and lower South.

Weigela (*Diervilla*)—Erect, free-flowering pink, delicately marked white, yellow, and shades of red. Prefers rich, humid loam although some var. require sandy or peaty loam. Of spreading habit. *D . . lonicera* is our southern native.

Willow (*Salix*)—The Willow and the Eucalyptus are indispensable in the north and south portions—the one supplanting the other according to climatic conditions. Most Willows are rapid-growing trees or shrubs, with long slender branches and lvs. Their catkins are ornamental and the color of the wood in winter most attractive. Most require moisture, although S . . *humilis** (Prairie Willow) and S . . *rostrata** prefer dry soil. S . . *discolor*, the "Pussy Willow" grows almost everywhere though is not native in the Southwest. S . . *nigra* (Black Willow)* being the commonly known and grown var. while S . . *Wrightii* with the shrub varieties (S . . *amygdaloides* "Peach-Leaf Willow," and S . . *longifolia** and S . . *taxafolia*)* grow on the upper Rio Grande and westward, as well as along streams throughout Texas. S . . *babylonica* (Weeping Willow) grows anywhere there is sufficient moisture. All may be prop. by cuttings or seed. The Desert Flowering Willow is not a *Salix* but is *Chilopsis linearis*—valued for its clusters of lovely pink-lavender, bell-shaped flowers borne in summer.

II. LOW-GROWING . . . CREEPING . . . SPREADING

Up to three (3) *feet in height*

EVERGREEN

*****Agarita** ("Agrito") (*Berberis*) ("Desert Holly")—Stiff, shiny foliage; fls. tiny, very fragrant, golden yellow. Berries red, blue or white. Good for hedges. Prefers dry, rocky hillsides. Transplant in November or December. Berries used for jelly and wine. Fls. attract bees. Roots and stems used to make yellow dye. B . . *repens*, B . . *swasyi* and B . . *trifoliolata* are native to Texas. Holly-like, greyish fol. very attractive. (*Mahonia*) *algerita*.

*****Apache Plume** (*Fallugia paradoxia*)—Small lvs. on slender, spreading branches. Rose- or apple-like, milk-white fls. Reddish plumose fruit. Prefers lime and semi-arid regions. Native to Southwest, hardy as far north as Massachusetts. Prop. readily by seed.

Thuja *orientalis ducidate,* or *Tetinispora leptoclada (Taxus cana-densis)* Yew—Arbor Vitae-like lvs. Attains about 2 ft. height. Prefers lime and semi arid hillsides; while *Taxus* prefers moist, sandy loam and has berry-like fruit. Both are widespreading and slow growing, and short-lived. *Taxus* will endure semi-shade.

NOTE: *See list of shrubs having varieties of varying heights for details and description of other low shrubs.*

DECIDUOUS

*****Anisacanthus Wrightii**—Grows about 3, sometimes 5 ft. tall. Should be cut back to 8 in. in February. Bears through summer and fall orange-red, trumpet-shaped fls. Shiny lvs. Prefers hot, dry regions. Is native to Texas.

*****Blackberries-Dewberries** *(Rubus)*—Handsome, cut-leaf fol. Single rose-like, white fls. Delicious fruit, cult. commercially. Prefer deep mellow loam (clayey). Canes must be headed annually to give maximum results in fruit. Prop. by suckers or cuttings. Valuable for informal hedges, sloping banks, etc. Native to Texas.

*****Castela Nicholsonii** (Goat-Bush) ("Amargosa")—Lvs. shiny green above and silver-grey under. Fls. scarlet or deep orange. Brilliant red fruit, stony. Of medicinal value, especially in jaundice and dysentery. Grows native, in semi-arid west Texas. Blooms in late spring.

*****Chaparral** *(Lippia lycioids)* ("Bee Bush")—The name *chaparral* is given locally to many quite different plants, including the Goat-Bush *(Castela)*, Agarita *(Berberis)*, certain of the *Acacias* and the *Lippias, Rhamnus caroliniana* and *Zizyphus obtusifolia.* Perhaps the Lippias are the most generally known as chaparral. It has small, aromatic, thorny leaves; mignonette-scented, white fls. very attractive to the bees. Grows in lime thickets, in low ground. Its pale, brittle branches are tipped with branched spikes of fls.

*****Coralberry** *(Symphoricarpus vulgaris) (Symphoricarpus orbiculatus)* (Indian Currant)—Bears coral or purplish-red berries on slender branches. Native to lime hillsides at edge of thickets in most of Texas. Grows readily from seed or shoots. Useful for informal borders or naturalizing on hillsides. Berries more highly colored in partial sun.

*****Coral-Bush, or Tree** *(Erythrina)* (Fireman's Helmet)—Light green lvs. on nearly leafless slender br. Long sprays of pea-like, scarlet fls. Slender coral beans. Prefers sandy loam. Excellent sea-side plant, 2–3 ft. tall. Thorny. Tender. Winter kills. Prune off tops to the ground each year. Perennial-like, or grows from seed. This plant, *E . . herbacea,* has a hardier, more shrub-like var. *E . . crista galli* that sometimes grows into a small tree— the branches die back and should be pruned to the trunk each year, to produce new growth.

Cydonia *japonica* (Flowering Quince) (Burning Bush)—Small lvs. Vivid, 5-petaled red tinged orange fls. Fruit quince-shaped. White and several pink varieties also available.

Hydrangea (Hardy)—Produces showy, large blue, lavender-blue or pink balls in late spring. Prefers moist, half humus half loam, acid soil; partial shade and protected location. Water freely. *H . . paniculata* is the hardiest of all varieties.

Hypericum (St. John's Wort)—Shiny, deep bluish-green foliage. Golden yellow fls. in late spring. Pendulous habit. Semi-hardy. Prefers moist, acid soil. *H . . americana* (Similar to Kerria) semi-erect. Withstands hot sun.

Kochia—See Shrubs from Seed and Cuttings.

Kolkwitzia (Beauty Bush)—2½–3 ft. Flowers are flattish clusters, pink with yellow throat. Seed covered with bristly hairs. Prop. by cuttings of green wood. Demands a great deal of moisture.

*Lawsonia *Inermis* (*Reseda,* or Henna)—Almost evergreen. Light green. Clusters of minute, very fragrant yellow or white fls. Lvs. produce commercial henna (the "cyprus" of antiquity), "camphore" of the Bible, also "Egyptian privet" or "mignonette"). Compact growth. Tender except in the Rio Grande Valley, or semi-tropics.

*Rose Mallow (*Pavonia Lasiopetala*) (*Hibiscus lasiocarpos*)— Swamp-mallow, perennial-shrub. Heart-shaped, velvety lvs. Rose-pink or rose-red, like small wild roses. Fr. like wine cups. Prefer rich, shaded ledges or lime hillsides. Especially good for shaded nooks of rock gardens. Native Texas.

NOTE: *See I. for additional low-growing shrubs.*

III. MEDIUM-HEIGHT SHRUBS

Three to seven feet

EVERGREEN

Abelia—Small lvs. turn in the fall. Tubular-shaped white tinged pink fls. One of the most satisfactory hedge materials. Blooms from spring until frost.

Aucuba *japonica variegata*—Dark green lvs. 4–8 ft. height. Any soil. Shaded positions. Dense shade. Secure cutting grown plants.

Bottlebrush (*Callistemon*)—Fls. have long bright red anthers that resemble a bottlebrush. Difficult to transplant. Prefers dry arid conditions; water sparingly. Attains about 4 ft.

Cape Jasmine (*Gardenia*)—Fls. waxy white, camellia-like, deliciously fragrant. Lvs. bright, shiny green. Should be planted on the south side of buildings and given protection from weather cold enough to frost. Prefers moist soil of rich, pliable loam. Prop. chiefly by cuttings.

Eleagnus (*Oleaster*)—Silver-grey lvs., underside bronze in fall. Fragrant silvery-white or yellow fls. Scarlet, or silvery berries. Prefers rich, neutral soil. *E . . fruitlandii* and *E . . Simonii* are especially adapted to the lime regions. 4–8 ft.

Myrtus *communis* (Roman, or True Myrtle)—Aromatic, small, green, glossy lvs. White fls. Blue berries all winter. Prefers acid-neutral soil. Slow growing. Spreading habit. Blooms all summer.

Nandina *domestica*—Shiny lvs., coppery-red in fall. Bright red fruit, in clusters. 5 ft.

Osmanthus *aquifolium* (*Olea fragrans*) (Sweet Olive)—Large, dark green, holly-like lvs. Fragrant, small white fls. 3–5 ft. Grows anywhere, prefers semi-shade. Prop. by cuttings. *O . . fortuni* withstands cold.

Senisa (Cenisa) (*Leucophyllum texanum*) (Barometer Bush) (Desert Sage)—Ash-grey foliage. Showy, bell-like lilac to pink-lilac purple, 2-lipped fls. appearing sometimes before (always after) rain. Sensitive to weather changes. About 5 ft. tall. Fls. sometimes pale lavender. Prefers lime regions.

DECIDUOUS

*****Alder** (*Alnus*)—Medium-sized, aromatic, light green lvs. Catkins followed by small nutlet. Prefers neutral to acid soil. 2–10 ft. tall. Native to Southwest.

*****Aronia** (Alder)—Ornamental foliage, red in fall. White flower-clusters followed by berry-like or pear-shaped, bright red fruit. Prefers neutral to acid soil. Upright growth. The purple, and the black var. require much water. *Aronia* (*arbotifolia*).

*****Bush Morning Glory** (*Ipomea leptophylla* or *fistulosa*)—Narrow lvs. Lovely pale lavender-pink fls. Seed covered with rusty hairs. 3–5 ft. height. Winter kills. Prop. by seed, plant in late winter. Native to Texas.

*****Callicarpa** (Beauty Berry)—Much-prized in Europe. *C . . americana* is native to Texas, called also "French Mulberry." Fls. are phlox-purple, pink, rose, or white—sometimes blue-lavender. Lilac-blue fruit, berry-like, produced in bunches along the stem, the size of small peas. May be grown, even in the North, in sheltered positions, if protected in winter. Prefers sandy loam, moist, even gravely neutral to acid soil. Lvs. large. Easily transplanted early in fall. Prop. by cuttings, layers or seed. *C . . purpurea* and *C . . americana alba* are the best known purple and white varieties. *C . . japonica* is the hardiest having pink fls. (*C . . Giraldii* being a slightly lower-growing var. of it). *C . . purpurea* is also known as *C . . dichotoma* and *C . . gracilis*. These are native to Texas, along streams in the low grounds of East Texas.

Cephalanthus *occidentalis* (Button Bush)—3–12 ft. shrub, sometimes small tree, has attractive, fragrant white flowered-head appearing in summer. Glossy willow-like foliage. Prefers sandy, moist soil, slightly acid. Prop. by seed or cuttings.

Clethra (Alder)—Slender green branches carry handsome spikes of fragrant white and pink fls. appearing in late summer. *C . . alnifolia* is the Sweet Pepperbush native from Maine to Florida. Prefer moist, peaty, sandy, acid soil. Prop. by seed or cuttings. Lvs. resemble the Alder. 3–10 ft. tall.

Kerria (Globeflower) (Japanese Rose)—Grows 4–8 ft. tall, and is as broad as high. Numerous short-branched, spreading, light-green stems. Slender, irregular-toothed lvs. turn yellow in fall. Fls. large (single and double var.) yellow, wild-rose in appearance. Demands well-drained, partially sheltered position. Prop. by cuttings or shoots.

*Lespedeza (Bush Clover)—Slender-growing shrub or herb. Greyish bronze foliage. Thrive in light dry soil. Late summer into fall blooming. Fls. pea-like rose-purple, and violet-purple. *L . . prairea* is native of Texas. *L . . japonica* is the one having white fls. Known also as *L . . albiflora*. Grow from seed but usually by division. Grows 3–6 ft. tall.

*Prunus *Reverchon* (Hog Plum)—Native Texas. Valuable for hedges. Fruit makes excellent jelly. Fls. white and very fragrant, appearing in early spring. *P . . tarda* is a taller variety. *P . . glandulosa* is much smaller and *P . . rivularis* has smaller fls. All are native to Texas, in deep wooded thickets in river bottoms, seldom in the open. Yellow-red fruits on chestnut colored twigs. Stems are grey.

Prunus *subhirtella pendula* ("Rosebud," Weeping Cherry)—A sport from "Beni Higan" ("Shidare Higan Zakwa") is very lovely, pyramid-shaped bush or low tree. Its habit of flowering before the leaves appear gives effect of a pink mist.

NOTE: *See I. for additional medium-height shrubs.*

IV. TALL SHRUBS . . . SMALL TREES

EVERGREEN

Camellia—Grow in sandy loam rich in humus and acid. Handsome foliage and showy fls. that are more profuse in moist somewhat shady places. Semi-hardy.

Cherry Laurel (*Prunus Laurocerasus*)—Shiny green lvs. Small white fls. and inconspicuous fruit. 3–30 ft. tall. Grows almost everywhere. In pruning take care to leave enough horizontal branches yet admit light to roots, as requires light to live. Most satisfactory upright shrub

Chinaberry (*Melia*)—*Melia umbraculiformis* (Texas umbrella tree) * and M . . *Azedarach* (Pride of India) are very rapid-growing ornamental trees or tall bushes. The umbrella tree has very dense dark green foliage has a rounded appearance like an open umbrella. Both varieties have clusters of fragrant, violet or lilac-colored fls. succeeded by yellowish transparent berries readily eaten by cattle and birds. Very hardy. Grows from seed or cuttings readily. Ornamental.

English Laurel—See CHERRY LAUREL.

Eugenia—See ROSE APPLE.

Feijoa *Sellowiana* (Pineapple Guava)—Showy grey-green lvs. White fls. with red stamens. Dark green fruit used in making jelly. Grows 3–8 ft. tall. Difficult to prop. (by cuttings). Prefers soil rich in humus, and moderate moisture. Does not thrive in tropical or in climate where sudden changes, but is drought-resistant.

*Huckleberry Tree-Bayberry Tree (*Vaccinum arboreum*)—Stiff, hard branches bearing lily-of-the-valley like white or pinkish fragrant fls. followed by blue-black clusters of berries. Grows 6–12 ft. and prefers sandy soil. Semi-hardy in north part of temp. zone. Native along the Gulf Coast.

*Mountain Laurel—There are two different families of plants that have a species (known as Mountain Laurel). One is native to the eastern part of U. S., i.e., where acid soil prevails. This is *Kalmia latifolia*, prefers moist sandy (but not clay or lime) soil; and foliage very attractive in contrast to yellow and red stem. Slow growth. Cult. similar to rhododendron. . . . The other is native to the Southwest, especially to Texas limestone hills. This is *Sophora secundiflora* "Frijollito" or Mescal Bean. Difficult to transplant. S . . *affinis* "Eve's Necklace" will endure neutral to slightly acid conditions. Its pods (like *Kalmia*) are black, whereas S . . *secondiflora's* are ornate silvery clusters that glisten. The coral-red, or maroon colored (sometimes yellow) seeds were used as currency by Indians, bartering a six-string of beans for a pony, etc., for they ground seed into powder for the highly intoxicating *mescal*, similar to whiskey in effect though more powerful. "Rain tree." Both plants, the *Kalmia* of the east and *Sophora* of the west are prized for their attractive foliage and fragrant, bonnet-shaped pink to white and rose to deep violet flower-clusters (sometimes cup-shaped, also).

Photina—Greek name referring to its shining foliage, large lvs. tinged red-scarlet to deep red in fall. Numerous scarlet berries. Thrive best in sun, in light sandy loam though will grow almost everywhere. Prop. by seed, cuttings or grafting. P . . *serrulata* is grown in lime regions with success. P . . *arbutifolia* (Tollon or Toyon) is native to California, New Mexico and Mexico, where it is much used in decorations and called Christmas berry. Semi-hardy. *P . . dentata* is also hardy.

Pittisporum (Pitch Seed)—Rather dense foliage, good hedge material. Prop. readily from cuttings. Orange-fragrant small fls. in clusters. *P . . undulatum* esp. fragrant. *P . . eugeniodes* hardy, rapid-growth, esp. adapted to lime shale. *P . . Tobira* withstands saline high winds. Deep green foliage. *P . . phillyraeoides* (Narrow-leaved) resembles weeping willow, esp. adapted to dry regions. Prop. by suckers. *P . . eriocarpum* is the white-leaf var. with yellow fls., but is tender. Fls. banana-scented.

Rhododendron—There are many kinds of Rhododendrons—evergreen, hardy deciduous Azaleas, and Indian Azaleas being the chief group classifications. All are lovely; and generally require partial, or semi-shade, moisture, acid soil (doing well under oak trees in many nurseries), peaty or porous loam and no direct rays of sun. As most of their root-systems are very shallow, care must be taken to treat them as they require to obtain maximum results.

Rose Apple (*Eugenia*)—A large group of tropical and semi-hardy shrubs with ornamental-ribbed smooth, dense and glossy green foliage. Fls. scarlet (black at maturity) greenish white, pale purple or deep purple with numerous yellow stamens giving the appearance of one-half of a fluffy ball. Fruits used for jelly, being spicy-acid, tomato-shaped the size of a large cherry. *E . . aromatica* is the commercial Clove tree. The *E . . Jambos* is perhaps the hardiest var. and its fruit is fragrant, rose-color and used both for jelly and in confectionery. Hardy as far north as San Francisco.

Sophora—See MOUNTAIN LAUREL.

Wax Myrtle—Shiny aromatic lvs. Thrives on coast, in sandy regions.

DECIDUOUS

Althea "Rose of Sharon" (*Hibiscus syriacus*)—6–12 ft. Fls. ranging from blue-purple to violet-red, white, flesh-color, rose-pink, in both single and double var. Lvs. rather light green, heart-shaped. Blooms in late spring through summer. Prop. readily from cuttings. Will grow almost everywhere. *H . . moscheutos, H . . lasiocarpus* and *H . . coulteri* are native to Texas and prefer moist, acid soil. Their roots are used in making mucilage. See also *Hibiscus* (page 52).

Artocarpos (Carab, or Breadfruit Tree)—See list of semi-tropical plants.

Azalea—See RHODODENDRON.

*Buckthorn (Indian Cherry) (*Rhamnus*)—Lvs. sometimes spiny, generally bright green, often large. Black or red berries—some yellow and a few white fls. inconspicuous. *R . . caroliniana* (Yellow Buckthorn) is native to Texas and *R . . cathartica* (White Hart's Thorn) prefers dry soil, also. The yellow var. is valued for its yield of yellow dye from its yellow wood. It grows on lime hillsides. *R . . Frangula* wood made into charcoal is used in making gunpowder. Its foliage is feathery, fruit red and is a valued shrub in the eastern states. Some species produce green dyes and fruits or bark used medicinally. Generally hardy. Majority prefer moist, neutral to acid soil. Prop. by seed and cuttings. Grow from 6–12 ft. tall. Used for hedges.

Bois d'arc—See MOCK ORANGE.

*Calycanthus (Sweet Shrub)—Pineapple-scented lvs. Large, fragrant, purple fls. (some reddish-brown). Native to southern states and also known as "Carolina Allspice." Bark is used as a tonic. Requires semi-protection from direct sun. Prefers moist, deep, rich soil, well-drained. Prop. by seed sown in spring, or by suckers. Semi-hardy.

Carab (Bread Fruit Tree)—See ARTOCARPUS in list of semi-tropical plants, page 56.

Caragana (Pea Tree) (Siberian Pea)—Bright yellow fls. Dark green wood. Lvs. like perennial-pea. Prop. by seed or cuttings. Flourishes even in light sandy soil. 10–20 ft. tall. Prefer sunny positions. Interesting seed-pods.

Cassia *floribunda*—See shrubs from Seed and Cuttings, page 63. *C . . Roemeriana*, page 122 (Senna).

Castor Bean—See shrubs from Seed and Cuttings, pages 63, 121.

Citrus (*Poncirus trifoliata*) (Bitter Orange)—See MOCK ORANGE. Poncirus Family prefers neutral to acid soil.

Crape Myrtle (*Lagerstroemia indica*)—The lilac of the South. Will not endure cold winters. Profuse bloom. The "watermelon-pink" var. possibly the favorite color. Fls. plumes of red, pink, purple, white. Rapid growth. Easy culture. Lives in almost all soil conditions. Blooms from early summer to frost. Perhaps most valuable of shrubs in the temperate zone. Dwarf varieties are being developed and introduced. The Crape Myrtle is ornamental both for its lovely blossoms and its red-tinged lvs. in fall.

*Dogwood (*Cornus*)—Lvs. medium-sized, whitish underneath. Fls. white-waxy or rose-pink appear on bare brightly colored (green or red) limbs and branches. Fol. assumes brilliant coloring in fall. Abhors lime. Prefers moist, neutral to acid soil and semi-shaded, protected locations. Blooms in late spring. Attains height varying from 10 to 30 ft. Prop. readily by cuttings or grafting. *C . . asperifolia* and *C . . florida* are native from Massachusetts to Florida and west to Texas. Slow growing. Habitat: in river or creek bottoms. Bark is a valued substitute for quinine. Wood is used extensively for spools, handles and especially for shuttle-blocks. The roots yield scarlet dye.

*Elder (Box Elder) (Elderberry) (*Sambuscus*)—Large, rather coarse shrubs, perennial-like. Spread by suckers and seed. Flower-heads are large, flat clusters of fragrant white or creamy fls. fol-lowed by red, black, green or yellow fruits, edible berries, small and valued for making wines or jellies. Prefers rich, humid soil. Some var. hardy as far north as Massachusetts. S . . *canadensis*, native to the south and as far west as Arkansas and Texas, has a number of varieties, all most effective both when in bloom and in fruit. S . . *caerulea*, similar, but grows looser and taller. S . . *racemosa* has red berries. S . . *Schweriana* (from China) has salmon-red fr.

Exochorda *grandifolia* (Pearl Bush)—Showy racemes of pure white fls. Slender branches. Thin, bright green foliage. Require sunny position. Prefer rich, loamy soil, well-drained. Prop. by seed and cuttings. E . . *racemosa* (*Amelanchier racemosa*) blooms in May. Is very hardy. E . . *Giraldii* has red lvs. E . . *Korolkowii* is the darkest green, most dense in fol. and most up-right in growth. Grow from 10–12 ft. tall.

*False Indigo (*Amorpha fruticosa*)—Fine feathery foliage. Re-markable for its dense, upright spikes of small unusually lovely violet-purplish fls. It has a white var. and one with pale blue fls. A . . f . . *albiflora* (white) and A . . f . . *caerulea* (blue). Is strong-growing, spreading, native to river banks of Texas, and prefers rich, moist soil—neutral. Will grow in sun, but with difficulty. Prop. usually by seed. 10–40 ft.

*Fringe Tree (*Chionanthus*)—Thrive best in somewhat sunny, moist-sandy soil, in semi-sheltered position. Large dark green lvs. Very fragrant, white fls. in loose panicles. Pendulous dark blue fruit in autumn. C . . *virginica* is native as far west as Texas, from Pennsylvania to Florida. Its root-bark is a tonic, reputed narcotic, and laxative.

Haw—See VIBURNUM.

*Hawthorn (Red Haw) (*Crataegus Crus-galli*) (Cockspur Thorn) —Small shiny lvs. Very long, sharp, almost red thorns. Clusters of exquisite white fls. apple-like in shape. Bright scarlet (or white) berry-like fruit. Prefers rich, slightly acid to neutral soil and moisture.

Honey Locust—(*Gleditsia tricanthos*). See pages 60, 61.

Japanese Persimmon (*Diospyrus*)—Ornamental fruit. May be trained espalier.

Locust—(*Robinia*). See pages 60, 61.

*Mimosa (*Acacia Greggii*)—Feathery foliage. Pink, bellshaped, fragrant fls. Fruit large strap-shaped pods. Hardy as far north as Washington, D. C. Similar to *Acacias*. Prefers neutral to acid soil. 8–15 ft. tall.

*Parkinsonia (*Retama*) (Jerusalem Thorn)—Yellow-flowered shrub. Reed-like branches, thorny green, giving it its Mexican name, "Palo verde," meaning green stick. Lacy, feathery, drooping foliage. Fls. in elongated drooping clusters. Will thrive in any soil. Evergreen in south, below freezing. Prefers moist situations. *P . . Torreyana*—native to Texas, withstands drought. Prop. by seed, and suckers or shoots.

Peach (Flowering) (*Prunus vulgaris*)—The flowering peach, in both single (*P . . Davidiana*) and double (*P . . Persica*) forms, have numerous shades of fls. from white, pinks, reds to deep purplish maroon. Most of the single var. are grown for the fls. that appear quite early, the fruits being of indifferent quality. There are a number of forms in the trees themselves, also compact, dwarf, pyramidal, weeping and purple-lvs. forms.

*Plum (Flowering) (*Prunus angustifolia*) (Chickasaw, or Mountain Plum)—Native from Del. to Fla. and west to Texas, forms a small, bushy-topped shrub-tree, reddish branches forming dense thickets. White fls. preceding lvs. Sometimes attains 8–10 ft. in height. There are several var. of this plum. *P . . Watsoni* (Sand Plum) *P . . varians* (yellow transparent) and hybrids valued for dry-region planting. More or less thorny.

Prunus—There is a wide choice of flowering and fruits found in the diverse *Prunus* family, including the Almond, Apricot, Cherry, Cherry laurel, Nectarine, Peach and Plum. *P . . angustifolia* and Redbud are especially lovely planted near each other.

*Poinsettia—See list of Semi-tropical plants, page 55; also EuPHORBIA on page 89.

*Redbud (*Cercis*)—Handsome, distinct foliage, heart-shaped, light green lvs. Lovely pink-lavendar fls. appear before the lvs.

Grows almost everywhere. Prefers rich, sandy somewhat moist soil especially when young. Prop. readily by seed. Grows very rapidly. Produces fls. in thick clusters hugging the stems, even when 3–4 yr. old, graceful little dwarf-tree-like plants. Fls. white, pink, and red. *C . . canadensis* (rosy-pink) *alba* (double white), *C . . chinensis* (purplish-pink), *C . . racemosa* (rose-pink) handsomest of all but semi-hardy, *C . . occidentalis* (pale rose) is also called *C . . texensis, C . . California* and *C . . renifoenis*. These are all native to America. The European var. is *C . . . Siliquastrum* (purplish rose) var. *alba* (white) has more nearly round lvs. and is a 40-ft. tree. All Redbud seedpods are long, flat and turn dark reddish-brown when ripe. The bark is of medicinal value for fevers, similar to quinine.

*Rose Acacia (*Robinia hispida*)—Bright green, graceful pinnate foliage. Fls. rose-colored, in racemes. Pod covered thick with hairs, bean-like. *R . . hispida nana*, one ft. tall, is the dwarf var. often grafted on other stems to give height. *R . . neo-mexicana* is the native var. found in the mountain canyons of West Texas. Its stems have prickles, stout, sharp and recurved, like the rose. Rose-colored fls. hang in showy clusters. It is locally called Mountain Locust or Pink Locust. *R . . Hartwigii* is a native to North Carolina and Alabama (acid to neutral soil) lvs. greyish and hairy underneath. Fls. rosy-purple; while *R . . vicosa* also native to Carolina and Alabama is a 40-ft. tree with dark reddish brown branchlets. Fls. pink with a yellow blotch on the standard.

*Sesbania (*Daubentonia*) (*Glottidium*) (Coffee Bean)—Short-lived shrubs, herb-like. Green-stemmed. Fls. bonnet-shaped. *S . . macrocarpa*, native to south and east Texas. Prefers rich, humid soil—acid. Requires a great deal of moisture; grows close to or in water. Fls. a brownish-yellow, broad petal folded over the

yellow lateral petals. Slender stems. Lvs. pinnate. S . . *longi-folia* (or *Daubentonia*) "Rattle Bush" is the var. having very poisonous seed and golden yellow fls. S . . *or Glottidium vesi-caria* var. has fls. tinged with brownish purple and pods are quite short. S . . *Cavanillessii* has showy racemes of bright yellow fls. All are native to Texas. Other Sesbanias in commerce come from abroad.

*Tecoma stans—See YELLOW ELDER.

Vitex (Sweet Lavender) (Chaste Tree)—Lvs. aromatic, light green with greyish fuzz on under side. Fls. in shades of white, blue and lilac. Hardy. Grow in almost any soil but prefer dry, sunny situations. Rapid growth from cutting or shoots. Very tall. V . . *negundo incisa* is recommended for western Texas and New Mexico.

*Yellow Elder (*Tecoma stans*)—Native to Texas, Arizona and New Mexico. Upright shrub. Yellow, fragrant, trumpet shaped fls. in large terminal racemes or panicles. Blooms late in fall and comes true from seed, flowering about one yr. old. Adapted to sandy, pine-land gardens; semi-arid lands. "Asperanza."

NOTE: *See I for additional tall shrubs. Also pp. 52–59 for trees.*

V. SHRUBS THAT ARE PERENNIAL-LIKE . . . WINTER KILL

*Artemisia (Wormwood) (Dusty Miller)—Feathery, silvery-grey, with white wooly underneath, lvs. Slender, branching stems also grey-white. Fls. inconspicuous. Grows everywhere, even in shade. Prop. by division. Grown for foliage, as a herb and for medicinal purposes. Some of the specific var. include Tarragon; Absinthe; Wormwood; Dusty Miller; Mugwort and Sage Brush. A . . *gnaphalodes* is native to Texas. May be dried and used in winter-bouquets.

*Buddleia (Butterfly Bush)—Rapid growing. Semi-hardy, spreading. Prefers rich, well drained, sunny location. Many var., most of them from China, one native to Texas and Mexico south to Brazil having orange-yellow fls. Fls. generally spikes of fragrant lilac, blue-lavendar, rose-lilac, or purple. B . . *asiatica* is the white var. B . . *Davidii,* with varieties and hybrids most widely planted.

*Datura—See page 118.

*Hibiscus (Mallow)—Rapid growing. Lvs. rather large, tropical in effect. Fls. hollyhock-like, in shades of rose, red, and white with red center. Thrives in any moist rich soil. Bloom in later summer and fall. H . . *Moscheutos* (Swamp Rose Mallow) is native from Massachusetts to Florida and west to Lake Michigan and (pages 39, 43) Texas. It is the best known native var. though there are several others. Generally listed as "herbaceous perennial." *H . . mutabilis* is the southern "Confederate Rose." *H . . rose sinensis* "Rose of Sharon" (Althea).

*Lantana—*L . . Camara*, having many varieties and hybrids, are all shrub-like perennials. Fls. verbena-like, are carried on upright stems—odor disagreeable to most people. Bloom profuse. Require sunny position, though not particular about soil and flourish even through heat and drought. *L . . Selowiana* (Weeping or Trailing) has slender twigs and is covered with rose-lavendar or blue-lavendar fls. until frost. Dark green lvs. tinge red with frost and are most attractive over rough walls or down lime hillsides. *L . . involucrata*, fls. light lilac or white on low bushy shrub. *L . . horrida* is native to Texas. Fls. yellow and orange-red as *L . . Camara*.

Plumbago (Leadwort)—Semi-hardy. Readily prop. by cuttings. Require sunny exposure. Fls. phlox-like flower-heads of light, sky blue (*P . . capensis*) the var. *P . . capensis alba* being the white var. most used. Lvs. small, soft and light green. Very tender. *P . . Larpentae* is very low-growing, almost a ground-cover, having dark blue fls. No soil preferences. Prop. by division. *P . . rosea* (var. *coccinea*, scarlet) long racemes of red fls.

Poinsettia—See page 55.

*Salvia (Sage)—Many varieties, varying widely in height, hardiness, type of growth and bloom-time as well as color and method of propagation. *S . . Greggi*—bushy, autumn-flowering, red (dark and rich), 1–6 ft.; *S . . Pitcheri*—(Meadow Sage) bushy, August to frost, true gentian blue fls. on slender long stalks, profuse. 3–4 ft. . . . *alba* (white var.) *S . . azurea*—like *S . . Pitcheri* but sky-blue fls. *S . . farinacea*—earliest to bloom, pale blue fls. 2–3 ft. "Heavenly blue" (page 95). *S . . ballotae-flora*—grown for lvs. for flavoring meats and seasoning. *S . . patens*—extremely tender, requires acid soil, vivid blue very lovely, requires sheltered position and care. *S . . splendens* (Scarlet sage) fiery red, perhaps most widely known var. Color distinctive though often clashes in garden use, hardy. Grown from seed (annual), dwarf var. compact growth 15 in. *S . . leucantha*—bushy perennial, deep purple fls. velvety, fall blooming, tender, 3–4 ft. "Mexican Sage."

VI. SEMI-TROPICAL PLANTS

SHRUBS

Acalpha (Chenile Plant)—*A . . hispida* (3–5 ft.) has green foliage and scarlet flowerets like fuzz on long trailing racemes; *A . . marginata*'s foliage is very unusual; while *A . . tricolor* (3–4 ft.) foliage is red.

Allamanda (Golden Trumpet)—Evergreen, broad, glossy green leaves. Fls. pure golden yellow. May be trained either as a vine or a shrub.

Alseuosmia *macrophylla*—New Zealand Honeysuckle or "Wax Bush," because texture of lvs. and fls. Grows 2–4 ft. high. Bright red spikes 3–6 in. Lvs. rich green.

*Bignonia—May be trained as vine or shrub. Fls. orange-red or yellow trumpets. Very showy.

Bougainvillaea—May be trained either as shrub or vine. Fls. very decorative cluster—bracts lavender, purple, maroon, salmon or white.

Carissa—A spiny shrub, excellent for hedges. Foliage very dark, glossy green. Fls. white, star-shaped.

Confederate Jasmine (*Trachelosperum jasminoides*)—Also called "Star Jasmine." A tender, evergreen, climbing shrub with very fragrant, five-lobed fls. Known also as *Rhynchospermum*.

Crape Jasmine—Similar to the well-known Cape Jasmine, though not quite the same. Fls. waxy white and lvs. glossy green.

Chinese Hat Plant (*Holmskioldia*)—Shrub of sprawling growth. Blossoms apricot-colored.

Croton—*C . . Torreyanus* "Vara Blanca," does well in dry regions. Fls. in long racemes. Lvs. light green. Many varieties of Croton. "Croton Tea." (Page 121.)

Dombeya—Similar to hydrangeas. Fls. lovely pink. Very tall; 12 ft.

Frangipani (*Plumeria*)—Very fragrant white blossoms with canary-yellow throats.

Geranium—Several var. Usually, in north, pot-plants. Given semi-protection are shrub-like in south.

Golden Dew Drop (*Durante repens*)—Fls. in lovely lilac racemes, followed by yellow berries. *D . . lorentzi* has white fls. *D . . plumeri* has blue fls.

Ixora—Dark green glossy lvs. Clusters of dark red, tubular fls. very showy.

Japanese Yew (*Podocarpus*)—Evergreen. Tall, slender-growing shrub.

Mangrove Black (*Avicennia nitida*)—Large, dark green smooth lvs. White fls. in terminal clusters, very fragrant. Grows very tall. Maritime evergreen. Attracts bees.

New Zealand Flax (Snake or Zebra Plant)—Ornamental grass-like. Lvs. white edged or green.

Oleander (*Nerium*)—Excellent for tall hedge, or in planting. Long narrow, evergreen lvs. Fls. white, red or pink showy clusters. Make lovely trees. 8–15 ft. Yellow Oleander: Tigers Apple.

Pampas Grass—Very ornamental.

Pepper (Brazilian) (*Schinus terebintheifolius*)—Brilliant scarlet berries. Large lvs. Rapid growth.

Persea (Avocado, Alligator Pear)—Valued especially for fruit. "Aguacote" or "Pagua."

Plumbago (*Capensis*) (Blue Leadwort)—Most satisfactory shrub. Bears wealth of phlox-like, sky-blue fls. (page 53). (2–6 ft.).

Poinciana (Bird-of-Paradise)—"Strelitzia." Foliage lacy small, willow-like. Fls. gorgeous pea-like blossoms with quite long, scarlet anthers. Called also "Tabachin," "Tavascheen," and "Barbados Pride." *P . . regia* is the famous Royal Poinciana. The so-called Dwarf Poinciana is really *Caesalpinia pulcherrima.*

Poinsettia (*Euphorbia heterophylla*) (*Euphorbia havanensis*) (*Euphorbia pulcherrima*)—"Christmas Plant," "Painted Leaf," "Flor de la Noche Buena," or "Flor de Navidad," "Flame-Leaf," so-called for its clusters of flaming red (sometimes pure white, or rose-pink). Lvs. or bracts at the top of stiff, upright stalks, bearing large ornamental leaves. Grows to 15 ft. and more in rich loam when given water and attention. Requires rest-period of several months. Re-set cuttings (in Valley) in January but water sparingly until May or June. Tender.

Russelia (Fountain-of-Firecrackers Bush)—Red fls. drooping like fountain. 2–3 ft. Very showy.

Shrimp Plant (*Beloperone*)—Evergreen shrubs bearing unusual racemes that appear like curled shrimp—red or maroon in the deeper tones, shaded to palest pink. 2–4 ft. Excellent for background or screen. Blooms most of the year.

Taza de Oro (Cup of Gold) (*Solandra Gutata*)—Large, very fragrant golden fls. Showy leaves.

Templetonia retusa (Coral Bush)—Bears large coral-red blossoms. Dark brown pods, opening to spill coral beans. Very attractive. Drought resistant.

Tigers Apple (*Thevetia*) (Yellow Oleander)—Very ornamental. Grows well in sandy soil. Is related to the oleander. Lvs. narrow and shiny. Fls. bell-shaped golden. Known also as "Lucky Seeds." Drought resistant. 15–25 ft. Can be pruned.

Thunbergia—Blossoms bluish-purple with white throats, hanging in clusters.

Viburnum (*odoratissimum*)—Evergreen, large glossy lvs. Very fragrant fls. in late spring. Very hardy shrub.

NOTE: In addition to the above that require semi-tropical conditions, the following shrubs also are grown extensively and seem to thrive. . . . "Asperanza" (*Tecoma stans* or Yellow Elder); Box; Callistemon; Camellia; Cape Jasmine; Crape Myrtle; *Datura arborea* ("Angel's trumpet"); *Erythina arborea* (Coral shrub or tree); Forsythia Hibiscus "Tulipan del monte;" *Malvaviscus Drummondii* "Manzanita" (Turk's Cap) native to the tropics, its crape myrtle; Lantana *camera* "Hierba de Cristo;" Mimosa; Pomegranate; Pittisporum; Poinsettia; Pyracantha;

Rubber plant (*Ficus*); Senisa (*Leucophyllum texanum,* "Ceniso"); Vitex; Desert flowering Willow. (See other lists for descriptions, etc.)

TREES

*Acacia . . Acapulcensis (Tepejuage)—Fast-growing evergreen. Fern-like leaves. Delicate yellow fls., fragrant, ball-like. Also classed as *Leucaena pulve rulenta.* 20–40 ft.

Amyris . . *Lantrisco madrensis* . . (Torchwood)—White flowers in spikes. Evergreen. Odor resembles myrrh.

Anaqua (*Ehretia elliptica*)—Good shade tree. Fragrant. Fls. twice yearly. Very small, brilliant orange fruit, attractive to birds. Can be trimmed to shrub-height. Wide distribution. 12–20 ft.

*Anacahuita (*Cordia boissieri*)—"Wild Olive." So-called for shape of fruit. Blooms nine months of year. Fls. white, crepe-like. Drought resistant. 10–15 ft.

Arcajuela (*Citharexylum Berlandieri*)—Fragrant white or yellow fls. in long spike-like racemes. Spiny shrub. Fruit, red berries becoming black with age. Also *C . . brachyanthum, E . . villosum.*

*Ash (Fresno) (*Fraxinus Berlandieri*)—Excellent shade tree. Only ash in U. S. truly evergreen. Rapid growth. Requires abundance of water. Transplants easily when young. May be grown from seed. 30–50 ft. Withstood hurricane of 1933.

Banana (*Musa sapientum*)—Rapid growth. Valued for fruit and tropical effect of large, long leaves. Should be protected from winds. Excellent for effects.

Bauhinia (ORCHID TREE)—Bears long racemes of white, orchid (lavendar), or yellow pea-like flowers. Likes water. 12–20 ft.

Camphor—Evergreen glossy bright lvs. Rich brownish red in fall. Tender.

Carab (Breadfruit Tree) (*Artocarpus*)—Ornamental, large thick lvs. Fls. in long spikes. Dense club-like catkin 10–16 in. long. Edible fruit (usually seed boiled). Branches fragile. Prop. by cuttings. Slow growth. Requires hot, moist air. Very tender. Milky-juiced. Also: *Ceratonia siliqua* "St. John's Bread"—*carob.*

*Catsclaw (*Acacia wrighti*) "Una de Gato"—Small, attractive, very thorny tree. Drought resistant.

Citrus—Include the Oranges, Lemons, Grapefruit, Tangerines, Kumquat, Loquat, etc.

*Chapote (Mexican Black Persimmon) (*Brayodendron texanum* or *Diospros Texana*)—Small evergreen. Fruit delicious, size of plum. Drought resistant.

Cherimoya (Apple Custard)—Related to Pawpaw. 12–20 ft. Large edible fruit. Prefers rich soil and good drainage.

*Colima (*Fagara Xanthoxylum*)—Evergreen with yellow wood. Ornamental, foliage and fruit, aromatic when bruised.

*La Coma (Ironwood) (*Bumelia angustifolia*)—Small ornamental tree, excellent wood for furniture. Round top. Blooms twice yearly. Fruit attractive to birds. Cardinals nest in its branches. Ancient "Chittim wood," or "Buckthorn."

Cypress (*Taxodium mucronatum*)—Large trees from Mexico. "Cipres." Require a great deal of water. Of the same family is the largest tree in the world, "Del Tule" in Oaxaca, Mexico.

*Ebony (Ebano) (*Siderocarpos flexicaulis*)—Excellent shade tree. Dark evergreen foliage. Grows rapidly. Flowers after every heavy rain. Requires *much water*, good drainage and fairly *rich soil*. Closely related to the Acacias. 10–20 ft. Withstood hurricane of 1933.

Elm (Olmo) (*Ulmus crassifolia*)—Excellent shade tree. Requires water. Evergreen. 20–60 ft. Drought resistant.

*Eucalyptus (Gum)—Most ornamental, useful shade tree. Grows very tall, and large. Bark distinctive, greyish. Flowers fragrant, attract bees. Endures heat, frost and most drought resistant. Wood and fruits used extensively. *E . . globulus* (Blue Gum) has lighter yellow wood than *E . . rostrata* (Red Gum). Both demand good soil preferably clayey-subsoil.

Grevillea (*Robusta*) (Silk Oak)—Symmetrical, pyramidal-shaped, excellent specimen tree. Fern-like lvs. Flowers comb-like, golden yellow, 6 in. long. Drought resistant.

Gum—See Eucalyptus.

*Hackberry (*Celtis occidentalis*) (*Celtis mississippiensis*)—Popular shade tree. "Palo Blancho." Withstands drought and winds. Deciduous. Small, reddish, berry-fruits. Quick growth. Subject to disease. 30–60 ft. Withstood hurricane of 1933.

*Huisache (Acacia (*Vachellia*) *farnesiana*)—Delicate foliage. Fragrant yellow balls attract bees. Flowers produce very high grade perfume. (See page 37.) Likes moisture. 20–50 ft.

Jacaranda *mimosaefolia*—Gorgeous blue clusters of fls. Tender. 20–30 ft. Also *J . . acutifolia* and *J . . ovalifolia*.

Jujube (Zizyphus)—Small tree valuable for fruit and foliage (yellowish green). *Z . . Rhamnaceae* is half hardy. Fr. dark red, almost black, edible. Grows in any soil. Prop. by seed or cuttings.

Juniperus—In variety. (See page 36.)

Kumquat (*Fortunella japonica*)—Lvs. narrow. Fls. small. Fruit orange colored and flavored.

*Laurel (Texas Mountain Laurel) (*Sophora secundiflora*)—Very ornamental. (See pages 40; 47.)

Loquat (*Eriobotrya japonica*)—Beautiful olive-green foliage, thick, glossy. Edible yellow fruit, size of plums. Symmetrical tree. Apricot or cherry flavored. "Biwa." Excellent for jams and jellies.

*Magnolia—(See page 37.)

*Mesquite (*Propopis juliflora*)—(See page 61.) Lacy foliage, willow-like. Also *E . . j . . glandulosa.*

Mexican Buckeye (*Ungnadia speciosa*)—Small deciduous tree. Lovely pink flowers.

Mulberry (*Morus*)—*Morus Kingon* is fruitless, deciduous shade tree. *M . . rubra* is the native red variety. *M . . alba* (white) and *M . . nigra* (black) widely grown also.

*Mimosa (*Albizzia julibrissin*)—(See pages 37; 61.)

Olive—Slow growth. Drought resistant.

Orchid Tree—See BAUHINIA.

Parkinsonia (Retama)—(See page 50.) 10–20 ft. Drought resistant.

Palms (*Sabal*)—Include Palmettos, Date, Sage, Fan, etc., wide variety. Most popular probably is S . . *texana or mexicana** (native), "Palma de Nichero." Withstood hurricane of 1933.

Papaya (*Carica*)—Fast growing, ornamental trees valued for fruits and foliage. Should be planted in groups, to cross-pollenize properly. Fruit melon-like.

Pecan (*Carya*)—(See pages 29; 60.)

Persimmon—See CHAPOTE.

Rue Tree (Ruta) "Herb of Grace"—Hardy. Perennial-like. Lvs. fragrant. Fls. yellow or greenish in great profusion. Has medicinal qualities.

Sapindus—S . . saponaria (tall herb); S . . *quillaja* (small tree), called "Soapberry;" and S . . *Drummondii* ("Jaboncillo") all have the peculiarity of producing lather hence the name. The fruit is round, orange-brown.

Silk Oak—See GREVILLEA.

Soapbark—See SAPINDUS . . *quillaja.*

Tallow Tree (*Sapium sebiferum*)—In fall leaves tinge maple-like. Almost evergreen.

Tamarix (Salt Cedar)—See pages 33; 40.) "Athel." Gross feeder. 20–40 ft. Very shallow root system. Drought resistant. Prop. from cuttings (must be *kept moist* to grow).

*Tenaza (*Harvardia Brevifolia*)—Small ornamental tree. Flowers fragrant, attractive and appear twice yearly.

*Umbrella Tree (*Melia*)—(See page 46.) Chinaberry.

*Willows—(See page 41.)

Vitex—(See page 52.)

*Zitherwood (*Citharexylon*)—Hard, durable wood used for zithers and fiddles. Also called *"Bois cotelet."* Flowers small white panicles. Berries gay—turn from green to red to black.

NOTE: *Plant or transplant both shrubs and trees preferably in December, although it may safely be done in November or January, often, by giving care, water and attention. Plants may be put out at almost any time provided abundance of water is*

*given and they are carefully balled before moving. Pruning seems
best during a long dry spell—spring-blooming in November and
December (sometimes as early as September, if not too hot),
etc. All gardening habits are compelled to be governed by the
weather.*

VII. TREES AND TREE-LIKE SHRUBS

It would be impossible to list all the trees that may be
grown in the South and West because they are legion, and
the great range of climatic differences as well as the varying
types of soil play such an important part in their determi-
nation.

Certain of the Oaks (*Quercus*), Elms (*Ulmus*) and Cedars   *Everywhere*
(*Juniperus*) will grow almost anywhere, yet many of the
trees and tree-like shrubs demand specific conditions—
usually soil-ingredients or the degree of moisture together
with the range of temperature—determines their hardiness
and suitability.

For convenience, grouping those that are locally hardy
under broad geographical divisions, the following most commonly seen trees are listed for ready reference in planning
landscaping premises. These lists do not attempt to be detailed, merely suggestive.

In the acid-soil lands of the Old South and west into Texas   *Prefer
Acid Soil*
those predominating include flowering Azaleas and Rhododendrons (often attaining the height of small trees); the
Cypress ("Arizona", "Italian", "Portuguese", "Majestic",
etc.) and *Chamaecyparis;* flowering white and pink varieties
of the Dogwood (*Cornus*); Magnolias; long and short leaf
Pines (*Pinus*); certain Yews (*Taxus*) and the Water Hem-
lock (*Thuja*) among the evergreens—while the deciduous
Ash (*Fraxinus americana,* white, and *F . . lanceolata,* green);
Beech (*Fagus*) and Birch (*Betula rubra,* red, and *B . . lueta,*
yellow) are found in the northern sections. The Chinquapin
(*Castenea pumila*) grows with the White (*Ulmus americana*)
and the Slippery (*U . . fulva*) Elms. The flowering Gingko
(Maidenhair-Ferntree); the Haws and Hawthorns; the Hazel
(*Corylus*) and Witch Hazel (*Hamamelis*); Larch (*Larex*);

both the Locust and "Honey Locust" (*Robinia and Gledit-schia*); Maples (*Acer*); many of the *Hicorias* (Hickory); the Red (*Q . . coccinea*) and Black (*Q . . velutina*) Oaks that demand moisture and prefer rich soil; and both the Sweet Gum (*Liquidamber Styraciflua*) and the Sour Gum (*Nyssa sylvatica,* or Tubelo) that demand deep, rich, moist soil as does the lovely Tulip Tree (*Liriodendron*); the *Ailanthus glangulosa* ("Tree of Heaven"); the "Bald Cypress" (*Taxodium disticham,* whose needle-like foliage is deciduous) all prefer acid to neutral soil.

*Prefer
Lime Soil*
Those that prefer neutral, or calcareous (lime) soil, generally found throughout central and north Texas into Oklahoma and Arkansas and in certain isolated areas in the Old South—include among the evergreen the Cedars (*Juniperus*) and in the southern portions the lovely pyramidal-shaped, feathery, drooping-foliage *Cedrus deodora* and *C . . atlantica glauce;* the Buckeye* or Dwarf Chestnut (*Aesculus octandra flava*); the Live Oak* and certain of the Cypresses . . . while among the deciduous are the two varieties of the Chinaberries (*Melia azedarach, umbraculiformis,* and *Melia floribunda*) both having fragrant, lavender flowers in clusters followed by tan-colored berries; Cottonwoods (*Populus deltoides*)* or Balsam Poplar with their birch-like limbs and light green leaves; the half-hardy Jujube (*Zizyphus*) and the Mimosa* *fragrans* (also *M . . borealis*) with its fragrant, fuzzy, rosy-pink balls and feathery foliage; the American Linden (Basswood, *Tilia americana*) that does not endure cold; Pecan (*Carya*) and Oaks; Persimmon* (*Brayodendron texanum,* 'Possum Plum) along the stream banks with the Willows (*Salix*); Sophoras*; and Black Walnut (*Juglans nigra*)*; the gleaming white limbs of the Sycamore (*Platanus occidentalis*) and Redbud (*Cercis occidentalis*) found all through the temperate zone, with various of the Pines and Elms.

The semi-tropics and coast-lands have many plants that will not grow anywhere else. (The principal ones of these are listed on pages 53–59).

In the desert and plains country, the vast prairie sections

the Mesquite (*Proposis juliflora*)*; the Desert Willow *Plains or* (*Chilipsis linearis*)* and the Scrub Oak (*Quercus ilicifolia*)* *Prairie* *Soil* predominate with *Pinus cembroides** (Pinyon) and the Jack Pine (*Pinus Banksiana*)*; the Aspen (*Populus tremuloides*) that turns such glorious yellows in the fall; the green Ash (*Fraxinus lanceolata*); various native *Chaparral** and *Condalias**; *Arbutus unedo* (Strawberry tree); several *Acacias** see page 37; the Greasewood (*Scarcobatus*)*; the Hop tree (*Ptelea trifoliata*)* with its clusters of greenish white flowers and yellow leaves; the Mountain Mahogany (*Cercocarpus*)* and Mountain Sorrel, or Sourwood*; and the *Juniperus chinensis neaboriensis.*

There are a number that seem to thrive throughout the *Shrubs* temperate zone, without much regard for soil or climatic vagaries. Among these are certain of the Arbor Vitae (*Thuja*); the Bois d'Arc (Mock Orange—*Maclura pomifera*)*; Buckthorn (*Rhamnus*)*; *Catalpa Bungei* (Umbrella tree) and *C . . speciosa* with their deliciously fragrant flowers; Hackberry (*Celtus occidentalis* see pages 29; 57); Honey Locust (see page 60); various Poplars (Bolle's, Carolina, Lombardy, White or Silver); the purple-leaved Plum (*Prunus cerasifera Pissardi*); the Red, White, Russian, and Weeping Mulberries; Rose* Acacia; Sumac (*Rhus*)*; the white-limbed Sycamore (*Platanus occidentalis*)* (called also Buttonwood); and the Willows (*Salix babylonica* or Weeping Willow) and the Flowering Desert Willow.

Among the tall shrubs or small trees there are the Altheas *Tall Shrubs* (*Hibiscus*); Cherry* Laurel; Crape Myrtle; Box Elder, or Ash-leaved Maple (*Acer Negundo*)*; the Eleagnus; *Lespedeza* (Bush Clover)*; and the Bush Honeysuckle (*Lonicera*) and the Tartarian; Ligustrums (*Privet*); *Osmanthus aquifolium*; Parkinsonia (*Retama*)*; Philadelphus; Photinia; Pyracanthus; Salvias*; Spireas; Syringa (Lilac); Tamarix* (Salt Cedar); and Vitex. *Anisacanthus*, Buddleia; Caragana; *Cydonia japonica* and Coralberry (*Symphoricarpus*)* are lower-growing but generally hardy, it seems.

The lovely Golden Rain tree (*Koelreuteria paniculata*) or Varnish tree, will endure all except acid soil.

Trees are greatly prized in regions where they are rare, or

difficult to have. It is, therefore, suggested that intensive feeding will be beneficial to insure success. One method is measure the diameter of the tree four (4) feet above the ground and allow three (3) pounds of plant-food for each inch of diameter . . . drill a series of holes eighteen (18) inches apart, the radius determined by where the outer leaves drip, and (preferably in March) water in correct ratio (that is the per cent of Nitrogen to Superphosphate to Potash) depends on local conditions. . . . Another method of determining the amount of food required or that can be readily assimilated is add (in feet) the height of the tree to its branch-spread, to the trunk-circumference (in inches), and the resulting figure will give the *number of pounds* of food needed. (See page 21.)

Evergreens

As many evergreens like acidity in the soil, to one-third the amount of earth they are planted in add one-third peat moss and one-third live-oak (or hardwood) leaves. If the soil is clayey, add some sand. A little tannic-acid stirred in at the roots, often is relished.

The general rule regarding planting trees is when the sap is down, ball, place in hole amply deep and wide (not to cramp roots) and water. Placing usually requires expert handling.

Targets

Scientific findings tell us that among the trees there are certain ones that are veritable lightning-targets, while others are more or less immune. In the order listed the following are most often struck—Oak, Elm, Pine, Poplar, Willow Ash. White Beech, Birch, Horsechestnut, or Holly are seldom scarred. As these latter are seldom grown in the southwestern region, the former list is of special interest, recognizing the extremes of weather conditions prevailing.

Hurricane

During the hurricane of 1933 in the Rio Grande Lower Valley those trees that survived best were the Ash, Hackberry and Palms—all natives to the region.

VIII. SHRUBS FROM SEED AND CUTTINGS

There is no greater joy to the true gardener than watching and tending plants from tiny seedlings to full-grown plant, shrub or tree!

Certain annual-like shrubs mature, grow quite tall, and **From Seed**
blossom freely in a single season. Among these are:

Cassia floribunda (Senna)—Golden yellow bonnet-shaped fls. in
  loose clusters. Also *C . . corymbosa.*
Castor Bean—Valued for decorative lvs., tropical in effect. Desirable for screens or hedges. Rapid growth. *Ricinus.*
Kochia (Mock or Summer Cypress)—Low-growing herb, with
  compact light green summer foliage, brilliant red in fall.
Tecoma Stans—Yellow Elder (p. 52).

While others, like Redbud, are of slower growth yet mature more rapidly than the conifers and broad-leaf evergreens.

Fall is the time to make HARDWOOD cuttings: Cut switches **By Cuttings**
of the current year's growth to eight-inch lengths, leaving
a bud at the top and a cut just below a bud for the root
end . . . top-cut slanting, bottom square.

Cut off all leaves. Tie into a bundle of 15 to 25 stems.

Bury obliquely, tops up, in a trench deep enough to cover
tops about two inches. Surround and cover completely with
sand.

Be sure to mark the spot as well as the bundle.

In February, dig up. At the base of each cutting will be
seen a callus (white rim). Place this cutting in its permanent growing position—about half its length above ground.
The greater percentage will grow.

With CONIFERS: Make cuttings similar to Geraniums,
leaving most of the leaves on the stem. Plant in sand about
October.

Leave ten to twelve months. Lift and plant in pots.

Plant in permanent positions after summer-heat has waned
(October or early November).

Plant Evergreens in August or first part of September.

The process of rooting cuttings has been greatly simplified
and accelerated by the discovery of P. W. Zimmerman,
Boyce Thompson Institute, New York, of a fluid commercially known as "Hormodin A."

IX. SHRUBS FOR SCREENS AND HEDGES

Hedges may be used as boundary markers and to form a frame for various *special gardens* (such as Rose, Perennial, Vegetable, etc.). They may be used as a screen from the street, or a neighbor's property, or as a division line to separate terraces or various sections even of small property. They may be used to screen or separate utility areas from the garden area, and to soften the harsh outlines of geometric patterns, necessary drives, etc.

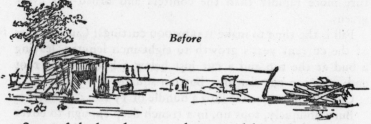

Before

Uses

Some of the best known and most widely used shrubs that may be kept low to medium in height include:

Abelia	Cydonia japonica	Nandina
Agarita	Forsythia	Polyantha Roses
Barberry	Kerria	Pyracantha
Box and Ilex	*Leucophyllum* (Senisa)	Spirea

Among the tall-growing varieties there are:

Arizona Cypress	Crape Myrtle	Ilex
Arbor Vitae	Cherry Laurel	Lilac
Bois d'Arc	*Citrus trifoliata*	Ligustrum
(Mock Orange)	Euonymus	Philadelphus
Cedars	Hawthorn	Privet
		Teucrium

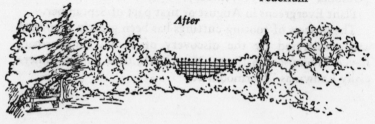

After

All shrubs, especially flowering shrubs, are gross feeders, *Shrubs Feed Shrubs* requiring fertilization to give maximum results. An all-round, dry, commercial fertilizer that may be applied to the top soil and worked in lightly is once each year—apply at the ratio of four and one-half tablespoonfuls to each two (2) square feet, or one (1) pound to every fifteen (15) feet of hedge . . . 100 pounds of bonemeal, to which add 50 pounds of cottonseed meal and 10 (ten) pounds of sifted (*hardwood*) wood ashes, unleached (or potash).

X. PRUNING

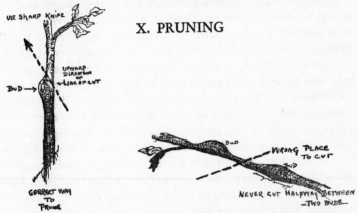

All new gardeners tend to allow shrubs and vigorous- *Value* growing plants to develop without restraint. They fear that through lack of expert knowledge they may do injury to a treasured bush or flower. However, nothing is of value unless it serves the purpose for which it was intended, so a shrub must be forced to comply with those purposes for which it was selected and planted.

Thus when and how to prune plants is one of the many *Relative Place* valuable lessons to be learned from the old English gardeners. Their years of experience have enabled them to use and keep within bounds their plant-colors, as an artist handles his palette, so that each individual specimen is forced to take its relative place in the garden picture. *How* to use plants *to advantage* and *so control* them that they occupy only the space allotted them denotes a Master Gardener.

To maintain grounds and foundations well balanced is always a vital consideration.

Privet, Ligustrum and Euonymus, if one wishes a low hedge, should be pruned to the ground every four or five years. Do not despair when the luxuriant growth is cut away, for the strong, established roots will send up a wealth of new lacy growth to delight the eye and keep the bushes thick and healthy. Where growth is abundant, frequent and severe pruning is necessary.

Evergreens

Evergreens are selected primarily for backgrounds, against which to display splashes of color, for their softening green is as distinct a color factor as white, which serves to blend groups of brilliant-colored flowers, so the shades of green are always needed to create harmony. Since all evergreens may not be directed into desired shapes, symmetry can only be secured by choosing those varieties which will permit of training. Valuable years of plant growth are lost when mistakes are made in the original selection. In shaping conifers and most of the broad-leaf evergreens, trim them in February-March but do not cut conifers beyond their needles. Broad-leaf evergreens, on the contrary, will sprout from bare branches, if it is necessary to be severe in shaping them.

Flowering Shrubs

While evergreens are only pruned for form and restraint, flowering shrubs should be kept trimmed for excellence of bloom, development of strength, and beauty of contour. Those flowering shrubs whose habit is to produce a number of canes, from the same root-stock, should have the old and hardened canes as well as all dead wood removed and *kept* removed. In this way the less matured branches will develop strength and vigor. In most cases these produce much more perfect blossoms. By allowing only enough canes to develop to give the bush symmetry without overcrowding, beauty of form is obtained.

In trimming, remember that the direction of the bud at the cut will be that of the new branch, and that too many branches in the center of the plant exclude required sun and air from the roots, causing a scarcity of foliage on the lower branches—an ugly leggy appearance.

When it becomes necessary to lower the top branches, never trim them all the same height. Cut them irregular lengths, though taking care not to be stubby, in order to give the shrub a more graceful, natural effect. To make a more dense growth, cut back tips of branches; and to induce wider growth, cut off old branches at the ground.

Shear evergreen hedges when growth is finished, usually early fall. Shear deciduous hedges once while dormant (for shaping); again as soon as the first spring growth has been made (to correct ragged look), and again when later growth produces same effect, at least three times a year.

Spirea, trimmed severely immediately after blooming, will give light and space to surrounding plants, as well as a greater wealth of bloom the succeeding season. This and several others of the early-flowering shrubs may be kept the desired shape and size by taking off those branches undesired *when the buds begin to swell*. These, put in water indoors, may be forced by the heat of the house to flower before those out-of-doors, and thus a double purpose is served.

Time

A simple key as to time of pruning flowering-shrubs is *all those blossoming in the spring* should be trimmed *immediately after flowering*, while *those that bloom in late summer or fall* should be cut back *after they lose their leaves* or during early winter.

Espalier

Training shrubs or trees espalier for ornamental display—especially where space is limited—has long been practiced, requires patience, and is an art.

Among those most readily adaptable and satisfactory:

Apricot—*Prunus armeniaca*—Cuttings grown for true flowering.
Citrus *trifoliata* (Bitter Orange)—*Poncirus*—Bears attractive, small orange-like fruit.
Crab Apples—M . . *floribunda;* M . . *angustifolia;* M . . *eleyi;* "Red Vein"; "Coronaria"; M . . *sargenti;* "Niedzwetskyana"; and M . . *scheideckeri;* are all good.
Eleagnus *simoni.*
Grapes—"Carmen" and "R. W. Munson." Not "Concord."
Magnolia *grandiflora*—Is both flowering and evergreen.
Pears—"Kiefer" and "Garber"—blight-proof.
Persimmon—(Japanese) *Diospyros*—ornamental fruit.
Plums—"Six Weeks"; "Gold"; "Abundance"; "Black Beauty"; "Burbank."
Pyracantha—*Lalandi* (*Crataegus coccinea*)—attractive red berries.
Wisteria—Cutting grown plants, only, bear perfect flowers.

XI. ACID-LOVING PLANTS, SHRUBS AND TREES

Some Acid-Loving Plants

The hardwood forests of the South and West are the habitat of many plants that must be most carefully nurtured elsewhere. Among these are the Dogwood, Rhododendrons, Cypripediums or Lady Slippers, Azaleas, Camellias, Mountain Laurel, Andromeda, Blueberry, Tar Flower, Pitcher Plants, Sundews, Sweet Bay, Bayberry, Ink or Gallberry, and many others, all of which will thrive in soil that is properly prepared.

Precaution Necessary in Lime Soil

Azaleas and Rhododendrons are among the most difficult plants to grow successfully in sections of the land, due to the fact that they demand the *superlative* degree of acidity in the soil in which they are to grow, and wherever lime, even in small quantities, is present the life of any, and especially this, acid-loving plant is endangered. Therefore those precautions that are taken to exclude the seepage of lime into the acid-soil bed (see page 12) are particularly advised when one attempts to have Azaleas in calcareous soil.

In sections where sand or clay is the predominant soil, the *In Sandy Soil* depth to which the hole that is to receive the acid-loving plant is to be dug varies from eighteen to twenty-four inches, dependent on the degree of compactness of the soil. Light sandy soil requires the removal of at least twenty inches more, a deeper hole. Break up the subsoil for about a foot in depth, and add to it acid, peaty soil, and some clay. Acid, peaty soil may be secured by various means, as natural muck (from marshes); peat-moss (in bales, usually); leaf-mold (from under *hardwood* trees such as Oak, Hemlock, Sweet Gum, Maple, Magnolia, Hickory, Cypress and some Cedars); well-rotted wood, bark or sawdust of these trees, to which is added some peat-moss and cottonseed meal. Clay soil *In Clay Soil* should be removed at least two feet in depth, forked well for at least ten inches deeper, and sand, together with the necessary acid, peaty soil, as above, added to bring it to the consistency of good loam. Both sand and clay, therefore, require about the same treatment, the chief difference being in the depth to be removed, for the proportion of the mixture to be replaced is the same. (See pages 14–16.)

This special soil mixture may be estimated as *Special Soil Mixture* follows: one part cottonseed meal to three parts sand, to which is added ten parts peat moss, or acid leafmold, or muck; and six parts rotted hardwood or bark of above named trees. Finely ground Sphagnum moss often is used without any mixture of soil. Or, another combination that is used, is one part clay, one part sand, and one part leafmold (acid) to two parts peat moss. Aluminum sulphate also may be spread over the surface (one-half pound to each square yard, approximately) and raked into the

Acidity Test

ground; or hemlock extract or tannic acid are satisfactory. However, the aluminum sulphate is indispensable as a safe, quick means of supplying and maintaining acidity in the soil, the correct degree being determined by blue litmus paper turning red after being placed (covered) in the soil for thirty minutes. The soil is then acid enough. (See page 14.) Sulphur is slower acting but is not quickly exhausted. Epsom salts also may be used.

Drainage and Protection

All acid-loving plants are exacting, also, in their requirements of adequate drainage. In some situations an elevated bed, sometimes on a gentle slope, is needed to obtain the best results from the plant. Yet care should be taken not to locate them in a spot that is too well-drained and dry. It is suggested that, as their habitat is usually in woods, a certain amount of shade and protection is their preference.

CHIEF ACID-LOVING PLANTS

Andromeda
Azaleas
Bayberry
Blueberry
Camellias
Christmas   Rose
   (*Helleborus niger*)
Cypress
Cypripediums
   (Lady Slippers)
Dogwood (*Cornus*)
Gentian
Hydrangea
Inkberry (Gallberry)
Iris *missouriensis*
   (and others of species)
      Maple
      Mountain Laurel
      Pitcherplant
      Rhododendrons
      Sweet Bay
      Sweet Gum
      Sundews
      Tar-Flower

Seasonal Bloom Cycles

COLOR HAS an appeal and an allure that few other things in life possess. Especially during those seasons when skies are drab and grey, or when rains drench the earth, a spot of loveliness that offers a subtle psychological attraction is one to which there is universal and immediate response. So, to create a garden in which at all seasons somewhere blossom, stem, or leaf satisfies the aesthetic senses is both a challenge and a delight. *The Quest for Continuous Bloom*

In some sections of the country accomplishment of this objective is relatively easy, in others it is well nigh an impossibility. Yet, all strive as valiantly and each is as proud of his degree of return as was the Royal Palace Head Gardener in Copenhagen of his puny, sickly, twelve-inch purple salvia (S. *leucantha*) that grows abundantly to several feet in height in Texas and in Old and New Mexico! *Dreams*

If it *were* so simple and so easy to achieve a cycle of continuous bloom would not most—if not all—of the fascination of gardening be lost? Only in the Elysian Fields can one hope to find that dream adequately fulfilled, but mortals here are spurred on by the dream to labor and to plan, and to still greater effort. *Ideals*

The great Linnaeus (Karl von Linné) in giving the world that immeasurable gift of classification of plant life, especially in the details of the seed-bearers of the families in the 19th to the 53rd Orders, has pointed out that the great families of flowering plants provide an infinite diversity in colors, heights, breadths, and time of bloom. Wherever one lives one may plan any number of specific combinations that should *Possibilities* prove a perfect garden—but—consider the weather, the soil, and the vagaries of the season!

The Seasonal Plants

What a curious thing it is that spring, summer, and autumn each seem to have a dominant and characteristic plant-material that is so identified with them that certain names spring to mind upon mere mention of a season! Early-flowering shrubs, bulbs, and pastel shades denote spring-time. Roses, Iris, and Lilies proclaim summer close at hand. Flowering annuals and perennials are summer's standbys; while autumn's glories in leaf and blossom closely resemble each other. The peculiar thread of dependability bound within these observations is the broad hint that just this hint outlines for general success in gardening for succession of bloom.

Early Spring Shrubs

The ribbons of color in Nature's earliest garden picture begin usually with golden bells and trumpets sounding the advent of spring . . . Forsythia (*spectabilis* and *suspensa*), sweet Bush Honeysuckle, Daffodils, and the starlike golden shower of Jasmine *nudiflorum*. Bursting into flame about the same time as the Crocus pops up beside the Scilla's bells is *Pyrus japonica* ("Burningbush") followed closely by Pussy Willows and the sweet flowering Pears and Plums (*Prunus Pissardi* with its feathery white sprays and copper foliage and *Prunus angustifolia,* one of the wild plums of the South-west) together with the various Spirea.

Low Plants

Close to the ground the Violets bloom in purple sheets and vie with Pansies for first place among the lowliest growing of the early-blooming plants. The wild, pale-blue Violets and the rare white ones are usually tenderer and perhaps therefore the more cherished. Alliums (white, rose, and gold) with Grape Hyacinths precede the various colored, true Hyacinth-bells and carry the purple tints and tones into the royal blues and the blues of the Lupine ("Texas Bluebonnet"), blending to the delicate lavender-blues of the beloved Triteleias of the Old South. Snowflakes (*Leucojum*), Snowdrops (*Galanthus*), and, where soil and climate permit, Lilies-of-the-Valley add their dainty white cups to the few plants that tolerate semi-shade, blossoming before the leaves of the trees are fully out.

Vines

Above, the pale lavender toward pink or pure white plumes of Wisteria perfume the air from trellis, or, trained to tree-shapes, droop as though lacy umbrellas. The Tulip-trees (Magnolia *Soulangeana* and Magnolia *stellata*) carry torch-like on bare limbs the deeper tones of purple and reddish-purple lined with creamy white, appearing in full loveliness well in advance of their leaves. Stocks and Wall-flowers in some sections weather the winter and are quite ahead of many others of the plants.

Phlox

Under trellises, pergolas, trees and other semi-shady places Vinca *minor* blooms and flourishes where other things are difficult to grow. It begins to bloom quite early and forms a satisfactory ground-cover. Yet there is no single family of plants that supplies as satisfactory ground-covers as the great Phlox family (P. *divericata, sublata* and the annual P. *drummondii*), while Phlox *paniculata,* the perennial hardy Phlox, is one of the most dependable plants of the summer garden, blossoming until fall.

Semi-Shade Plants

Many of the bulbs and lilies will also grow in the semi-shade, under the Dogwood (*Cornus*)—pink & white—the Southwestern native Haws, the Black Haw (*Viburnum prunifolium*) and the Red Haw (*Craeteagus Crus-galli*) attracting the bees with their fragrant, clustered white blossoms.

Lilac

Where soil will permit and climatic mildness favor Camellias, Azaleas, night-blooming Jasmine, Gardenias, and Florida Bignonia reward the fortunate gardener with a wealth of color and fragrance. Lilacs, too, have long been favorites, and many a pioneer woman, if fortunate, has barely kept alive and brooded over her beloved Lilac as her new home was located further and further Southwestward from her northern home-site. Lilacs and many of the flowering shrubs seem to enjoy most the blankets of snow that melting slowly keep them moist from autumn to spring. Where snows are infrequent or absent watering brings wealth of bloom, also to spring-flowering bulbs and Daffodils, carrying down additional nourishment when a light covering of well-rotted manure has been scattered over them in the fall.

Photina and Cherry Laurel are early a mass of delicate snowy white, closely followed by Ligustrum and Privet. Redbud carries masses of color over areas where Rhododendron and wild Azaleas and other acid-loving plants will not survive. Its distinctive coloring does not blend with flowering Peach, Cherries, Almonds, Apricots and Crabapples (*Bechel* and *purpurea adanhamensis*) whose pinks, rose and reds complement each other.

White Cydonia, Pomegranates and the golden Kerrias add their pastel contributions to the early picture, blending in harmony with the age-old favorite Iris *florentina* and I. *germanica* (white and blue)—the glorious blues of the bulbous Iris, late golden Daffodils (Narcissi) and the many-colored Tulips planted in drifts about a pillar, "Lady Banksia" Rose or a Hugonis' clear yellow beauty.

Swelling into leaf the Bignonia and Virginia Creeper's burst of growth is as delicate in coloring as is the blossom. The Belgian and French Honeysuckles perfume the spring air, announcing midspring's advent.

Single annual Pinks (*Dianthus*) in fringed and many variants of coloring with a host of other annuals are indispensable to use in filling in the gaps and lacks between bloom-periods of perennials, shrubs and bulbs, and in that period before the Lilies and Roses come. In fact throughout the seasons.

Columbine (*Aquilegia*)—one of the loveliest of the delicate, pastel-hued plants—appeals to all. The long-spurred varieties (Mrs. Scott Elliott strain)—a great improvement over the wild varieties, blends beautifully with the lovely Louisiana Iris* and the feathery delicacy of the Tamarix (Salt Cedar).

Mid to late spring provides many flowering shrubs and trees that rival the bouquet of flowers at their feet—Weigelia, Honey Locust*, Ailanthus ("Tree of Heaven"), the two kinds of Chinaberries and the Catalpas (umbrella and upright), Mimosa, Acacias* (nine being native to the Southwest), Flowering Desert Willow*, Poinciana*, Parkinsonia*, with Kolkwitzia, the Brooms (*Genista* and *Cystis,* the former the "Planta-genet" of the age of Chivalry), Red Osier (*Salix*), Philadelphus, Syringa, Vitex, Paulownia (that should be shielded from strong winds) and Nandina among those commonly grown.

No tree in the southern part of the temperate zone is as *Magnolia* stately or is more beloved than is the Magnolia *grandiflora*. Where it can be grown it lends a degree of elegance that nothing else seems to replace or to rival, flowering sometimes with the pageant of Iris, sometimes after they are spent. Magnolias and Jasmine are traditionally coupled as are Roses, Iris and Lilies.

Cycles of bloom vary so with the season, vary with temper- *Cycles of* ature and moisture-range, and vary vastly with the compo- *Bloom* nents of the soil. One cannot draw accurate pictures, but must be content to suggest, outline, remind or reminisce. These suggested combinations of color ribbons for spring into summer cannot be but panoramic, lightly skimming over the great field of plant-life—nor do they pretend to be exhaustive or localized. By suggestion of quality, texture, color-blends and combinations in general, one is stirred and the imagination aroused to creative endeavor. Where specific plants or families of plants do not thrive, there can usually be found others, closely resembling, that will satisfy.

Where one cannot have Magnolias, Oleanders, and Hibiscus *Substitutes* what could be lovelier than watermelon-pink Crepe Myrtle throughout the summer into the fall? tall Altheas or lower growing Abelia? or in the belt just north of these Buddleia, Eleagnus and the Daphnes?

Summer and late spring brings in hosts of flowers that *Plant* flourish only in specific sections—many thriving only in the *peculiarities* east and north, that cannot be successfully grown in the south and west. Conversely some—especially the western plants, seldom survive removal from their preferred habitat —notably members of the Yucca* and Cacti*. On the other hand Coralberries*, Sumac* (Rhus), Daisies, Asters, Perennial Sweet Peas and Sarsaparilla vines (that bring berries for winter or foliage in autumn in addition to their flowers), seem to accommodate themselves rather readily to almost all conditions.

Climbing
Roses

Of the vines and trailing or semi-trailing plants that grace arbors or gateways and provide charming approaches to garden spots Roses have always held first place, and some of these have had that valuable quality of intermittent bloom from midspring to fall—notably the old-fashioned, soft pink "Empress of China." While the glory of spring bloom only cannot often be approached by the fall bloomers that repeat, who would be without a *Paul's Scarlet*, a *Silver Moon* or a *Mermaid* willingly? The lovely old Cherokee has as its

additional value amenability toward training as hedges, while *Thousand Beauties* will cascade down hillsides or embankments. It has been found that climbing roses or polyanthas may be grown where bush and other Roses refuse to live, which is valuable to know when planning a garden.

Clematis

In certain sections nothing replaces the rich blues and rose colorings of the Clematis (*paniculata*, etc.), while for dependability the *Convolvulacea* (among the best known being the "Heavenly Blue" and the "Scarlet O'Hara" morning glories) for spring and the Bignonias ("Trumpet Vines" in orange yellow and near-scarlet tones) from summer to fall.

Coolness

What a contrast is the dainty Trailing Lantana that hangs gracefully over a wall in a mass of cool, delicate lavender bloom so grateful in the heated season, with its cousin the sturdy, coarse Lantana of bush height! What a joy the carpet of gay Portulaca unmindful of heat, relishing full sun!

Lilies

By careful selection of varieties the Daffodils, then the Hemerocallis (Daylilies), then the true Lilies may carry the early gold coloring throughout the cycles of spring and

summer into the autumn—deepening to rich orange here
and there for variation as the seasons progress, adding to
their charm. Most attractive planted with these are those
plants that have the rose or lemon-cream tones (in spring
the Dianthus or Phlox *drummondii*), the blues and lavenders
or violets (as the Plumbago in summer), and against the
orange colorings of fall the contrasting pale tones are again
satisfying, or perhaps the rich deep purple of *Salvia leucantha**, the Mexican or Spanish sage, the lavender hues of
Physostegia ("False dragonhead"), or fringed Petunias.
Among the indispensables of any garden are the Petunias
and Verbenas, that often survive mild winters and come
into bloom quite early, sometimes accompanying the Larkspur and Poppies of mid-spring, or Cornflowers and Campanulas (Canterbury bells) or Digitalis (Foxglove) of late
spring—Marguerites, Delphinium, the brilliant "Standing"
or "Tree-Cypress" (*Gilia rubra*)*, and the Gladioli.

Summer follows quickly the passing of the loveliest of the *Summer*
Lilies—the stately Regale. The yellow and bronze flowers of
the Calliopsis* supersede the Coreopsis, in turn to give way
later to the Klondike Cosmos. The coarser, hardier plants
in general seem to be those that brave the heated season—
Zinnias, Daisies, Cannas, Sunflowers* (Helianthemums of
many types and kinds), Scabiosa, Sweet William, Lantana—
that usher in the Ageratum, Marigolds, 'mums and Dahlias
of fall bloom.

Early fall is glorified by the renewed burst of life in *Fall*
numbers of plants—notably the Roses and those of the annuals that have been cut back after the spring flowering
season. Of the climbing plants what could be more beautiful
than festoons of "Queen's Wreath" (*Antignon*—Coral vine),
a tender importation from Mexico, like rose lace patterns
against the blue skies!
The ribbon of color through the heated season seems to
grow more and more intense as though building up to the
climax of that final burst of glory—Autumn. Velvety Sal-

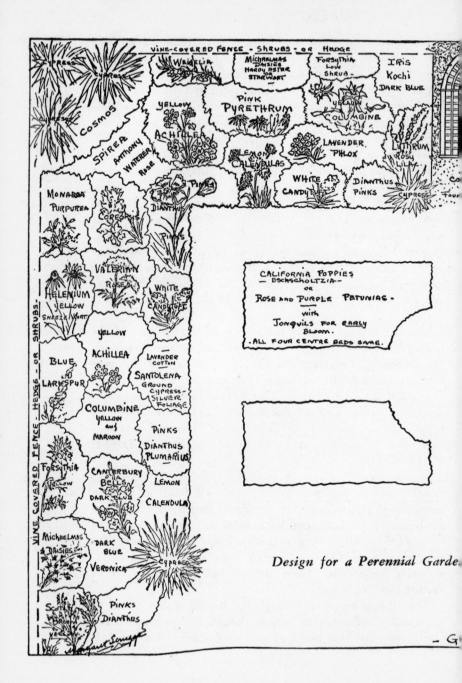

Design for a Perennial Garden

— G

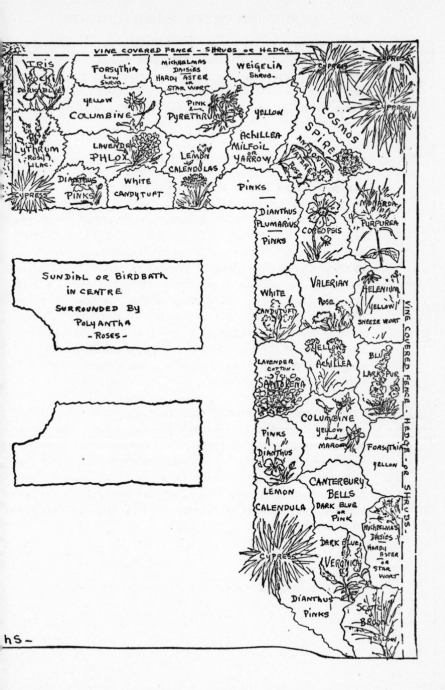

phiglosis cups among a mist of Michaelmas daisies, Heleniums bordered by Sweet Alyssum (that blooms again if cut in the spring), tall lavender to purple spikes of Liatris ("Blazing Star") rising well above the dainty Monarda and the flat (rose, white or yellow) heads of Yarrow (Achillea)—what could be more enchanting!

Winter

As autumn grows to a close and the first flurries of snow begin to prepare the garden for its rest period, evergreens (such as the Cedars, Yews, Pines, Firs, Junipers, and the Broad-leafed Evergreens) provide a rich foil for the scarlet or orange berries of Holly, Yaupon*, or Agarita*, Barberries, Nandinas, Hawthorns, Elders, Pyracanthas, Coralberries* and many others, upon which the birds delight to feast. Some of these shrubs that are berry-bearing as well as some that are not have the additional desirable quality of stem or leaf-coloring throughout the winter, such as the Red Osier and others of the *Salix* family, Rhamnus "Buckthorn," *Robinia viscosa*—just to mention a few—that are so brilliant one does not miss the blossoms of spring, summer and fall, but enjoys the winter garden equally as much in its place in the seasonal cycle of bloom.

Seasons in Persian Rugs

Of man's handiwork Persian rugs, perhaps, most closely resemble the wealth of Nature's bloom cycles in their choice of colorings, for their weavers live so close to Nature and for untold generations their traditional patterns indubitably have been founded on that which Nature exhibits. Shall we liken Kermanshahs to spring, Kurdistans and Bockaras to summer, the wild rich Kazaks to autumn and the rare old Bergamas to winter?

GARDENS OF PERENNIALS

It would be difficult to design a garden that would apply to the various separate sections of the temperate zone. The pictured "Design for a Perennial Garden" shows plants that flourish under moderate conditions. Nearer the semi-tropics other plants would have to be substituted, likely (plants that thrive there), while in the mountain regions and further north the same type of garden could be created with yet another group of totally different plants, selected because they have definite preferences.

Those living in the cooler sections will notice the absence (in the pictured garden) of Hostia (Plantains), Bleeding Hearts, Mallows, various Phlox varieties, the stately Delphinium, Hollyhocks, the Oriental Poppy and others considered indispensable to their gardens.

In the far South, however, practically all those pictured will grow, with perhaps the exception of Geraniums and Hibiscus of their dependables and Petunias, Verbenas, Plumbago and Snapdragons that rank with them as perennials rather than annuals.

In the semi-tropics it is interesting to note that where one finds the same plants often as are found further north, the chief difference lies in the time of planting (almost all done in September) and in the very different time of coming into bloom, as well as the duration of the bloom season.

Hosts of Gay Flowering Plants

PERENNIALS

No GARDEN, be it ever so small, is complete without its hardy border, its beds of perennials and annuals.

*Value of
Perennials
in Gardens*

Perennial plants are most satisfactory, for they start growth with the earliest hint of spring and from the time the first flowers come in March and April, there is a succession of bloom until late Fall. The garden-lover looks forward to these recurring seasons as joyously as the visit of an old friend is anticipated.

Every garden, of course, needs a definite design and a green background, either a vine-covered wall, or shrubs, mostly evergreens with a few flowering shrubs interspersed here and there for color. This placed, one can begin with the planting of perennials. And what a fascinating occupation, for keep in mind that a series of pictures are to be created, the scheme of each season blending into the next as the cycle advances.

*Key to
Choice of
Perennials*

Therefore, choose plants with regard to height, color and season of bloom, placing them in uneven groups of three or fives. By all means avoid straight lines. Could anything, for instance, be lovelier than a mass grouping of lavender Phlox and tall yellow Snapdragons with clumps of orange California Poppies, and Pinks in front of them, serving as a low border to complete the picture? *Monarda purpurea* supplies an excellent lavender to bloom with the rose Loosestrife (*Lythrum roseum*). These two plants do well and bloom during the hot days of late June and July.

*For
Continuous
Bloom*

To have continuous bloom, place a grouping of summer or late fall-blooming plants in between or in back of spring-blooming ones, so as the one is finished, the others will follow. This succession of bloom creates a bright and changing pageant.

Whether the herbaceous border has or has not a background of shrubs, place those tall-growing plants (such as Hollyhocks, hardy Asters, Helenium, Goldenglow, Helianthus and Larkspur) in the back of the bed; the medium-height plants, of course, in the center; and, as a border, the low-growing or edging plants of different colors, selecting those that will give a continuance of bloom. *Tall Growing Perennials*

Do not make the mistake of planting your perennials too close to each other, for they must be left undisturbed for at least four years to acquire their full beauty, and need room to develop into large clumps. (A good rule to follow is from one to two feet apart, according to height.) For this reason, and the most important one in planting perennials as well as annuals, prepare the beds thoroughly (according to the articles on soil and propagation). *Correct Spacing and Planting*

Even in a moderately mild climate almost all perennials or annuals can be grown if the beds are properly prepared, the soil enriched with the proper plantfood, and the plants (Delphinium, Peonies, Phlox, Columbine, etc.) placed in a location (such as the east side of the house, garage or in front of a tall hedge) where they may be shielded, especially from the burning afternoon sun. Good drainage is also very essential.

Every fall and every spring put a mixture of bonemeal, dried sheep manure and wood-ashes around perennials; lightly cultivate this in with a small hand-trowel, and then water thoroughly.

Do not make the mistake of watering all plants every day, and never just sprinkle; but water *thoroughly*, letting the water soak down to the roots about twice a week in very dry weather. This causes the roots to go down and not to come to the top to be baked by the hot sun. Twice a week, *soaked thoroughly*, is enough and then *only* if they need it. *Amount of Water Required*

Most perennials are propagated by root division (Peony, Phlox, Delphinium, Daisies, Hardy Asters, Salvias, Achilleas, *Propagation by Division*

Chrysanthemums and others). A few, some Pinks and all Carnations, are better "layered." This is done by covering the woody stalk with dirt. Shortly it takes root, and then can be planted to itself. Those that can be propagated by seed are listed in the catalogues. (See p. 132.)

Time to Plant or Transplant Perennials

Always transplant or plant perennials in the fall, preferably about the end of October. If transplanted in the spring they do not get the proper root growth necessary to take them throughout the long hot summers. For this reason many perennials have not been grown successfully that would have thrived had they been planted in the fall. If seeds of perennials are started in August, in a partly shaded bed or cold frame, kept moist, they will be large enough by the end of October to transplant to their permanent place in the border. Thus they will become rooted enough before cold weather to withstand the winter, and form large clumps by spring, blooming most of the summer.

Early Flowering

In early Spring, as you go down the flagstone path, with what eager eyes you look over your beds to see the clumps of Peonies, Pyrethrum, Columbine, *Cheiranthus allionii, Glaucium* (the Horned Poppy), Anchusa, *Campanula* (Bellflower), *Trachelium, Adenophora* (Ladybell), *Physostegia virginiana* (the early blooming Dragonhead), *Cammassias, Valerian officinalis rubra*, Pinks, Coreopsis, *Baptisia australis, Thermopsis montana, Helenium Hoopesii*, early Daisies and others springing up between the clumps of Tulips (giving them a soft carpet, as it were). Just about three weeks later all these perennials are a *mass* of bloom, forming a wonderful picture, together with huge clumps of Iris.

Each day one exclaims, "Could anything be lovelier?" but as the days pass on and the later perennials burst into bloom, it is hard to decide which picture is really the loveliest.

May and June bring forth more bloom, a miracle of beauty and color—*Achillea filipendulina, Achillea millifolium, Monarda didyma, Monarda purpurea, Lythrum roseum* with its spikes of rose pink flowers, Hemerocallis (the double and single Daylilies) send their tall spikes of bloom well above the purple *Phlox*.

This pageant lasts well into July, only to be replaced by *Salvia leucantha*, *Salvia farinaceae*, and *Salvia azurea* with their tall spikes of velvety-orchid and sky-blue that harmonize so beautifully with the *Helenium autumnale* and Riverton Gem. The stately Goldenglow, with its bright yellow clusters of flowers, is a background for *Physostegia virginiana*. On into September and October, with clumps of Ageratum, annual Klondike Cosmos, and Michaelmas Daisies. As we reach late October and November, the garden retires in a blaze of glory supplied by the wonderful Chrysanthemums in rose-pinks and crimsons, yellows and bronzes!

Summer and Fall Flowering Perennials

Skillful planning will enable you to use the same ground several times so that places occupied by Tulips or any spring bulbs may be a blaze of color in the late summer or fall with lovely annuals, for the root-systems of most annuals do not disturb or interfere with the bulbs or perennials dormant below them.

Plan Planting

Surely there are rich rewards in a perennial garden and much quiet joy!

Perennials

HARDY HERBACEOUS PLANTS

Plant	Color	Height	Time of Blooming	Remarks
*ACHILLEA—EUPATORIUM.. filipendulina (Yarrow)	Yellow	3 to 4 ft.	End of May and June	Showy perennial; valuable for cut flowers; should be cut back after flowering. Needs full sun.
*ACHILLEA — Millefolium.. (Yarrow)	Rose	3 to 4 ft.	End of May and June	Showy; valuable for cut flowers; should be cut back after flowering. Full sun; spreads rapidly.
ADENOPHORA—Ladybell... (Potanini)	Blue Purple	3 ft.	End of May and thru summer	Resembles Campanula; increases rapidly.
ANCHUSA—Alkanet....... (Dropmore) azurea	Blue	4 ft.	Early summer	Tall spikes of sky blue flowers.
ANCHUSA Myosotidiflora	Blue	12 in.	Early spring	Dwarf perennial; clusters of blue flowers resembling forget-me-nots
†ANEMONE.............. japonica—Windflower	Mixed Colors	2 to 3 ft.	Fall	Do better in partial shade. No afternoon sun; well drained location. Tender.
ANTHEMIS.............. tinctoria	Yellow	1 to 2 ft.	June and July	Succeeds in poorest soil; finely cut foliage; large yellow daisy flowers on tall stems.
†AQUILEGIA—Columbine..	Various Colors	3 ft.	May and June	Partial shade; prefers oaks and cedars; ordinary good garden soil; add a little peat moss, oak leaves or leaf-mold; prefers acid yet rich soil.
*ASCLEPIAS—tuberosa..... Butterfly Weed	Orange	1½ to 2 ft.	July	Sandy soil, full sun. Do not disturb after once planted.
ASTERS—Michaelmas Daisy	Various Colors	3 to 5 ft.	Fall	Any good soil; full sun.
*BAPTISIA — australis...... False-Indigo	Dark Blue	3 ft.	May	Lupine-like flowers; rich soil; sunny location.
BOLTONIA—asteroides...	Pinkish White		Aug. and Sept.	Aster-like; blooms in profusion.
CAMPANULA—Medium.... Canterbury Bells	Various Colors	3 to 4 ft.	May	Semi-shade; requires protection, as do delphinum.
CARNATION ALLWOODII...	Various Colors	2 to 3 ft.	May and June	Half Carnation and half Pink.
CENTAUREA.............. montana	Violet Blue	2 ft.	June to Sept.	Good cut flower.
CHEIRANTHUS—(Siberian Wallflower—Allionii)	Orange	1 to 2 ft.	April, May and June	Similar to Wallflowers; splendid border plant; good drainage.
CHRYSANTHEMUMS........	Various Colors	2 to 3 ft.	Fall	Culture given in article by Mrs. Marcus.
CHRYSANTHEMUM— (MAXIMUM) (Shasta Daisy)	White	2 to 3 ft.	Summer	Deep rich soil; sunny position; divide alternate years.
COREOPSIS............. (Tickseed)	Yellow	2 to 3 ft.	End of May and June	Sunny position; well drained soil.
DIANTHUS—Pinks......	Various Colors	2 ft.	May and June	Sunny position; well drained soil.
†DELPHINIUM.......... (Larkspur)	Blue	3 to 4 ft.	May and June	Very rich soil; specially prepared; likes lime; no afternoon sun; semi shade.
†DIGITALIS............. (Foxglove)	Rose and White	4 to 6 ft.	May	Biennial; neutral soil; prefers protection from afternoon sun; east exposure.
*EUPATORIUM............ Hardy Ageratum	Bluish Lavender	2 ft.	August and September	Any ordinary soil.
†GERBERA..............	Mixture	2 ft.	May	Full sun; prefers moist, peaty soil; needs protection in winter.
‡GAZANIA..............	White, Yellow Orange	1 ft.	April	Borderplant; sunny position.
GYPSOPHILA............ (Baby's Breath)	White	2 to 3 ft.	Summer	Any well drained soil; prefers lime and sunny position.
HELENIUM.............	Yellow	3 to 4 ft.	Aug. and Sept.	Any ordinary soil; full sun.
*HELIANTHUS........... multiflorus	Yellow	3 ft.	July	Any ordinary rich soil; full sun.
HELIOPSIS.............	Yellow	2 to 3 ft.	July	Any ordinary rich soil, full sun.
HEMEROCALLIS.......... (Day Lilies)	Yellow and Orange	3 ft.	May, June and July	Spreads rapidly; full sun or shade.
HIBISCUS.............	White, Pink and Red	3 to 4 ft.	All summer	Full sun; forms large clumps.
HOLLYHOCKS............	Various	4 to 6 ft.	Spring	Full sun.
HYDRANGEA............	Various	4 to 6 ft.	Spring	Semi-shade.
HYPERICUM—St. John's Wort..............	Yellow	2 to 3 ft.	June and July	Semi-shade.

†Requires special care.   *Native.   ‡Grown extensively in El Paso.

Perennials

HARDY HERBACEOUS PLANTS—*Continued*

Plant	Color	Height	Time of Blooming	Remarks
LATHYRUS............ Perennial Sweet Peas	Pink and Rose	Trailing Plants	All summer	Any ordinary soil.
*LIATRIS........ .... Gay Flower	Rose and Purple	3 ft.	July	Sunny location; grassy linear leaves; ordinary soil; spikes of rosy-lavender flowers.
LYTHRUM ROSEUM... .... Loosestripe	Rose	3 to 4 ft.	June and July	Does well in any good rich soil; in any location. Forms huge clumps, so allow plenty of room; tall spikes of rose flowers.
MATRICARIA.... .... Feverfew	White	2 ft.	June	Rather low growing for border.
*MONARDA—Bee-Balm.... didyma rosea	Rose-red	4 to 5 ft.	June and July	Forms big clumps; any good garden soil; sun or partial shade.
MONARDA.. .... purpurea	Lavender	4 to 5 ft.	June and July	Forms big clumps; any good garden soil; sun or partial shade.
*OENOTHERA.......... .. (Evening Primrose)	Yellow	2 to 3 ft.	June to September	Sunny, rich soil, though will grow on limestone, rocky hills.
PEONIES..............·.....	Various	3 ft.	May	Shade from afternoon sun; rich soil. Do not plant too deep.
PENTSTEMON............ Any variety	Bluish Lavender & Scarlet	2 to 3 ft.	May and June	Foxglove-like in shape; any good garden soil; full sun.
PINKS.................	Mixed	1½ ft.	May	Easily grown; full sun.
PINKS (Dianthus).........	Mixed	1½ ft.	May	Easily grown; full sun.
*PHLOX—Hardy	Various Shades	2 to 3 ft.	June and July	Very rich soil; do not cultivate too close to plant; water freely; shade from afternoon sun.
PHYGELIUS CAPINSIS....... Cape Fuchia	Scarlet	2 to 3 ft.	June	Pentstemon-like flowers on tall stems; sunny location matures; hot, dry weather.
*PHYSOSTEGIA............ virginiana	Pinkish-Lavender	3 to 4 ft.	August	Sunny location; tall spikes.
PLATYCODON—Balloon flower (graniflora)	Blue	3 to 4 ft.	July and August	Well-drained location; leave in same location indefinitely.
PYRETHRUM............	Mixed	2 to 3 ft.	May and June	Any location; rich soil; plenty of water in dry weather.
RUDBECKIA—hortensia... (Goldenglow)	Yellow	5 to 6 ft.	Aug. and Sept.	Free flowering; sunny location; excellent cut flowers.
*RUDBECKIA—Coneflower. (purpurea)	Purple	3 ft.	July	Purple coneflower.
*SALVIA................. 1. azurea............. 2. farinacea.......... 3. Pitcheri 4. leucantha	Blue Blue Blue Blue Orchid	3 to 4 ft. 3 to 4 ft. 3 to 4 ft. 3 to 4 ft. 4 to 5 ft.	Aug. and Sept.	Sunny location.
SANTOLINA............ (Lavender Cotton)	Yellow	8 to 12 in.	May	Sunny location.
†SCABIOSA..............	Mixed	2 to 3 ft.	June and July	Well drained; sunny location; good rich soil.
SEDUM.................	Mixed	1 to 2 ft.	Aug. and Sept.	Sunny location; well-drained soil.
STATICE................	Purplish Blue	1½ ft.	June and July	Sandy loam; sunny location.
STOKESIA............... cyanea	Blue	18 in.	July and August	Well drained; sunny location; sandy loam; put ashes around crown in winter.
SWEET WILLIAM.........	Mixed	14 in.	April	Free flowering; sun or semi shade.
THERMOPSIS............. caroliniana	Yellow.......	2 to 3 ft.	End of May	Lupine-like plant.
VALERIANA............ officinalis rubra	Rose	2 to 3 ft.	May and most all summer. If faded flowers in September, cut off.	Dry summer border; prefers limy soil.
VERONICA.............	Blue	2 to 3 ft.	May and June most all summer.	Good ordinary soil

†Requires Special Care.   *Native.

PERENNIALS GROWN IN NEW MEXICO

Achillea	Platycodon	*Artemesia
Ageratum	Statice	*Gaillardia
Anthemis	Shaster Daisy	*Physostegia
Campanula persicifolia	Valerian	*Phlox
Petunias	Veronica	*Verbena

This information was furnished by Professor Adlai Feather of State College, Mesilla Valley, New Mexico.

PERENNIALS—BIENNIALS

*Achillea (Yarrow)—Many uses have been found for this feathery-leaved plant, whose brilliant pink, rose, orange, yellow or white flat-topped flower-heads are so attractive and ornamental. As an herb it was used by the mighty Achilles at the siege of Troy, and since then medicine has found a number of uses for its leaves, stems and blossoms. It prefers a moderately moist, rich soil and a sunny position.

*Ageratum (*Eupatorium*)—The fluffy blue and rose-lavender flower-heads of this easily grown, fall-blooming plant much prized both for its range of shades of blue and for its varying heights—dwarf, medium and tall varieties being available. *A . . lasseauxii*, introduced from South America, has handsome vivid rose-colored flowers. All varieties may be grown from seed quite easily, sown out of doors in spring.

*Amsonia—The lovely terminal spikes of plumbago-blue that rise from this rather shrub-like bush in March and April make the "Blue Texas Star" a valued addition to the garden, for it will grow in any good soil and requires only a moderate amount of moisture. The four native varieties, named for Amson the noted American physician, have each adapted themselves to the exacting soil requirements of the four principal types of soil—acid, lime, neutral and adobe.

Artemesia—See page 52. DUSTY MILLER, WORMWOOD, SAGE BRUSH, TARRAGON.

*Asclepias (Butterfly Bush)—The rough, hairy, leafy stems of this most beautiful milkweed spring erect from a deep, tuberous root and bear at their summit umbels of brilliant orange-scarlet flowers in May. Named for the Greek God of Medicine, its various medicinal qualities have long been recognized. Swaying in the sun this handsome plant is most attractive to butterflies, its waxy mass of pollen being greatly relished by them.

*Asters—Delicate and dainty-looking as these fall-blooming, amethyst, golden, blues of many hues and white appear, they are quite sturdy and hardy. Many varieties and heights are native in Texas, and have found their way to the gardens of the world, generally known as Michaelmas daisies.

*Baptisia (False Indigo)—Indigo-blue flowers in long racemes spring above delicate bluish-green bushy foliage, borne on milky, grey-green stems in magnificent, lupine like clusters, in May. *B . . australis* (blue) and *B . . tinctoria* (bright yellow) are better known than is *B . . leucophaea* (cream-colored). All are native to Texas and all yield dye, the roots being also valued medicinally. The plant grows much taller after the blooms die.

*Boltonia (False Chamomile)—Large, single, aster-like flowers

borne at the tip of long, daisy-like stems are a mass of blossoms
in the fall. *B . . asteroides* is pure white, while *B . . latisquama*
is pink tinged lavender and has a dwarf variety . . *nana. Boltonia* is tall-growing, generally.

*Callirhoe (Poppy Mallow)—Fringed, rosy-crimson or wine-
colored, poppy-like flowers borne on long, slender stems rising
from the axils of dark green, finely divided foliage—produced all
summer and fall—give this semi-trailing perennial a unique place
in the garden scheme. It grows widespread on the hills, throughout Texas and is the subject of legend the world over.

Datura—(See page 118.)

*Eryngium (Sea Holly)—The deep purple, ornamental, spiny
bracts that tip the thistle-like cone-shaped flower-heads of this
plant—with its thin, deep-cleft foliage and stems covered with
hair-like, needle-sharp spines makes this fall-blooming plant both
unusual and attractive. Cut at the right time, it may be dried
and is much used in winter bouquets.

*Euphorbia—These plants of very diverse habits and appearance
are mostly hardy, thriving in the open, and, in Texas, weed-like
in their profusion in their native habitats. *E . . marginata*
(Snow-on-the-mountain) is annual, but *E . . heterophylla*
(Poinsettia, Christmas Flower, or Painted Leaf) is a gorgeous
shrub in the Rio Grande Valley, and *E . . corollata* is a most attractive perennial, with showy white appendages, preferring light
soil and fairly dry situations. Euphorbias are all milky or juicy
and are cultivated for their curious shapes, ornamental foliage
or unusual characteristics.

*Evening Primrose Family (*Oenothera*)—This large family boasts
many types, heights, habits of growth, and shades of yellow,
rose-pink and white flowers of varying size, poppy-like in shape
and quality of petal, usually. Texas has most of these varieties
in greatest profusion. Best known in the garden, perhaps, are
O . . missouriensis (large yellow flowers on semi-trailing plants,
becoming most attractive seed-pods). *O . . Hartmannia
speciosa* (large fragrant white flowers with small foliage; excellent for massing—variety . . *rosea* having rose-pink blossoms);
O . . caepitosa (dwarf variety with pink or white blossoms,
crinkly-petalled *O . . fraseri* (dwarf with yellow flowers) and
O . . fruticosa (tallest, perhaps, and of stocky form bearing
bright lemon-yellow flowers).

*Gaillardia (Indian Blanket) (Firewheel)—These bright yellow
and red perennials, biennials and annuals grow readily and are
hardy quite far north. Of the many native Texas varieties there
are those that have become suited to all climatic and soil diversi-
ties. *G . . grandiflora* of commerce is the *G . . pulchella*, whose
dwarf var. is called "Goblin," and the var. in which the yellow

predominates is known as *G . . sulphurea oculata* ("Mr. Sher-
brock"). *G . . picta* and *G . . aristata* (annuals) are distinguished for their deep red centers. *G . . chrysantha* (bright
yellow) prefers semi-acid sand as does also *G . . lanceolata* (red
tipped petals). There are many combinations in the petals,
varying from all-yellow, yellow-tipped on red (vice versa)
bright red, carmine to deep fire-reds or maroons and many so-
called hybrids that have been developed from the original plants,
valued additions to the garden from early summer until frost.

*Liatris (Blazing Star) (Gay Feather)—These tall, erect, showy
herbs produce long racemes of flowers on wand-like spikes—in
shades of lavender, purple, bright rose-red or white. *L . .
pycnostachya* (rose-purple), *L . . spicata* (purple), *L . .
scariosa* (deep purple), *L . . punctata* (lavender)—in fall, and
may be dried for winter bouquets. They vary in height from
dwarf (8 in.) to more than three feet, being determined both
by type and situation, responding to rich soil and moisture if
given in moderation. These plants are native to the South and
Southwest.

*Lobelia (Cardinal Flower)—This exquisite, intensely red flower
has wide distribution. Its massive flower-spikes are set with
glossy, cardinal-red blossoms. It has long been in cultivation,
requiring a great deal of moisture and peaty, or acid soil and
preferring half-shady places. *L . . syphilitica* differs from *L . .
cardinalis* (red) in the vivid blue hue of its flower-spikes and
has a var. . . *alba* that bears white flowers.

Monarda (Fragrant Balm)—*M . . didyma*—named for the Spanish writer on medicinal plants, Nicholas Monardez, this showy
plant of the horsemint family produces a profusion of pale rose-
lavender, rose-purple, maroon, scarlet, and deep purple flowers,
very striking in mass-effects. Prefers dry, sunny well-drained
position. Called also Bergamot or Oswego Tea.

*Penstemon (Beard Tongue)—The glossy leaves and pastel shades
of rose-lavender to white tinged with purple found in the native
P . . cobaea contrast with the scarlet of *P . . torreyi*, the
blue, lilac or white of *P . . angustifolius,* the bright blue to
purplish of *P . . glaber* all native to the dry hills of the Southwest. A number of hybrids have been developed from these, all
lovely variations of the canterbury bell-like spikes of the native
var.

*Phlox—The Phlox family boasts annual and perennial varieties.
Among the daintiest of the perennials, preferring rich loamy
semi-acid soil and partial shade is the *P . . pilosa,* whose nar-
row leaves and habit of growth as well as preferences is similar to
P . . divaricata (fragrant, deep-blue or pinkish-blue flowers).
P . . . subulata (Moss Pink) is almost a ground-cover growing

tufted and matted and bearing a profusion of light blue, lavender, pink or white flowers on very slender stems and almost covering the fine, light-green foliage. *P . . drummondi,* the annual
Phlox, has many shades from brilliant scarlet to rose to white
and shades of cream and yellow. It is indispensable in the garden
for early spring bloom, and is followed by the many varieties of
Hardy Phlox (perennial) whose handsome massed flower-heads
give splashes of color for many weeks.

*Physostegia (False Dragonhead)—On upright, wand-like tall
stalks the lavender, purple, rose or white flowers appear like a
succession of graduated, wee bells ranging to an abrupt point or
peak. The leaves are long, narrow, toothed and the lower ones
tinged purple. *P . . virginiana* (and its hybrids) is much better
known than *P . . denticulata,* a lower, more slender plant. Both
are native to the temperate zone. *P . . virginiana* var. *speciosa*
is the tall form, while var. *alba* is the white-flowered and *P . .
gigantea,* the giant form with deep rose (tinged lavender) flower-
spikes.

Poppies—See p. 93.

*Queen Anne's Lace—There are two plants called this name, both
native. Chervil (*Chaerophyllum*) sweet-scented herb, biennial,
(though sometimes perennial or annual) has a flowerhead of
white, many-rayed umbel-formed florets; both lvs. and fls. are
lacy in appearance. Slender, erect stems. Tuberous roots, carrot-
like, though grey or blackish-color. Edible. The *Daucus* differs in
that its flowerhead is borne on a sturdier stalk, not branching;
and the seeds have hooks that attach themselves to clothing.
Some var. have blood-red or violet colored roots. Both plants
are very ornamental, *Daucus* being much coarser in texture; may
readily be grown from seed.

Ruellia—Slender stemmed herbs, bearing lovely blue, bell-like
flower-cups resembling petunias prefer semi-shade. *R . . pe-
dunculata* (Bluebell)* is deep rich blue. *R . . drummondiana,**
bluish-purple with white markings (sometimes all white). *R . .
occidentalis* (Wild Petunia)* all grow from seed or cuttings.
R . . Harveyana—native to Mexico and the Texas border, has
violet or lilac flowers. *R . . amoena* from South America, has
bright red fls. as does also *R . . formosa* (scarlet) though it is
tender. All prefer rich soil.

Salvia (Sage)—(See pages 53; 115.)

*Texas Plume (*Gilia rubra*) (Tree cypress)—This brilliant, showy
plant deeply resents domestication. Named for Philip Gil, the
Spanish botanist, it is by some termed a bi-ennial, but often
blooms the first year grown from seed. It is sold under the name
of *Gilia coronopifolia* by some. Its glorious scarlet flowers dotted
with yellow are borne at the tip of tall, swaying stalks bristling

with myriads of needle-like leaves. Plant seed in early fall where the plants are to grow. Difficult to move plants.

*Tradescantia** (Spider Wort)—Named for John Tradescant, gardener for Charles I of England. This plant likes partial shade and rich loam though will grow in poor soil if watered. Its violet-blue, rosy-lavender and deep blue three-petaled flower-heads in roseates are most attractive among the long, lance-like leaves. It grows very rank in Texas, and wherever enriching, moist conditions exist.

*Yucca**—There are many kinds of Yucca (Spanish Dagger, etc., see page 37). Although perhaps the most generally grown varieties are the *Yucca treculeana,* whose sword-like leaves and showy white flower-heads rise to tree-like form; *Y . . filamentosa* (Adam's Needles) whose leaves are narrow and flower-stalks of cream-white bells loose and lovely; Red Yucca (*Hesperaloe parviflora*) whose very long, curving, graceful stalks (red at the ends) bear most of the summer into the fall; bell-like coral-red flowers (a var. having purple flowers is native to New Mexico); and the Dasylirions (Sotol) the var. *D . . texanum* being commonly called the "Sotol" and *D . . wheeleri,* the "Spoon Cactus."

SEMI-TROPICAL

The word "perennial" has more than the usual meaning for the gardener in the semi-tropics, some being treated like shrubs, that require timely pruning, etc.; others like annuals planted in the fall to enjoy the blossoms in late winter or early spring; some blossom almost continuously, renewing themselves (such as Periwinkle, Tithonia, annual Zinnias, etc.); others grow gigantic when there are frequent rains or exceptionally mild seasons (Tithonia, Cosmos, Ageratum, etc., requiring support!). Those that renew themselves many times are not as fine quality as those that are secured from seed or plants from the north; but as the parent plant finishes its cycle of life it is gratifying to have tiny plants springing up to replace it.

DROUGHT-RESISTANT PLANTS

Among the native plants that thrive and are generally drought-resistant are:

Ageratum—6 inches to 4 ft., blooms all year. Blue flower-cluster-heads.

Bluebell (Gentian) "Swamp Lily"—Poppy-like heavenly-blue cups that appear in April to June, following heavy rains, otherwise only in the low lands or swamps.

Coreopsis—6–24 inches. Yellow daisy-like flowers. When no freeze blooms all winter until late summer.

Gaillardia—6–24 inches. The outstanding plant. Brown, orange and yellow flowers.

Primrose "Cowslip," or "Buttercup"—3–12 inches. Pink cups blooming in February to May.

Poppy "Mexican Poppy"—(*Argemone*) "Thistle Poppy"—White, pink, yellow, dark red or wine (no scarlet). 1–4 ft. December through April.

Salvia—6–24 inches. November to May. Shades of blue and red.

Verbena—3–10 inches. Shades of pink-lavender to blue-lavender, not deep purple.

Among the commonly grown cultivated plants are:

African Daisy—1–2 ft. Very hardy. Lavender flowers.

Begonia—6–12 inches. All colors. Blooms all year.

Carnations (Dianthus) (Pinks)—1–2 ft. All shades. Bloom all year.

Chrysanthemums—All shades. November to March if no freeze.

Cosmos—Yellow, pink, orange (not deep). 2–5 ft.

Daisies—Including Shastas. April–June.

Geranium—All shades. Require good drainage, sun and grow 1–4 ft.

Hollyhock—3–4 ft. Blooms all year. Single pink or red most used.

Periwinkle (*Vinca*)—Excellent for dry locations. Deep pink, white.

Peppers—Various ornamental peppers, nearly every variety.

Perennial Phlox—2–3 ft. Lavender-pink flowers.

Poppies—There are a number of plants called poppies that are of very different families. Among those grown are:

"Prickly Poppy," or "Mexican Poppy" . . . . *Argemone*

"Horned," or "Sea Poppy" . . . . *Glaucium flavum*

"Plume Poppy" . . . . *Bocconia*, or "*Tree celandine*"

"Oriental Poppy" . . . . *Papaver orientale*

"Tulip Poppy" .... *Papaver glaucum*
"Water Poppy" .... *Hydrocleis nymphoides*
"California Poppy" .... *Eschscholtzia*
"Shirley Poppy" .... *Papaver rhoeas*
*"Primrose Poppy" .... *Oenothera*
"Mexican Tulip Poppy" .... *Hunnemannia*

Sea Lavender (*Statice latifolia*)—6–18 inches. Orchid variety only, 2 ft.

Snapdragon (*Antirrhinum*)—All shades. Bloom February to May.

Sweet William—Blooms all year. 6–24 inches.

Tithonia—Blooms all year. 3–8 ft.

Violets—Late winter to May.

Yellow Golden Glow—4–6 ft. July to September.

DELPHINIUM

Delphinium, although most temperamental, can be grown even in extreme climates. In the Southwest some find that they are best treated as annuals, planted each fall, in extremely rich soil as they are gross feeders. As experience has proved that either cow or sheep manure, if placed close to this plant, causes root-rot to develop, it is recommended that bonemeal be used.

Dig the soil about eighteen inches deep and spade under sand, peatmoss, and tobacco dust. Then put in the plants. Do not plant too deep. Do not cover the crowns.

Every spring and fall scatter a handful of lime around each plant, and a week or so later a handful of bonemeal with some superphosphate. Coal-ashes put around the crowns in the fall will help protect the plants during the winter.

Water thoroughly twice a week during summer. When summer heat comes, mulch the bed. Delphinium thus cared for often may be had most successfully.

CHRYSANTHEMUMS

To know the history of the origin of the Chrysanthemum *Origin* is not at all necessary to its successful production. But, rich with age and legend, it holds a certain fascination, and stimulates the desire for a more intimate knowledge of a flower that survives, not only because of its history, but because of its beauty and charm.

The Chrysanthemum originated in China, being mentioned *Japan's National Emblem* as early as the time of Confucius (in his *Li-Ki*) and it was developed to its present state of beauty by both Chinese and Japanese florists. Japan even adopted this flower as its national floral emblem. It was introduced into Europe about 1790, being sent to England by Mr. Cels, a French gardener.

At the time that the first Chrysanthemums were being *Classification and Name* shown in Europe, the botanists had difficulty classifying this new bloom. Some said it belonged to the Anthemis family, while others contended it was surely of a Pyrethrum genus. Finally it was agreed to call it "Chrysanthemum" from *Chrysos* meaning golden and *Anthos* meaning flower. Well named, it is, too, for of all flowers can you think of a more cheerful one than this "Queen of Autumn"?

The pompon variety, one of the hardiest types, has sprung *Early Introduction Into Europe and America* from the blending of two small flowering varieties of the "Chusan Daisy", introduced by Mr. Fortune in 1846. The French gave them the name Pompon because the pompon on the soldier's cap resembled the flower so closely. To Peter Henderson goes the distinction of introducing the Japanese varieties into America, others following him in rapid succession.

The types, varieties and colors have increased immeasur- *Many Types Have been Evolved* ably, and success in their cultivation has become so certain that choice of variety becomes really a matter of one's taste. It is wise, however, to remember that for exhibition purposes, of the three varieties—Early, Early Mid-season and Late—use only Early or Mid-season varieties for outside planting. For garden varieties, this rule does not apply, for any variety selected may be used there.

It is most important to use nothing but the healthiest plants, as there are so many things to guard against, i.e., over-forced, side shoot plants, over-fed, midge-infected and stem-rot. So the first recommendation is to be sure of your stock.

As to soil, regardless of the location (acid soil, limestone soil or semi-acid soil) the Chrysanthemum will do well *if* the soil is properly prepared *before* planting. 'Mums are *gross feeders* and must have fertile soil. The roots, too, are near the surface, hence require generous watering, but good drainage. Soil should be fairly heavy rather than too sandy, equally composed of two parts of black dirt (or topsoil), one part well-rotted cow fertilizer, one part sandy-clay loam, thoroughly blended. Where possible, beds should be raised six

inches above grade to allow for drainage, as this helps to keep the ground from becoming sour. If one has very poor soil to deal with, just dig a little deeper so that your carefully prepared rich soil will be available in greater abundance to nourish these greedy feeders. In planting, it is advisable to have them twelve inches apart in each row and the rows at least twelve inches apart or more if possible, as 'Mums need good air circulation on all sides. The time to plant 'Mums is spring. Lift clumps, pull apart, and replant—discarding the woody center.

Adequate means of support are necessary, any number of ways being available, such as wire (or frame) stakes, bamboo rods, etc., placed when the time arrives when support is required.

Liquid fertilizer, made from fresh cow manure, is applied (see p. 19) every ten days *until* the color begins to show (beginning only after the plants have attained *twice* their original height at time of planting). In using liquid fertilizer, first water the plants thoroughly, wetting all the foliage, and soak again immediately after fertilizing. If this plan of watering before and after is not followed, the liquid fertilizer is apt to burn the roots and foliage. For a single, intensive feeding, dig a trench around the plant—about three (3) inches from the stem—and allow slow seepage (it is suggested from a bag-hose, a long narrow tubing made from fairly coarse-woven material attached to the hose) of five (5) gallons of liquid fertilizer (see page 19) to every twenty-five (25) plants or approximately one-fifth (1/5) of a gallon to each plant. *But* to gain results from this, the ground must be *kept* loose—worked almost daily—during the whole preceding season of growth as well as following this feeding. Work lightly.

For garden purposes, protection is rarely provided; but, after the buds begin to show color, it is vital, for exhibition purposes, to keep dew and rain and frost off the beds. The plants can stand very low temperature, but the frost and dew, particularly, are injurious to the buds. *Protection*

Disbudding, tying, watering all come in for their share of attention *regularly* and much depends on this regularity. Disbudding (or pinching off all buds on a stem except those designed for maturity) is regulated by the number of blooms desired on a plant. For bedding purposes, little disbudding is absolutely necessary, but for exhibition purposes, it is essential to confine the number of buds left on the plant to about two blooms. Disbudding must be done continuously to insure success. *Disbud for Large Flowers*

Watering must be done unstintingly. A thorough watering, using a pretty stiff pressure, is most beneficial and necessary to keep the leaves free from dust, to keep the plants healthy and to help control Aphis, Red Spider and Mealy Bug. Care should be used not to wet the buds that are showing color. *Watering*

There are several insect pests and diseases that must be guarded against, so that the foregoing hints on culture, if followed, leave only two or three more dangers to combat. The hardest to control is Mealy Bug which attacks the leaves, and the Black Aphis which sucks the sap from the tender shoots. Both are controlled by nicotine sprays. *Pests Insects*

Midge, or Stem Rot, is not to be controlled by spraying or insecticide. Pull up any plants affected and destroy by burning and applying a light application of hydrated lime to the soil where the plant was pulled. "Quasol" (and other similar remedies), diluted to specific directions is also helpful. Midge *Stem Rot* or Stem Rot is the Chrysanthemum's worst disease. It shows itself only at blooming-time (by turning a sickly yellow and wilting over night). Should the leaves turn yellow from over-feeding, however, give the plants an application of copperas water.

Old Fashioned Varieties Again Popular

The original Chrysanthemum, as it was introduced, was of the hardy type but for many years the florists' variety has completely overshadowed the old-fashioned kind. The trend of taste is swinging back now to give the original single and pompon style an equal chance and many gardens will again be graced by the cheerful flowering of the *Pyrethrum aureum* or Golden Feather, *Anthemis coronorium* or summer Chrysanthemum, *Arctotis grandis* or African Daisy and the many, many varieties of Pompons, besides other members of the Compositae.

The dwarf Chrysanthemum "Amelia" is most interesting, beginning blooming in June and continuing until frost. Its clusters of pink flowers remind one of the old-fashioned Azaleas.

Chrysanthemum Koreanum: Important additions to the fall garden are the *Chrysanthemum Koreanum* whose unique value lies in their extremely early flowering. The blossoms are daisy-like in appearance, in white and brilliant colors, and are borne on wiry stems that make them excellent cutting flowers.

Propagation is by division (in the spring)—although they resent yearly disturbance. They require little care, being neither affected by drought, nor heat of summer, nor cold of winter. They require no staking, or winter-covering. Any but the poorest soil satisfies them.

The first introduced were single and lovely. But the double ones have proved to be equal in brilliance, importance, and beauty.

Types of Chrysanthemums: The several types of chrysanthemums differ so greatly in the character of their flowers that for convenience in identification the entire chrysanthemum family has been arbitrarily grouped under a number of descriptive headings. These group-names have large, medium and small types—both in size of blossom and in height of plant. Among the most important of them are Pompons (Incurved and Reflexed), Anemone and Pompon-anemone, Button, Daisy (including small and large Single), Ragged (or Hairy), etc.

Hybridizers have centered their efforts toward creating summer-flowering varieties, so that there may be a wider choice in time of flowering. In making selections, note the time given to expect blossoms, that the cycle of bloom may thus be extended.

Cascade Chrysanthemums: A most interesting effect can be gained by training a certain type of Chrysanthemum to grow downward, making a shower effect, and forming what is called Cascade Chrysanthemums. There are a number of varieties susceptible of being trained in this manner, particularly those with small daisy-like blossoms, for it is the multitude of blossoms that create the shower effect.

Among these *Takamakie,* yellow; *Shoji,* red; *Sakurogari,* lavender; *Momo-Nonaka,* pinky salmon; *Mikageyema,* white; make medium-sized plants; while *Kiho,* yellow; *Entei* and others make larger specimens.

Directions for Training

When the plant is about twelve inches high, place beside it a wire stake, or light flexible bamboo rod, four or five feet long, at an angle of forty-five degrees. Tie the main shoots to this and keep the lateral growth pinched off, except the six or eight runner-branches that are to be allowed to mature. Gradually lower the rod until the buds appear, when the support must be removed, allowing the plant to fall downward in a shower, sometimes as much as six or eight feet, taking extreme care not to snap the brittle stems.

To secure uniform development an even distribution of light over the plant should be controlled, by placing it beside a wall with the support pointing north. After the buds appear a southern exposure is needed to bring them to their proper maturity.

Since Chrysanthemums require the short-length day to blossom (see page 142), it is suggested experiments be tried using paper hoods for each individual plant (or canvas cov-

9561

ering over a number) when desiring to force an early bloom —in or out of doors.

*The
Japanese
Legend
of the
Chrys-
anthemum
Varieties*

Legend: Japanese folklore lends to the "Queen of the Autumn" an interesting legend of its origin which surrounds it with an atmosphere of romance. One beautiful moonlight night a young girl, wandering in a garden, gathered a blossom and began to pull off the petals one by one to see whether her lover cared for her or not. Suddenly a little elf stood before her and, after assuring her that she was passionately adored, he added, "Your love will become your husband and will live as many years as the flower you may choose has petals." He then disappeared and the maiden began her search for a flower which should have the greatest number of petals. At length she picked a Persian Carnation and with a gold hair pin she separated each petal into two or three parts. Soon her deft fingers had increased the number of folioles of the corolla to three times the original number and she wept with joy to think of the happiness she had been the means of assuring her future husband.

And so the *Ki-Ku,* as the Japanese call the chrysanthemum, was created hundreds of years ago in a garden with the moon shining over the flowers, the streams, and the little bamboo bridges.

ANNUALS FOR A SEASON

*The Ideal
Garden*

THE IDEAL garden contains a balanced proportion of the various kinds of plants suitable to its special location. Shrubs for backgrounds and in those spots where dignity and strength are needed; bulbs for early blooming and later to supply the beauty and elegance that only the Lilies can give; and perennials for constancy and dependability of bloom. Yet no garden can be independent of the Annuals.

*Reserve
Seedlings*

The gardener with forethought selects a sheltered but sunny spot where, early in the spring, the seeds are planted, or if space does not permit, prepares the seedpans or "flats", knowing full well that when the bulbs die down or for some unforeseen reason the best-loved perennials wither and die, these cheerful, quick-growing little plants will brighten the bare places.

Petunias, that can supply one with almost any color desired; the Chinese Forget-me-not (*Cynoglossum*) with its sprays of lovely blue flowers; and the *Eschscholtzia*, best known as California Poppy (which *can* be transplanted *with care*) are a group of rather low-growing plants most dependable for the reserve supply. *Petunias*

Annual Forget-me-not

Annuals can be found to supply almost *any* need. An entire garden *can* be arranged using *only* this type of flower. But to do this, one must carefully plan the arrangement, and study the height and time of blooming of each variety to be used. *Wide Variety of Choice*

The beds and borders must be prepared the fall preceding the year of bloom; for many seeds, such as Larkspur, with its double flowers of white and shades of blue and pink; Cornflower (*Centaurea*) or Bachelor Buttons, the newer of which includes a wide range of color; Candytuft and all types of Poppies, and annual Phlox (*Phlox drummondi*) should be planted in the fall, that they may make sufficient rootgrowth to insure a long period of blooming. Once planted, most annuals will drop their own seeds, and will not need replanting for several years. After that, the flowers seem to deteriorate, and fresh, new seeds should be secured. Select only the largest and finest blossoms, mark them, and allow *them* to mature for seeds! By keeping all other seedpods removed, the plant will bloom longer and more profusely; the season will be prolonged; and the undesirable types will be eliminated. *Prepare Beds for Larkspur*

Poppies

Save Special Seed

Phlox, one of the first of the annuals to blossom, continues to flower until early summer. It is most effective if a large area is provided where shades of but one color are used . . . for example, the lightest tones of pink shaded to red. *Do not buy packets of mixed seeds.* Selected colors give better results, larger blossoms and more true to shade. Phlox *thrives* in poor soil, and Clarkia, also. *Phlox*

Larkspur in drifts of pink and shades of blue give a marvelous effect. The double varieties are almost as lovely as *Larkspur* their cousins, the temperamental Delphinium. Red Poppies, and blue and white Larkspur are lovely growing together, but the Poppies must predominate.

There are a whole host of lovely flowers whose seeds may be (see page 130) planted in the spring in the place they are to occupy all season, although many of these do not resent being transplanted. Clarkia and annual Scabiosa are most interesting, but in the Southwest they are not very well known.

A number of the annuals are specially valuable as their time of blossoming can be controlled by judicious planting. For instance, Cosmos planted in the fall will bloom much earlier than if the seeds are sown in the spring. Calendula is equally adaptable. Other plants can be found that have a number of varieties that bloom at *various* seasons. Stocks, Coreopsis and Asters exemplify this type.

Snapdragons often live through the winter, so are in effect perennial, but are not really dependable as a garden flower, because they are very tender and subject to pests and disease.

"Painted-leaf", or annual Poinsettia, and Kochia are excellent as shrub substitutes; while Four o'Clocks, annual Hollyhocks, Bush Morning Glories, and a large spidery plant called Cleome,* give height where desired. Cleome has a profusion of odd, white or rather pale, blossoms that need to have lavender and red-purple Petunias beneath them to enhance their delicate beauty.

Petunias are so valuable! In addition to the single, there are gorgeous double varieties. All drop their seed like Larkspur and Poppies, but cannot always be counted on to come true to color.

The Verbena, another dependable annual, has been greatly improved, the newer varieties having softer shades and larger florets. It is not generally realized that with liberal winter-covering (see page 139) a bed of Verbenas *may* be preserved from year to year.

It is difficult to recognize a number of the old garden favorites, for the new varieties are so much larger, their season of blooming is longer, and even the range of color has been enlarged.

Candytuft and Sweet Alyssum divide honors with annual Ageratum and garden Pinks (*Dianthus*) as border plants.

Nasturtiums, single and double-flowered, continue to hold first place in the hearts of new gardeners; they give the greatest profusion of gay blossoms when planted in new, rather poor soil. The tall-growing varieties require more space, unless given a support over which they may be trained, yet their reward for the extra care is an abundance of much larger and more colorful blossoms than to be secured from the dwarf varieties. *Vivid Nasturtium.*

Marigolds can be planted among them to carry the blooming-season into the fall, as they have the same coloring. Notable among them is a variety whose leaves do *not* have an unpleasant odor, and the fact that they offer such a wide selection of types from which to choose. *Fall Colors*

The brilliant tones of the autumn leaves are often reflected in the blossoms of the late-blooming annuals. The vivid red Cockscomb (*Celosia*), the decorative Castor Bean* and bright-orange Tithonia (the largest and tallest of the annuals), many of the Zinnias, and the fall-blooming, orange Klondike Cosmos (of which Hardie's early-flowering *Orange Flare*, originated by David Hardie of Dallas, received the unanimous choice of all the judges in the All-American competition for new varieties in 1935). *Versatility of the Zinnia*

It is interesting, also, to note that a surprisingly great number of the dependable garden plants, not native as far north as Texas, have come across the Rio Grande—from Old Mexico. Among these are the Dahlias, Marigolds, *Argemone* (Prickly Poppy), Tithonia, *Russelia* (popular for patios and gorgeous in hanging baskets and window boxes), and the Zinnia.

Argemone alba (white Prickly Poppy) and *A . . rosea* (dusky-red) are rather tall-branching, stout-stemmed plants with many needle-like spines on the stalks and leaves. They enjoy good soil and will reseed themselves if undisturbed. The foliage, greyish in tone, hugs the cup-like blossoms so that they appear as a host of butterflies alighted upon the branches, half hidden among the leaves.

The Cassias*—shrub-like in growth (see page 63) provide beautiful, showy, golden-yellow splashes of color in the late spring and are prized for their velvety leaves, also.

The almost flat, thistle-like, rose-lavender blossom-heads of the "Star Thistle" (*Centaurea americana*)* or Basket Flower, make a fine display rising above their rather coarse leaves. They propagate readily and grow about three feet tall. These are lighter in color than the plumed biennial *Cirsium austrinum* (Thistle)* whose leaves are more or less spiny and flowers rose-purple to deep purple, both the leaves and stems silvery-looking. Hummingbirds line their nests with the down of the seed-pods of these thistles.

It is not generally known that the annual *Coreopsis* (variety . . . *tinctoria**) is what is called "Calliopsis". This tall, graceful plant bears a profusion of yellow flowers— usually with red at the base of the petals and yellow centers borne at the tips of wand-like, wiry stems. They are fine for cutting and increase the color-range of the perennial *C . . . grandiflora* pastel-shades of pink, white, lavender, etc., and are succeeded by the deeper yellow-orange of the fall-blooming Klondike Cosmos.

For height and color in the back of the flower bed, where there is room for sufficient spread there is no hardier family than the *Helianthus*, whose types vary as widely as the Zinnia of today. *H . . . maximiliani** grows from two to eight feet and is as showy as the Hollyhocks. *H . . . mollis** is much shorter, has downy foliage, blooms earlier, and bears a wealth of lemon-yellow flowers in contrast to the golden disks of the taller variety. All of the sunflowers and goldenrod (*Solidago*) take room for spread but are most effective if used advisedly. Planted in the same section of the garden with the various Salvias,* create interesting contrasts in color and texture.

It is amazing how many of the dependable garden flowers are denizens of the Southwest and how many of them have not been greatly altered by cultivation or hybridization. There are a few, however, that have been greatly enhanced in beauty, size, color-range and height. Those that remain relatively unchanged usually demand more room than the average gardener is willing to allot them, for they often retain a look of the untamed in their sprawling habits, or are coarse in texture, or flamboyant in vivid coloring, or size of bloom. Definitely these *belong* in the natural, or informal garden!

ZINNIA CULTURE

Just as every family boasts of one outstanding member, so the Zinnia must be the pride of the whole tribe of the annuals! It is the one outstanding plant to be used for all purposes. It can be planted early to be a part of the spring border, or the seeds may be sown in the reserve bed to fill in the bare spaces. *Versatility of Zinnias*

In late May it can be planted among the Larkspur and Poppies to surprise one with blossoms soon after the other plants have been pulled out. Or, the seeds may be planted where they have some shade—during July and August—for the late season's flowering.

When Zinnias are several inches high, the ground may be loosened and a fertilizer added to nourish the plants, to encourage them to produce larger and better blossoms. *When to Feed*

*Wide
Choice
of Colors*

The fact that the Zinnia, like the Gladiola, rarely fails to bloom six weeks after planting, makes it invaluable to the gardener. The blossoms that were merely tolerated in days gone by because of their harsh colors have been so cultivated until now the loveliest of shades can be secured to harmonize with every color scheme.

*Of Many
Heights*

There are varieties to supply every need; very tall bushes with enormous blossoms that rival the Dahlias, and even a low-growing type with exquisite miniature flowers!

Zinnias, as listed, diminish in height, and in size of blossom —(1) Giant-flowered; (2) Dahlia-flowered; (3) Picotee; (4) Chrysanthemum-flowered; (5) Dwarf; (6) Lilliput, or Pompon.

Yet, with all its good qualities, few people really *love* the Zinnia.

Those who are sojourning for a time in a location that is not permanent, need not therefore be deprived of the joys of owning a garden. There are quick-growing annuals and vines *to fill every demand;* and Iris acquired can be moved from one location to another at *any* season.

PLANTS FOR SPECIAL USES

Fall Bloom or Berries

Shrubs
Abelia
Althea
Bush Morning Glory
Crape Myrtle
Dusty Miller
Flowering Willow
Ilex *decidua*
Ligustrum and Privet
Poinciana
Sumac (Rhus)
Vitex
Vines and Trailers
Cypress Vine
Morning Glory
Perennial Pea
Petunia

Queen's Wreath
Scarlet Runner Bean
Thunbergia
Trailing Lantana
Verbena
Bulbous Plants
Canna
"Rain Lily"
"Spider Lily"
Tuberose
Water Lilies
Annuals and Perennials
Ageratum
Alyssum
Calendula
California Poppy
Chrysanthemum

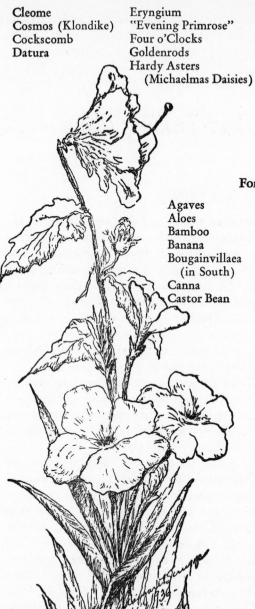

Cleome
Cosmos (Klondike)
Cockscomb
Datura

Eryngium
"Evening Primrose"
Four o'Clocks
Goldenrods
Hardy Asters
  (Michaelmas Daisies)

Hibiscus (Mallow)
Lantana
Liatris (Gay Feather)
Marigold
Mexican Prickly Poppy
Petunias
Plumbago
Roses
Salvias
Snapdragon
Sunflowers
Zinnias

For Tropical Effects

Agaves
Aloes
Bamboo
Banana
Bougainvillaea
  (in South)
Canna
Castor Bean

Catalpa Tree
Chinaberry Tree
Coleus
Crinum
Datura
Elephant Ears (Caladium)
Fig Tree
Fountain Grass
Geranium
Gourds
Grapevines
Hibiscus
Locust Tree
Mullein
Magnolia
Oleander
Ornamental Pepper
Pampas Grass
Palms
Palmetto
Papaya
Rubber Plant
Sycamore Tree
Trumpet Vine
Yuccas

Old-Fashioned Favorites

Cape Jasmine (Gardenia)
Martha Washington Geranium
Moss and Brier Rose
Tuberose

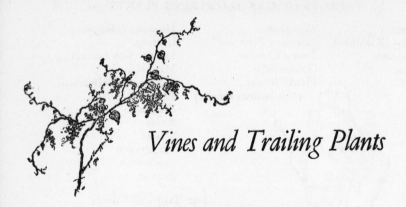

Vines and Trailing Plants

Choice in Vines

RESTFUL CORNERS, gay arbors and sheltered nooks, or the welcome shade of a lacy trellis—all suggest clambering green things—sometimes studded with flowers, sometimes rich with berries or fruit, often merely one of the soothing tones of green. One may choose from the host of possibilities a Climbing Rose instead of a Vine, or a Honeysuckle, that also must be trained, may appeal or be more suitable in coloring and fragrance for a special purpose than one of those plants that cling. The range of choice in the field of climbers is as varied as is that of any other classification of plants.

Securing Small Plants Advised

If early bloom is desired, with accompanying deep shade in summer and fall, the Wisteria's delicate panicles of lavender or white, one of the first flowers to appear in the spring, come before the leaves are scarcely out. The Jasmines, in variety, range in color from white to yellow, while Clematis may be had in white, rosy-carmine, and deep, rich purple. These all are most successful when small plants are secured, rather than try to grow them from seed or cuttings. Moon-

Tubers

vines that are tubers and the gorgeous Mexican Morning Glories, too, should be gotten from the nurserymen. An old-fashioned favorite, the delicate-flowered Madeira vine, with its showers of white stars, and the fall-blooming, rosy-carmine racemes of the Queen's Wreath (known also as "Mexican Love-Vine," the *Antigonon leptopus*, "Rosa de Montana," or Coral Vine) are the tubers which require protection in the northern part of our section of the country. (See page 110.)

Most of the Morning Glories (*Ipomeas*, in variety), the members of the Pea family that climb (Sweet Peas, etc.), the Runner Beans and the Kudsu Vine all grow from large seed that give best results if soaked in water over night before planting. They range in color almost the round of the color-wheel. Our native Passion Flower (or "Maypop"), with its lovely blue flowers, should be more generally used. It is as easily grown from seed as the Mimosa, or Sensitive Plant with its delicate puff balls of rose, or yellow. *Soak Large Seed*

Balloon Vine (Love-in-a-puff, or Hearts-Ease), the native Coral Bean and the Dwarf white Morning Glory, thrive here in their native habitat, reseeding themselves. Everlasting or Perennial Peas, the Dolichios (Hyacinth or Jack Bean), Weeping or Trailing Lantana, Thunbergia and Dutchman's Pipe are all grown easily from seed—the latter not requiring rich soil or space conditions.

The Silver Lace Vine is a vigorous grower that gives best results from small plants. Its showy sprays of white are as effective as the Cobaea (Cup and Saucer Vine, or Cathedral Bells), which, like the Balsam Apple, and the Balsam Pear, grow rapidly and well from seed. A curious fact about the Cobaea is that in planting the seed must be placed *edgewise*, and be *merely covered* with light soil. The Canary-Bird Vine with its sprays of yellow, unusual flowers that are so valuable as decorations for they keep so long after cutting, also grows rapidly from seed. Our native Woodbine, or as it is better known, Trumpet Vine, with its orange-scarlet or yellow flowers is of vigorous, though woody, growth and flourishes in almost all conditions, growing best, however, from small plants. *To Secure Small Plants Recommended*

Another native plant that is very ornamental, used often in decorating, is the small and shiny-leafed Smilax that climbs high, so can be secured in very long sprays. Gourds and grapes in variety are also decorative both in leaf and fruit, being especially effective on arbors and trellises. Boston Ivy and English Ivy have no fruit or flowers and are of slower *Non-Flowering Vines* growth; while the Virginia Creepers (*H .. Engelmanni, H .. quinquefolia and H .. heptaphylla*), the latter the native Texas variety, grow rapidly and differ from each other largely in size of leaf. All these grow best from small plants, not seed, and are valued for their foliage, and in the color range of tones, or in the fall-coloring of their fruit or berries. *Ficus repens* and *Euonymus Radicans* both are evergreen and glossy leaved.

VINES

(*Not Native*)

Legend: (S)—Grows from Seed; (P)—Secure Small Plants.

Antigonon leptopus (Queen's Wreath or Mexican Love Vine) (P). Rose-scarlet, pea-like sprays, blooms in the fall; Rosa de Montana, also Coral Vine.

Balsam Apple (*Momordica balsamina*) (S). Fine green leaves; apple-like fruit.

Balsam Pear (*Momordica charantia*) (S).

Boston Ivy (*Ampelopsis tricuspidata veitchi*) (P). Shiny leaves; no flowers.

Butterfly Runner Bean (S). Rose flowers.

Canarybird Vine (*Tropaeolum canariensis*) (S). Yellow flowers.

Cardinal Climber (*Ipomea Quamoclit hybrida*) (S). Star-shaped scarlet flowers.

Cobaea splendens (*alba*) (S). Bell-shaped purple flowers.

Confederate Jasmine (*Trachelospernum*) (P). Star-shaped white flowers.

Clematis *paniculata* (P). C. *Jackmann*, blue; C .. *Texensis*, scarlet; C .. *Crispa*, white flowers.

Cypress climber (*Ipomea Quamoclit*) (S). Star-shaped red and white flowers.

Dutchman's Pipe (*Aristolcchia sipho*) (S).

English Ivy (*Hedera gracilis and Hedra helix*) (P). Waxy leaves, no flowers.

Gourds in variety (S). Ornamental climbers.

Grapes in variety (P).

Ground Ivy (*Creeping Charlie*) "Gill on the ground" (*Nepeta*)

Ground Myrtle (*Vinca Minor*) (P). Ground cover; blue flowers.

Honeysuckles in variety (*Lonicera*) (P). White and yellow, red and orange flowers.

Jack Beans (Hyacinth Bean) (*Dolichos*) (S). Clusters purple and white flowers.

Jasmine nudiflorum (P). Yellow flowers.

Jasmines in variety (P).

Madeira (*Mignonette*) (*Boussingaultia basilloides*) Tuber; delicate white flowers.

Moonflower (S). Large white flowers.

Morning Glories in variety (S). Rose, blue, white flowers.

Morning Glories blue (*Ipomea rubrocaerulea*) and Mexican Blue (S). Blue, yellow flowers.

Perennial Pea (*Lathyrus*) (P). Lavender-rose flowers.

Petunia. Semi-climber; many colors in flowers.

Pueraria (*Japanese Kudzu*) (S). Rose purple flowers.

Scarlet Runner Beans (*Phaseolus multiflorus*) (S). Scarlet flowers.

Silver Lace Vine (*Polygonum aubertii*). Small white flowers in clusters.

Thunbergia in variety (S). Yellow-orange flowers. Open sun.

Weeping Lantana (*Sellowiana*) (S). *Indolucrata*, Native. Semi-climber; lavender flowers.

Winter Creeper (*Euonymus radicans or Euonymus kewensis*) (P).

Wisteria *chinensis* (P). *W. Floribunda Macrobotrys.* Sky-blue flowers.

W. Magnifica. W. multijuga. Pale lavender blue flowers.

NATIVE VINES LISTED IN COMMERCIAL CATALOGS

Legend: (S)—Grows from Seed; (P)—Secure Small Plants.

Ampelopsis heterophylla (Texas Virginia Creeper) *quinquefolia* (P). Flowers greenish and inconspicuous; berries dark blue, in clusters. Very attractive to all the birds.

Balloon Vine (*Cardiospermum halicacabum*), Love-in-a puff or Heart's Ease (S). Flowers white. (S). Prefers moisture.

Bignonia (Trumpet Vine) or Woodbine. (Tecoma) (P). *Campsis Radicans. Chamberlynie. Speciosa.* Flowers *orange-scarlet*, vigorous, woody growth. *Yellow. Lav-* ender. "Red" Trumpet Vine. (*Tecoma grandiflora*). Flourishes under all conditions. Full sun.

†**Clematis *coccinea* (*Viorna*),** "Red Leather Flower". (P). Flowers red, hidden in very thick foliage. Native. Grows in shade; limestone regions or riverbottoms.

Coral Bean (*Erythrina herbacea*). (S). Flowers scarlet.

Cross Vine.

Evolvulus (White Trumpet Vine) *Sericesus.* (S). Dwarf Morning Glory. Flowers solitary, grows in dry, open places. Poor soil.

---

†NOTE: All Clematis require light, well-drained, loamy, *very* deep soil. They are gross feeders, and require a great deal of water. In times of drought water slowly and deep. Bugs are *very* fond of them!

Mimosa (Sensitive Plant) *fragrans.* (S). *Borealis,* Western variety; *stigillosa,* Gulf Coast. Flowers pink, fuzzy balls, similar to huisache, and yellow balls. Grows on dry, gravelled limestone hills.

Passion Flower (*Passiflora*) "Maypop". (S). Flowers dark blue. Will grow in arid regions.

Portulaca (Flowering Moss) Ground cover trailer. (S). Flowers, rose, red, blue, yellow and lavender; leaves fleshy. Will grow in arid regions; does not climb.

Rattan Vine. (P). No flowers. Very prolific grower.

Sarsaparilla (Carolina Moonsee). An evergreen with small, shiny leaves, used for decorating. Scarlet berries.

Smilax. (P). *Glauca* (Catbrier). Climbs high.

Virgins Bower (Clematis). Flowers deep scarlet.

Southwestern Native Plants
of Garden Value

Continuous Bloom

ONG HAS THE colorful Southwest been noted for its wealth of beautiful wild flowers. This vast region presents a continuous pageant of bloom from early Spring until frost tinges the leaves many hues and the brilliant winter-berries gleam on the hillsides and prairies.

Appreciation by Botanists

One of the first explorers in the sixteenth century, writing home, marveled at the natural beauty of the land and its abundance of plant growth. Tradition says these sixteenth century Spaniards and French Crusaders brought to this land, from the Holy Land, the lovely blue Lupine, our "Blue-bonnet". It has, since, carpeted the land, and, like the verdant hills of its native Syria, is freely interspersed with golden-yellow Daisies, Buttercups, Coreopsis, rich scarlet "Wine cups", and brilliant red tree-cypress ("Texas Plume" *Gilia-rubra*).

In many cases it is still rather difficult to determine the habitat of some of our most widely scattered plants. It has been argued that armies surging back and forth for the past four hundred years have scattered the seed in transporting food for their cavalry. Freight-trains, too, traveling the length and breadth of our prairies, have transported seed in the grain, and packing, in their strings of boxcars (and recently the highway beautification has had its part in transporting plants often far from their native haunts).

Later, in the first part of the nineteenth century, thousands of seed and plants, native to the Southwest, were collected, mounted and shipped to the great botanical centers of the world by Berlandier, Drummond, Charles Wright, Lindheimer, Lincecum, Fendler, von Roemer, Prince Paul of Wurttemberg, Edward Buckley, Wislizenus, Jacob Boll, John Drinker Cope and Julien Reverchon, working for such internationally famous botanists as Dr. Asa Grey of Harvard, Dr. George Engelmann of St. Louis, Prof. Louis Agassiz, Prof. William J. Hooker of Glasgow (later Sir William Hooker of Kew) and other great European collectors and experimentalists.

Source of Many Varieties

Today, more than most people realize, many of those flowers most treasured by gardeners in every land have been developed from the wild denizens of the "prairie country." A few varieties remain just as they were first seen in Nature's Garden, while others have been superseded by more attractive hybrids, whose colors and manner of growth are often quite different from the parent stock.

Probably our best known, most appreciated flower is the Phlox Drummondii (see page 90), the seeds of which were introduced by Thomas Drummond into Europe in 1835. The flowers of one of the two distinct groups of these annuals are more rounded, while those of the others form tiny stars. The several plants vary also in height (being dwarf, intermediate, and tall), and in the range of their colors.

In popularity, the Gaillardia is second only to the Phlox. Marked effects of cultivation, however, are seen in its size and form, although nothing of its brilliant coloring has been lost.

Because of the fact that plants indigenous to a country will thrive better there than will any importations, an effort has been made to secure a comprehensive list of those that are offered in the catalogues of commercial growers.

Comparatively Few on the Market

The potential value to the gardener of these sturdy bushes and flowers that are so peculiarly adapted to climate and soil conditions is only beginning to be appreciated.

W. A. Bridwell of Forestburg, Texas, who has spent more than thirty years studying native Southwestern plants, has said:

"A fact not known to many gardeners is that our natives are much more adaptable than xerophytic plants from other countries.

"Another fact unrecognized is that Texas probably has more bulbous-rooted wild flowers than any other state in the Union. So far as I know, the Fern, *Cheilanthes tormentosa*, is found in no other state; and we have the finest Amsonia to be found anywhere.

"We have the largest assortment and the most brilliant bloomers of the great family, *Euphorbiaceae*, except South Africa.

"Our Cacti also are wide in range.

"Our Wild Plums are the finest to be found.

"The exquisite Southern Maidenhair Fern (*Adiantum capillus-veneris*) is more plentiful here than anywhere else; and the same is true of the purple Cliff-brake (*Pellaea atropurpurea*).

"In *Eustoma russellianum* we have the most gorgeous-flowered Gentian known, and in *Sabatia campestris* and *Erythraea Beyrichi* the most brilliantly colored.

"Our native Barberry (*Berberis trifoliata*) (Agarita) is evergreen, and grows where those from Asia and the Pacific Coast wither and die.

"We have the largest assortment of Gay Feathers, Liatris *punctata, scariosa, squarrosa* and *pycnostachya*.

"The finest Lobelia (Lobelia *splendens*) reaches a development that is finer here than in other parts of the West.

"In Penstemmon *grandiflora* and Penstemon *cobaea* we have the biggest and finest on earth.

"Our Salvia *pitcheri* is the finest hardy sage known and our *Rosa foliolosa* is the only wild rose fit for a rockery.

"In Ephedra we have one of the strangest plants known, and it comes to us from prehistoric times unchanged.

"In one thing only I have to haul down the Texas flag. The New Mexico Phlox (*Mesoleuca*) is one of the finest natives on earth, and undoubtedly the finest Phlox for rockeries. It bears clear pink, white throated flowers, as big as silver dollars, blooms all summer long and the plant is so small you can cover it with your two hands. It may possibly lap over into West Texas, but I know of none native there."

Mrs. Lee Newbury, another authority on native plant-material, to whose research this book is largely responsible for its comprehensive data on native plants *of garden value*, has said:

"That prominent member of the beloved *Lupine* (pea) family, *Lupinus texensis* (Bluebonnet), is known and admired by everyone, especially those who have been fortunate enough to see a hillside covered with their beautiful blue blossoms. Too rich soil or too much water causes rank foliage growth at the expense of flowers. They bloom best in well-drained soil, in full sunshine.

"To allow them to reseed, the plants must be undisturbed until the pods have popped open, but if seed is planted it is best to soak them overnight before they are sown, and for best results this should be done no later than September.

"It is said our Bluebonnets will not grow (except by replanting) across the Texas border. Perhaps this is because they are often a biennial that lies dormant a season. It is true they sometimes will flower the first season, sometimes will not even germinate.

"Our Gaillardia,* Solidago (Goldenrod),* and Calliopsis (*Coreopsis tinctoria*) are used extensively. Our native Penstemon (*cobaea*) (Beard's Tongue or Dew Flower) is a very handsome plant, a biennial usually. These will grow and multiply rapidly once they have become established in the garden.

"The Coneflowers are 'indispensable in the hardy border,' Dreer says, thriving everywhere. *Rudbeckia* (orange) has a large brown cone surrounded by ray-florets usually bright yellow or orange, while *R . . pallida* having narrow ray flowers. *R . . hirta* is the 'Blackeyed Susan.' *R . . bicolor* prefers acid soil, while *R . . subtormentosa* is a perennial having ashy-grey leaves and stems, and *very* hairy. The Purple Coneflower is '*Brauneria*' of the Echinacea family, closely related to the Rudbeckias. Its ray-petals are quite long, drooping, and a lovely rose-purple to deep purple, its cone also being a bit different in shape. There is a rare native having yellow rays. Similar to these, though smaller flower-heads, are the *Ratibida* (Niggerheads).

"All the ray-petal florets are indiscriminately called 'daisies' by those who are not botanically inclined. There are, however, some eight or nine distinct daisy varieties native to Texas that make an assortment for the garden that is unequaled. Berlandier's daisy has woolly leaves on white stems, yellow petals on flat disks that turn from green to red or dark purple when mature, and prefers acid soil rich and moist. Engelmann's daisy and Lindheimer's are both yellow and seem to thrive almost everywhere.

"The Huisache, Butterfly or Honey daisy, (variously called) *Amblyolepis stigera*—has large, fragrant, yellow flowers borne on bluish-green, milky-veined stems, with long, narrow foliage. Growing *en masse*, its fragrance is delicious. It is not particular about soil or conditions.

"The Paper daisy, whose yellow ray-flowers pale and turn paper-like with age, has densely soft, woolly foliage and, like the Rock daisy (*Melampodium cinereum*), is somewhat low growing, an inhabitant of the mountainous part of Texas that easily adapts itself to the plains or prairies, neither being choosey about their habitation. The Rock daisy is white.

"The Actinella (*Tetraneuris linearis*), 'Monitoto,' also yellow and woolly, flowers much earlier than the Paper (*Baileya multiradi-*

ata) or the Rock daisy, and has an unusually long flowering period and is remarkably drought-resistant.

"The Bluff daisy (*Laphamia lindheimeri*) is low, shrubby and noteworthy for its capacity to grow out of pockets or crevices in almost vertical walls. Its gay yellow blossoms are often so profuse the foliage is about covered by them.

"Wax-like yellow flowers opening in late afternoon give the name 'Sleepy daisy' to the *Xanthisma texanum*, the annual whose seed are commonly recommended as extremely hardy plants. They grow everywhere, it seems.

"The Texas variety of the commonly known Shasta daisy, or Marguerite, is the *Aphanostephus skirrobasis* (white flowers with yellow centers), while *A . . humilis* has smaller, more numerous rays borne on very slender stems, and *A . . ramosisimus* will grow and flourish during droughts on rocky hillsides, both the latter two varieties having a decidedly purplish tone to the under part of their white petals.

"*Datura* (Angel's Trumpet, or Trumpet Flower), with its large, fragrant, trumpet-shaped flowers (white or pale yellow), resembling huge morning-glories borne on woody, shrub-like bushes with decorative leaves, is one of our handsomest plants. *D . . meteloides* is a perennial and prefers moist, low ground as does *D . . stramonium* (grown extensively in East and South Texas for its medicinal qualities and uses). *D . . quercifolia* is the West Texas native. Their erect buds resemble okra, while the seed-pods are burlike and thickly beset with stout prickles. They are erect when green but tip groundward as they ripen and split to scatter the seed.

"The fragrant white and yellow Nicotiana are invaluable in the garden, especially after sundown.

"Is there a daintier, lovelier plant than the yellow or the deep-rose-purple Oxalis, with its exquisite heart-shaped leaves?"

Many of the plants listed with an asterisk (*) are perennials, some annuals and a number are bulbous. Most will thrive in sandy, even in lime-impregnated loam; in unobstructed sunlight; where there is positive drainage and sufficient water in the early period of their growth to insure adequate root-growth. Then, too, practically "all of these plants will endure temperatures ranging from fifteen degrees Fahrenheit *below* to one hundred and twelve degrees *above*, and humidity that varies from muggy rainy years to desert-like dryness" (such as experienced in 1930–31).

TRANSPLANTING

It is many times expedient to transplant native plants, that is, where there is great abundance and sufficient roots, or seed that will assure the continuance of natural growth; or where the plants would be destroyed in the path of construction, or building activities. When this is true, the following rules should be carefully observed:

First: An effort must be made to give the plant the *same type of soil* it has enjoyed in Nature's garden, remembering that many times wild things *thrive only* in close proximity to other wildlings, including those that surround the plant. *Dig deep enough* that the taproot (should there be one) is not injured or broken, lifting the *clump* out *as a whole!*

Second: See that the plant is given the *same amount of sunshine or shade* to which it has been accustomed.

Third: Transplant wildflowers, or shrubs, *at the same season* that it is advisable to move like varieties of cultivated flowers.

TO PRESS SPECIMENS

In lieu of a special Botanical Press when on field expeditions, experience has proved this the best manner to preserve all types of plant-life. . . . Place them in wet or dampened newspapers, turning in the ends of the paper to exclude the air until they can be transferred to fresh, dry newspapers, and be placed under heavy weights. *Carefully* lay out the specimen to show the flower, or that characteristic specially desired (passing a slightly heated iron over the paper covering it, is suggested as an aid in preserving color) before placing under pressure. Do not bruise in handling!

NATIVE PLANTS AND HERBS THAT CHARM AND HEAL

THE LORE AND LEGEND OF SOME VARIETIES OF SOUTHWESTERN VEGETATION

We are told that our superstitions are but degenerated forms of scientific facts, and that Science is continually learning from Superstition. The Mexican who sows Fennel in

Science or Superstition

his garden knows that "to sow Fennel is to sow sorrow," but he offsets this act by planting Rosemary and Blue Sage at his door, the former symbolic of happiness and the latter indicative of long life.

Herbs in Legend

It is said that Charlemagne forced his soldiers to wear Houseleek on their clothing as a measure of good luck; that the young, pious Crusader, Louis VII, courted the favor of the Iris which has "a sword for its leaf and a lily for its heart," according to Ruskin; and where is the old-fashioned American mother who tied a bit of asafetida about her offspring's neck during periods of contagion? A modern poet writes thusly of the native plants—

> *For flowers, like men, are finest when*
> *There's least of the wild remaining.*

Not everyone will agree with this viewpoint. Whatever the mission of plants and flowers, it is interesting to note that to certain of them there have always been attributed particular mystical powers and curative properties. Nature, with her "infinite variety," has seemed to have a definite fondness for the wildling.

Herbs in Medical Usage

While the various opposing medical schools have been warring among themselves as to the cause and cure of disease in the human body, natural and primitive man has been drawing successfully throughout the ages from the vegetable kingdom for his food and medicine; and witches, sorcerers, conjurers and others with some knowledge of the curative value of plants have plied their trade to their own purposes.

The Southwest grows literally hundreds of medicinal herbs and shrubs which have for long been used advantageously by the natives, and through this connection considerable knowledge and much folklore has been handed down. Leaves, flowers, roots, and in some cases the seeds, are the parts of the plant that are used for medicinal purposes. Boiling water, or alcohol are the mediums of infusion.

The following are but a few of the more important native medical herbs (many grown, or gathered, for commercial purposes):

Blue Sage (*Salvia farinaceae*)—First discovered in South Europe, is one of the most prolific, most common and most beautiful of the Southwestern blue flowers. There are several varieties, each blooming at a different season, which gives a rather continuous blue cast to the landscape. A delicious and refreshing tea is made from the leaves which, together with the whorls of small flowerets, should be carefully gathered and dried *during the blossoming season*. It is also much utilized as a seasoning for meats and dressings. It is tonic, astringent, expectorant and diaphoretic.

Butterfly Weed (*Asclepias tuberosa*)—Milkweed family, also called Pleurisy Root, as the name implies, is much used for diseases of the lungs and pulmonary organs.

Castor Bean (Palma Christi) (*Ricinus communis*)—Spurge family, yields an oil that is widely known as a cathartic, and as a lubricant for machinery. The plant was first introduced as a medicine in 1764 by Peter Cavone of the West Indies.

Croton Tea (Tea Plant and Mexican Tea) (*Croton monanthogynus*)—Spurge family, is a rusty colored, aromatic weed whose leaves are gathered while still in blossom and used for tea by the Mexicans. The dried leaves and stems when ground are employed as flavoring or as a condiment for meats, and the well-known Croton Oil is obtained from a variety. It is diaphoretic and sudorific.

Damianita Mexicana (*Chrysactinia mexicana*)—Is pitted with oil glands, and is at once aromatic and resinous. It is a tonic, stimulative and laxative.

Dog-Toothed Violet (Adder's Tongue) (*Erythronium albidum*)—A perennial of short flowering season, usually from March to May, according to locality, and the flowers and leaves wilt soon after being picked. The bulb, which is edible, was roasted and enjoyed both by the Indians and the early settlers. As a property it is emetic, emollient, and antiscorbutic when fresh, but when dried, it is nutritive.

Horsemint (*Monarda dispersa*)—Mint family, is a perennial that got its name from a Spanish authority on medicinal plants, one Nicholas Monardez. Hoarhound (*Marrubium vulgare*); Skullcap (*Scutellaria drummondii*); Wild Bergamot (*Monarda fistulosa*); and several of the Pennyroyals are near relatives, and members of the Mint family that are useful in the preparation of curative teas. Other herbs which are utilized in infusion are the Wormseed (*Chenopodium anthelminticum*), naturalized from Europe; Balsam Groundsel (*Senecio balsamitae*); Watercress (*Nasturtium officinale*) as a salad is rich in Vitamin E; Plantain (*Plantago occidentalis*); Wild Parsley (*Ptilimnium laciniatum*); and the Violet (*Viola missouriensis*). *Other Herbs*

Mexican Wormwood (*Artemisia mexicana*)—Grows abundantly here. It is from a close relative of our Artemisia that the Frenchman gets his *absinthe*. Medicinally it is anthelmintic, tonic and narcotic.

Mistletoe (*Phoradendron flavescens*)—A parasite growth, is similar to the Old World Mistletoe which the Druid priests kept in their homes; and the Indians chew the leaves to cure toothache.

Moth Mullein (Velvet, or Blanket Mullein) (*Verbascum thapsus*) —Figwort family, a stout biennial whose straight, tall, wooly stem grows alternate, big hairy leaves that lie close to the ground mostly, is indigenous to lowlands and moist places. According to tradition, the Romans of the 14th Century sprinkled the powdered seeds and roots on water to induce fish to bite, and they also dipped the stalks in suet, allowed it to dry and used them for procession torches. About the same time the Greeks were utilizing the leaves, which they soaked in oil, for lamp wicks. Roman women dyed their tresses to a golden hue in an infusion of the flowers. Germans carried flambeaux for festivals, mullein stalks covered with pitch. Humming birds employ the hairs from the leaves in their nest building, and primitive folk used the dried leaves and flowers for a smoke. The plant is demulcent, diuretic, anodyne and anti-spasmodic in effect.

Senna (*Cassia roemeriana*)—Senna family, was first used as a medicine by the Arabs. The Redbud (*Cercis Occidentalis*) belongs to this family, and the old settlers claimed its bark would relieve chills and fevers. The tender buds of a kindred variety are in demand in England for salads. The leaves make a valuable, mild and effectual tea. It is cathartic in principle.

Wild Carrot (*Daucus pusillus*) (Queen Anne's Lace)—Is lovely as well as useful. The carrot dates its domestication to the prehistoric period. It is reputed to have been used in Rome in Pliny's day, and the early Spaniards believed the root to be an efficacious remedy for rattlesnake bite.

Wild Lettuce (Sow Thistle) (*Lactuca canadensis*)—Chicory family. Herodotus speaks of its being eaten as a salad in 550 B.C., and the old Roman served it at his table. The plant's milky juice yields an opium substitute that is used by the medical profession. Caterpillars and other insects feast on it, but the animal world leaves it untouched. Verily, "one man's meat is another's poison!" It is narcotic and demulcent.

Yarrow (Milfoil) (*Achillea millefolium*)—One of the most useful of the native herbs. Has figured in the literature, mythology, folklore and medicine of many lands. Its potency as a love charm, its efficacy as a witch's brew, its curative property as a doctor's remedy and its aesthetic value to the garden have made it notable. It is astringent, alterative and diuretic.

Among the medicinal herbs none was more treasured by the early settlers than the lovely Mountain Pink (*Erythraea Beyrichii*) known as "Quinine weed." They gathered the plants while in bloom, dried them, and put them to soak in good brandy; administering a tablespoonful three times a day as a remedy for chills and fever. *An Early Fever Remedy*

Other medicinal herbs that flourish in the Southwest are: *Narcotics* Nettle (*Solanum caroliniensis*); Pokeberry (*Phytolacca decandra*); Golden Rod (*Solidago serotina*); Eryngo (*Eryngium Leavenworthii*); Foxglove; Beard-tongue (*Penstemon cobaea*); Sunflowers (*Helianthus*); Wood Sorrel (*Oxalis drummondii*); the Kansas Sunflower (*Brauneria*); Black Nightshade (*Solanum nigrum*); and the Jimson Weed, or Thorn Apple (*Datura stramonium*), Joe Pye Weed (*Eupatorium*).

Among the definite narcotics to be found here are Purslane Speedwell (*Veronica peregrina*); Herb-of-the-Cross (*Verbena officinalis*); Bitter Corn Salad (*Valerianella amarilla*) and a small, dry-looking grayish-green weed (*Nicotiana repanda*), commonly known as Indian Tobacco, which frequents city lawns and adjacent fields. What a stiff, soulless little thing the latter plant is! And yet, along with all the others, it has a place in the Universal Scheme.

This article lays no claim to exhaustive detail; nor does it deal with the plants from the standpoint of medical efficacy; neither does it recommend their use medicinally in any form. It features only those plants and herbs that are themselves classified under the head of Herbal Materia Medica, or such as are related to plants so listed, and those that have food value, with regard for interest and appeal, that are indigenous to the South and Southwest.

HERBS† FOR SEASONING . . . FROM SUNNY SPOTS

Anise (Sweet)
Artemesia Absenthium (Wormwood)
Artemesia Dranculus (Tarragon)
Balm (Sweet)
Basil (Sweet)
Bee Balm
Caraway (Sweet)
Catnip
Dill (Sour)

Fennel (Sour)
Leeke
Marjoram (Sweet)
Menthas (Mint Family)
Poppy Seeds for pastry
Parsley (Sweet)
Rosemary
Sage and Savory
Tansy (of rank growth)

† . . . Sow these seeds on a cloudy day.

Propagation

THERE ARE several ways by which the amateur gardener may successfully propagate plants and thus increase his garden by his own efforts without resorting to the professional grower; by seeds, divisions, layering, cuttings, grafting and budding. Those who can successfully raise plants by these various methods can bring new beauty to their gardens as well as share with flower-loving friends.

I. SEEDS

Many scientific experiments have been and are still being made on raising plants from seed, and the lay-gardener now has a chance to take some of the guesswork out of seed germination.†

---

†SEED GERMINATION—"The Plant Physiologists have worked steadily for thirty years on the different problems of seed *germination*. There are three types of seeds: (1) Those that start to grow promptly under ordinary germinative conditions. Most plants of commonest culture belong here. (2) Seeds that are alive but are hindered from growing by something outside the embryo, such as hard seed coat, or the need of high temperature, or light, or increased or decreased oxygen supply. Of these factors, hard-coatedness is the one most apt to trouble the amateur gardener since the Legumes suffer from it and that family is vastly important, especially in the South, where the flora is very rich in pod-bearing trees and plants. Some of the members of this family start with no trouble, but if delays occur the first thing to look for is a hard coat. Seeds of Peas, Broom (*Cytisus spp.*) Lupine, Locust, Wisteria, and Red Bud (*Cercis*) are among those that may give trouble. Any method of breaking, scratching or wearing away the seed coat so the water can enter will promote the growth of these seeds. Soaking, rubbing between pieces of sand paper, or in the larger seeds filing with a three-cornered file are all good methods. (3) Seeds in which the embryo itself is dormant at the time when the seed is ripe and must go through other changes before germination can take place. It is of the greatest importance to learn to handle this group because it is the special characteristic of the families to which many of our finest ornamentals and fruits belong; the Dogwoods, the Barberries, some of the Honeysuckles such as Viburnum, Snowberry, Honeysuckle itself and

*Growing
Conditions*

Several factors enter into this. *First of all,* the seed must be alive; *second,* the soil must be carefully prepared to suit the special type. The proper amount of sun or shade, as well as a suitable temperature, materially influences growth. It is important also that they be neither too damp, nor too dry.

FLATS

*Place to
Germinate
Seeds*

The ideal way to germinate seed is, of course, in a greenhouse where temperature and moisture are evenly maintained. Under ordinary conditions, however, this is not possible, but any of a number of containers may be used. Probably the best is the porous seedpan, next to which is suggested the use of "flats", or wooden boxes (about thirteen by twenty-one inches, being three or four inches deep). One may also use flowerpots, bulbpans, or even cigar boxes, with rare seeds placed in half an eggshell. Put a half dozen small holes, and pebbles or clear sand, in the bottom of the flats or cigar boxes, for drainage. If the flats have been used before, a wise precaution is to whitewash the inside to prevent possible fungus growth.

*Soil for
Raising
Seed*

Probably the ideal soil for raising seed is equal parts of sand, leaf mold, and loam. Some prefer equal parts of peatmoss and loam. Garden soil with sand and a little bonemeal, thoroughly mixed, may be used; or sandy loan with a little bonemeal, for the first transplant. Whatever soil is used should be sifted through a four-inch, or finer sieve.

Elder, and—most important of all—the Rose family where we find the Rose, both the species and the hybrid forms; Pear, Apple, Cherry, Plum, Strawberry, Spirea, and Hawthorn.

"Seed with dormant embryos after-ripen, or get ready to grow, most rapidly if they are kept moist and cold until certain changes take place in the embryos that permit germination to start. If the climate of a place is such that during the winter there will be 75 to 90 days when the temperature of the surface of the soil is just above freezing, seeds sown out of doors in the fall will get *enough cold* weather to start them in the spring. Where winters are too cold or not cold enough nature may be helped by placing the seeds in containers of moist peat and setting the whole thing in the *icebox.* Keep moist but not wet for two or three months, then take the seeds out and sow them as usual. Many will start when treated this way that would never start if planted, as soon as when ripened, in a warm greenhouse. Remember that in order to germinate seeds right moisture conditions are most important."

PERSIS S. CROCKER, of Yonkers, N. Y.

After placing one-half inch drainage in the container, fill it with well-saturated, prepared soil to within one-half inch or less of the top; and pack down well with a brick, or block of wood.

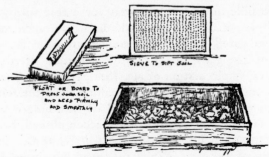

SIEVE TO SIFT SOIL

FLOAT OR BOARD TO PRESS DOWN SOIL AND SEED FIRMLY AND SMOOTHLY

Recently it has been discovered that many plants' diseases are carried in the seed. This is easily prevented by the use of a commercial fungicide and should by all means be a part of the business of seed planting. Put a little of the powder in an open-mouthed bottle, or fruit jar, and shake the seeds about in it before planting. *Plant Disease Preventatives*

Seeds sown in "flats" or other containers *may* be broadcast, or sown in shallow drills, thinly, if care is taken not to plant them too deeply. Small seeds need barely be covered. Very fine ones need not be covered at all, but merely pressed firmly into the surface of the soil. These very small seeds may be mixed with sand to prevent crowding. A good rule for larger seeds is to plant them to a depth equal to twice or three times, never more than five times, their own diameter. After planting, moisten the surface of the container well with a gentle spray. *Depth to Plant Seeds*

In order to keep the temperature even, it is well to place glass, paper, or lath over the containers. Old burlap is apt to contain fungus disease. *What Cover to Use*

As soon as the seeds have germinated, begin to raise the covering, and increase the supply of air until the young plants are ready for full sunlight.

Even moisture is most essential, and should be given from underneath whenever possible. One pot may be set into an- *Moisture Needed* other with the larger one packed with peat-moss, which should be *kept* wet; or the seed or bulbpan may be put into a flowerpot saucer. Flats may be set into containers of galvanized iron or other cheap metal. If watering from below is not possible, use a rubber spray, or a rose spray on the hose.[1] If glass is used to cover the flats, too much moisture will be indicated by excessive condensation on the undersurface of the glass which may be carefully lifted at one corner to give circulation of air. (See page 125.) Great care

Care of Seedlings

should be taken in watering the seedlings that the soil is not packed by the force of the water. Early morning is the best time to water. After germination is accomplished, bring the young plants into full sunlight *gradually,* and give them an abundance of fresh air. While they may have been kept in the shade or even in the dark before sprouting, it is best to remove the glass and put them in bright light as soon as they are up. Shade during the hottest part of the day.

OPEN BEDS

Seeds Sown in Open

To prepare an open bed: Spade the ground, water, allow the earth to dry, and water again. Before the second spading, put a thin layer of bonemeal on top. If heavy black soil predominates, put three inches of sandy loam on the surface before seeding.

Such seeds as Poppies, Annual Phlox and Larkspur should be broadcast in the fall; Sweet Alyssum and Portulaca should be sown in shallow drills or broadcast in early spring. Utmost care must be taken not to cover the seeds too deeply.

Time and Method to Follow in Transplanting

Transplanting (see page 119): Most annuals need be transplanted only once, most perennials twice. Seedlings should be transplanted when the second pair of true, or characteristic, leaves appear. It is best to throw away all weaklings and use only the healthiest plants, except in the case of Petunias which sometimes produce finest flowers from smallest plants. The seedlings should be carefully lifted in order

[1] . . . "As glass heats up so much, it is better to use paper, lath screen, or best of all, cheesecloth, and water through the cheesecloth."—PERSIS CROCKER.

not to injure their roots and, especially in the case of most annuals, should be placed in their permanent beds. One is repaid at this point by spreading rich, prepared soil about the roots of the seedlings. Press the soil down firmly about the roots, then water with a fine spray. Use shingle or cardboard protectors against the sun, if the transplanting cannot be done in cloudy weather. It is nearly always advisable to remove some of the foliage, especially if the plant has not been grown in a pot, or if the transplanting is done in warm weather. Scratch the ground around the small plants before it becomes thoroughly dry to insure aeration and looseness.

Plants should be set out far enough apart to allow for their full growth and to prevent disease in the garden. *Distance Apart to Place*

Allow distance between plants equal to one-half their mature height. Thus plants which grow three feet high should be set out one and one-half feet apart, and those which grow only one foot high should be set out six inches apart.

Most perennials need to be shifted twice. The only difference in the transplanting of annuals and perennials is that perennials are moved to a second "flat" instead of to the open ground. Put a handful of bonemeal to each second "flat" of soil. In raising perennials from seed, a shade of some sort is advisable. It is suggested that a shelf which holds *Perennials Care*

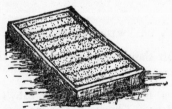

about six "flats" be attached to the back of a building, over which a light screen of unbleached domestic should be hinged, operating with a small rope and pulley, to protect the seedlings from storm and sun alike.

After the small plants are well started, either in the second "flat" or in the open bed, water them every ten days with weak manure-water. (See page 19.) *Forcing Growth*

The roots of plants play an important part in their existence, be they taproots or fibrous roots. They hold the plant
in position and draw sustenance from the soil. Taproots are
highly developed in such plants as the Poppy and Mignonette,
and care must be taken in transplanting not to injure them.
Too deep cultivation in a garden may injure the fibrous roots,
resulting in loss of bloom, and is, therefore, to be avoided.

ANNUALS . . . "WHAT TO PLANT IN SPRING"

Annuals which may be planted in March or April:

In Flats (OR *Open*[1] *Beds*) are: Ageratum, Alyssum, Arctotis,
Calliopsis, Cosmos, Cockscomb, Forget-me-not, Globe Amaranth,
Hollyhocks (a biennial), Marigold, Periwinkle, Petunia, Portulaca,
Blue and Scarlet Sage (*Salvia*), Scabiosa, Verbena, Salpiglossis,
Klondike Cosmos, Annual Pinks (*Dianthus* Annual), Baby's Breath,
Torenia.

In Flats in the House: Feverfew, Dahlias and Zinnias.

In Open[1] *Beds:* Scarlet Runner Bean, Candytuft, Cypress Bean,
African Daisy, Four o'Clock, Moonflower, Morning Glories, Nasturtium.

Valley Note (*semi-tropical*): Seeds to plant in spring for summer-flowering: Balsam (*Impatiens balsamina*), Bachelor Button
(*Gomphrena*), Blanket flower (*Gaillardia*), Calliopsis, Clarkia,
Cockscomb (*Celosia*), Cosmos, Datura, Four o'Clock (*Mirabilis
jalapa*), Geranium,† Marigold,‡ Petunia,† Portulaca, Salvia,† Nico-
tana, Zinnia.

ANNUALS . . . "WHAT TO PLANT IN THE FALL"

Annuals which should be started after the first soaking
rain in September:

In Flats OR *Open*[1] *Beds:* Sweet Alyssum, Baby's Breath, Arctotis,
the Centaureas, Balsam, Chinese Forget-me-nots, Petunias, Pinks,
Snapdragons, any Daisies, Blue Salvia, Coreopsis, Pansies, Annual
Poinsettias, Tithonia.

In Flats: Calendula, late African Marigold.

In Open[1] *Beds:* Bluebonnet, Candytuft, Anchusa, Clarkia, Daisies, Cosmos, Stocks, Four o'Clocks, Larkspur, Mignonette, Phlox
drummondi, Cockscomb.

---

[1]Where climate permits.
†Indicates start in flats. ‡Transplant in January.

For Late Fall Bloom: Sow Zinnias and French and African Marigold in "flats" or open beds.

It sometimes pays to take a sporting chance on hardy annuals, such as Zinnias, and plant a few about the fifteenth of February, for very early bloom. Likewise, one may fill in some empty (see page 10) spots in the Autumn garden by planting French and African Marigolds and Zinnias in July. If the proper time for planting annuals has been neglected, good Summer bloom may be obtained by planting Annual Baby's Breath, Poppies and Larkspur the last of April or the first of May in the beds where bloom is desired, and Dahlias for Fall bloom may be started out-of-doors at this same time.

What May be Planted in Late Spring

Valley Note (semi-tropical): Depending on the variations in the weather, planting time ranges from late August (if there have been rains) to October (when no rain has cooled the ground sufficiently, and produced the needed humidity in the air). As a general rule the last week in September or the first week in October is safe.

Plant in fall: Ageratum, Alyssum, African Daisy (*Arctotis stoechadifolia*), *Gypsophila paniculata* (Baby's Breath), Butterfly flower,† (*Schizanthus*), Candytuft, Chinese Forget-me-not (*Cynoglossum*), Cornflower (*Centaurea*), Shasta Daisies,† Delphinium,†

---

†Indicates start in flats.   ‡Transplant in January.

Hollyhocks, (*Althea rosea*), Blue Lace Flower (*Didiscus*), Queen Anne's Lace (*Daucus carota*), Larkspur, Love-in-a-mist (*Nigella-damascena*), Marigolds (*Tagetes‡ and T . . . erecta*, or African; *T . . . patula*, French), Mourning Bride (*Scabiosa*), Nasturtium (*Tropaeolum*), Pansy (*Viola‡ tricolor*), Periwinkle (*Vinca*), Petunia,† Phlox, Pinks (*Dianthus*), Poppy (*Papaver*), and California poppy (*Eschscholtzia*), Shirley (*Rhoeas*), Painted tongue (*Salpiglossis*), Snapdragon (*Antirrhinum*), Statice, Stocks,† Strawflower (*Helichrysum bracteatum*), Sweet Pea (*Lathyrus odoratus*), Sweet William (*Dianthus barbatus*), Verbena.

Plants which reseed themselves easily are: Ageratum, Bluebonnet, Calliopsis, Coreopsis, Cornflower, Cosmos, Feverfew, Four o'Clock, Gaillardia, Larkspur, Poppies, Petunias, Annual Phlox, Portulaca, Queen's Lace and Annual Poinsettias.

PERENNIALS AND BIENNIALS

Time to Plant

The best time for planting perennial and biennial seeds is midsummer, but some of them *may* be started in April or May (Foxgloves, Columbines, Hollyhocks, Gaillardias, Bluebonnets and the Campanulas). Some perennials, like Pansies, Sweet William and Snapdragons should be treated like annuals, be planted in the late Summer or early Fall.

II. DIVISIONS

Those plants that do not set seed, or do not come true from seed, may often be divided at the roots, to form new plants and to avoid overcrowding. This is also a short cut to obtain promptly blooming plants.

How to Divide Roots

Whenever possible, gently separate the roots, using a spade or knife only when necessary. Some plants may be propagated by separating the *stolons* or *suckers* which are formed on the old plant as trailing branches underground.

Bulblets are formed in the case of some Lilies, notably the Tiger Lily, in the axils of the leaves on the stems; *bulbels*

†Indicates start in flats. ‡Transplant in January.

within the root scales of the old bulb as in the case of Narcissi and others; and corms, in case of Gladioli. These may be removed, and brought to blooming size through several seasons of growth.

Rhizomes, the underground stems which are formed on Iris and Lilies-of-the-Valley, bear roots and eyes from which the plants develop; and may be divided and planted, if care is taken to have at least one eye in each portion. Shallow, horizontal planting insures the best results.

Runners which root at intervals are sent out above ground by some plants, and spring up as new plants. These may be divided and set out in other places.

Some perennials, such as Violets and Coreopsis, form groups of *new shoots.* These need to be divided to secure new plants and to prevent crowding.

III. CUTTINGS

Three safe methods of increasing without variation varieties which do not come true from seeds are: by propagating from cuttings; from layers; and by grafting and budding.

Cuttings may be made from most perennials, roses and *Time* from trees and shrubs, either evergreen or deciduous. They may be made from leaf, stem, or root, according to the type of plant being propagated, and at any time of the year, although the early spring months are considered safest and best. There are two kinds of cuttings—soft wood and hard wood.

LEAF CUTTINGS

Leaf cuttings may be easily made from such plants as the Begonia, Succulents, and some forms of Cactus. One method is to take a whole leaf, cut it through the veins and put in a glass jar[1] filled with moist sand. Place the leaf so that the

---

[1]Generally, jars run up the heat too much unless the whole is kept shaded. I like much better to surround the cuttings with the sides of an old flat . . . lay over it one or two layers of cheesecloth, then water frequently. In putting the cuttings into the ground, place them almost parallel to the surface of the earth so that three inches of a four-inch cutting is buried, and the top leaves

veins will come in contact with the sand. The glass jar will keep the sand from drying out. Many cacti root very easily if the leaves next the stem are allowed to lie in moist soil.

STEM CUTTINGS

Stem cuttings are the type most often used by amateur gardeners. They are a safe and sure method of increasing stock and are to be heartily recommended for trial. It is best to cut off a piece about three inches long at the end of a stalk. Pull off all but the top leaves and put the slip in a bed of sand. Keep it well watered and well shaded until the roots are formed, after which it should be transplanted to a bed of loamy soil. The stem with its newly formed roots constitutes the new plant. The process will take on the average about three weeks. Because the food stored in the cells of the slip is only enough to maintain life, it must not be overtaxed, and hence, all but the top leaves should be removed.

SOFT-WOOD CUTTINGS

Cuttings from perennials are best made in Spring and Summer. They may be taken from Arabis, Chrysanthemum, Clematis, Coleus, Dahlias, Geranium, Hollyhocks, Delphinium, Lobelia, Phlox, Pinks, and others.

ROSE CUTTINGS

Rose cuttings may be made longer than perennial cuttings, usually from six to eight inches long. These cuttings, after being planted, should be covered with a glass fruit jar which should not be removed until the plant shows vigorous growth.

HARD-WOOD CUTTINGS

Shrubs and trees, such as Hydrangea, Spirea, Pomegranate, Althea and Crape Myrtle may easily be rooted during the

---

are in contact with the soil—lay them so the bottom of the leaves are on the soil—that cuts down evaporation, and keeps the cuttings fresh—a very important rule. Take lots of cuttings. If you want twenty plants get a hundred cuttings, and you are much more apt to succeed.—PERSIS CROCKER.

Spring months. Cuttings of mature flower-stems, six or eight inches long, may be planted (an inch or so being left above the ground) and thoroughly watered. If the cuttings are made in the Fall, they are best tied together in bunches, completely buried in damp soil or sand, and mulched. They are ready for planting in the Spring. (See page 63.)

EVERGREEN CUTTINGS

Evergreen Cuttings, made preferably in the Summer, will also root if the lower leaves are removed and the stripped portion planted in moist sand. They should remain in the cold frame until they are to be moved to open beds, in the Spring.

ROOT CUTTINGS

Those plants which do not form a mass of roots, but have thick, fleshy roots, may be propagated from root cuttings. Divide the root into pieces an inch or so long, plant in a flat of good soil, and keep watered and shaded until they root. This will take place in about a week. Root cuttings are best made in August or September, from such plants as Japanese Anemone, Oriental Poppy, and Plumbago.

IV. LAYERING

The process of *layering*, employed especially with the Pink (*Dianthus*) family, is a simple and certain way to reproduce the original plant. It consists in rooting a part of the plant without detaching it until it is rooted. If young shoots are fastened firmly to earth, preferably near an eye or joint, and covered with earth, they will form calluses from which roots will soon develop. (See page 63). The new plants may then be separated from the old and moved to their permanent positions. Besides Pinks of various kinds, Magnolia, Jasmine, Holly, Verbena, Dogwood, Honeysuckle, Juniper, and others, may be propagated in this manner.

V. GRAFTING AND BUDDING

Grafting and budding both mean the union of the growing tissues of two plants. *Grafting* is the insertion of a twig bearing one or more buds of one plant into the growing wood of the other. *Budding* is the insertion of a single bud beneath the bark.

The *scion* is the part which is inserted into the *stock* or rooted portion, which supplies food for the scion. Although the bark and wood tissues of the scion and the stock are knit together, each retains its identifying characteristics.

The chief reasons for grafting are to perpetuate certain varieties, and to enable certain plants to live in different soil under conditions otherwise unfavorable to them. The stock is made to support an entirely different flower or fruit from that which the scion produces after it has grown.

Time

Grafting should be done in the Spring after the sap begins to rise and is successful only in plants which form a layer of bark covering the wood. It is necessary that the *cambium* layer, or that tissue lying between bark and wood of both scion and stock, *be in contact*.

Seedlings may be grafted, thus propagating certain kinds of ornamental trees and shrubs; young trees (such as oranges or other fruits) and the trunk and branches of older trees, *if* the choice of stock is always made from closely related families. Thus Apples, Pears, and Quinces will unite as will Flowering Quince, Hawthorn and Photinia. Many Conifers also, such as Arbor Vitae, Juniper and Cypress may be grafted.

After the graft is made, it should be waxed with grafting wax to prevent evaporation. It may be applied at each graft, either by hand or by means of strips of cloth dipped in the wax and tied tightly about the union. This process is a delicate one, requiring accuracy of touch and much practice; and a great deal can be learned from the books and nurserymen.

VI. COLD FRAMES

There are various ways of circumventing the seasons and gaining time and size and quickness of bloom. Hot Beds, cold-frames and small greenhouses will accomplish this.

A hotbed in warm climates is not as satisfactory as a cold frame.

The cold frame is so called because there is no artificial heat. A good size is nine by six feet, ten inches high in front and eighteen inches high in the back, with three glass sashes. Within this frame, excavate to a depth of one foot. Mix with the topsoil, sand and manure, (leaf-mold or compost) as follows: One wheelbarrow of topsoil to one-half a barrow of sand and one-half a barrow of manure. Mix well; sift; and replace in the frame, allowing it to settle thoroughly before planting.

Sashes may be secured with double glass, with a space between that acts like a thermos bottle, holding the heat. Sashes should be attached to the frame with hinges at the top, and must be opened during the day, except in freezing weather. Use bricks as props, turning on the various sides according to the warmth of the day.

This is an ideal way to start plants for the hardy borders, to be transplanted when the danger of frost is past. Where a great number are needed to give a mass effect, the cold frame is much the most satisfactory way to propagate them, and very much less expensive than buying them by the dozens.

Seedlings in the cold frame become acclimated and develop better than plants shipped from a distance, so that often flowers may be had that have hitherto been thought impossible for a location because of the climate.

One of the dangers of a cold frame is dampening off of the seedlings. This may be controlled by sterilizing the soil and by watering sparingly.

VII. GARDEN SECRETS

In setting out small plants in the open ground care should be taken in lifting to keep as much dirt on the roots as possible. Gently press well-pulverized, soft dirt around the roots—set in holes just large enough to contain them—fill with water—firming the plants with additional dry dirt.

Winter Protection

Winter protection is necessary in certain sections for a number of plants, particularly for Queen's Wreath (*Antigonon*), Cannas, Chrysanthemums, Plumbago, Lantanas, Salvia *leucantha* and Verbenas. A small shovelful of barnyard manure usually affords sufficient covering and has the added value of providing fertilization, but it has been found that sheep manure, used as a winter protection is too strong.

Mark your garden tools plainly to avoid loss!

To test seeds' fertility: Scatter seed on a brick or sheet of blotting-paper, and float (on a wood shingle) in a pan or dish of water, covered with a piece of clear glass. Keep in a warm room. The number of seed that sprout will determine the ratio of probable germination.

Small branches of Euonymus, placed in window boxes to supply a background of green, will frequently take root, if kept sufficiently moist, and can be used later to replenish hedges, etc.

Time of Planting

Amateurs are often confused by the apparent conflicting advice as to *Time of Planting*.

Fall

The advantage of planting seed in the fall is that a deeper root-system is established, insuring a much stronger plant, finer quality, and much longer season of bloom.

Spring

However, a certain amount of success may be secured from planting seed in the Spring, remembering that all seed to be sown in the Spring should be in the ground by St. Patrick's Day.

Rule

An easy rule to keep in mind is that Spring-flowering plants should be sown in the Fall; Summer and Fall-flowering plants should be sown in the Spring.

Poppy seed must lie in the ground many days before they germinate, so plant them as early in the fall as possible.

Calendulas and Dianthus sown in September in the cold frame are much earlier than those planted in the open.

It is not generally known that Dahlias may be grown from seed. They will bloom the first year if started in March in the cold frame. Sow the seed *thinly,* in rows. Sprinkle sand over them, and tamp them with a small, flat board. (See page 169.)

Transplanting Petunias and Verbenas ... plant on a slant; and as the stem grows peg it down with hairpins, covering with soil. Each joint will take root, making a mass-planting in a short time from *very* few plants.

An interesting fact is that often the color of a blossom *Color* may be determined by the stem of the small seedling. This is especially noticeable with Snapdragons.

TIME-TABLE OF PLANTING

In Fall

All leaf-losing trees, shrubs, fruit trees, roses, and hardy herbaceous border plants.

Evergreens are most successful if planted in fall.

Divide Iris in *early* fall. May be transplanted in clumps at any season in Southwest.

Divide Hemerocallis.

Divide, or transplant most perennials.

Divide Hardy Phlox.

Seeds sown in fall (page 128).

Plant most bulbs.

In Spring

Choice evergreens *may* be planted as late as April, if balled.

Divide in early spring
   Artemesia.
   Chrysanthemums.
   Crinum.
   Daisies (Shasta).
   Hardy Asters (Michaelmas Daisies).
   Japanese Anemones (Windflower).

Seed sown in spring (page 130).

Seed sown in summer (page 131).

COLOR NOTES

More brilliant color—especially the yellows of roses—may be secured by watering in a solution of one ounce of *nitrate of iron* (*copper sulphate* or *copperas*) diluted in two gallons of water, which is better than a solution of *nitrate of soda.*

Anything iron (nails, iron filings, etc.) in the soil around the plant will deepen pinks and reds.

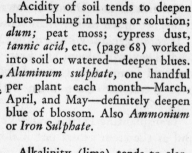

Acidity of soil tends to deepen blues—bluing in lumps or solution; *alum;* peat moss; cypress dust, *tannic acid*, etc. (page 68) worked into soil or watered—deepen blues. *Aluminum sulphate*, one handful per plant each month—March, April, and May—definitely deepen blue of blossom. Also *Ammonium* or *Iron Sulphate*.

Alkalinity (lime) tends to clarify whites.

Cut flowers placed in water that contains dye (from crepe paper, *mercurochrome, indigo,* bluing, ink or water-colors, for instance) will assume deeper, or extraordinary hues.

Superphosphate (really dissolved bonemeal) is not only a good general fertilizer—produces more bloom and increases brilliancy of color.

To increase blossoms. The phosphates:
Superphosphate
Potash
Phosphorus
Nitrate of Soda
scattered around plants and watered in will cause them to bloom more freely.

VIII. EFFECT OF LIGHT ON VEGETATION[1]

The greatest factory in the world is the green leaf of the plant. In it, in light, the carbon dioxide of the air, with water and the inorganic compounds of the soil, is manufactured

[1] EDITORIAL NOTE—The scientific basis for this section is found in work being done at Boyce-Thompson Institute for Plant Research at Yonkers, N. Y., by

into starches and sugars—carbohydrates of one sort or another—that form the basis of all the foodstuffs of all the world. Every animal must draw its sustenance from plants in some way, for animals cannot manufacture the foods they need. In their bodies they arrange plant foods into animal materials; but the green plant alone can take gases from the air, mineral matter and water from the soil, and then, activated by the tremendous energy of the sun, can transform these inorganic materials into organic energy suitable for plant and animal food.

Photo-Synthesis

Foods made by the plant may be used at once in the processes of growth, flowering and setting seed, or the plant may store the manufactured materials in its body. The plant body, built up by this food storage, gives us wood with all its uses, coal, natural oil and gas, besides all the things into which these may be divided. It is the stored foods that tie up the sun's energy and hold it until a new process releases it. The source of energy in this great factory is light, and the process of food-making taking place in the green leaves is called *photosynthesis*, "Building up by Light."

Factors in Rate of Plant Growth

The rate of plant growth is limited not only by the peculiarities of the plant itself but also by external factors, such as light intensity and duration, carbon dioxide supply, temperature, and water supply. In nature a plant rarely has an opportunity to grow at its maximum rate. Possibly many would grow a little faster if the days were a little moister, or warmer, or the sun a little brighter. In a greenhouse these conditions can be varied and are easily controlled, so scientists have long been able to tell us what are the highest and lowest temperatures that a given plant will endure, and also what temperature leads to the greatest development.

Dr. John M. Arthur and his associates. Much of the valuable information which is being secured from the experiments conducted by the scientists at the Boyce-Thompson Institute will be of vital assistance to plant growers in the Southwest, as their deductions explain why certain plants that flourish in other locations fail to thrive here. This Institute was founded in 1924 by the late Colonel William Boyce-Thompson, and has already become famous for its findings on seed germination, on the control of blight, on locating the cause of mosaic disease, and on the speeding up of growth and fruiting of shrubs and plants. This article has been contributed by Persis S. Crocker, wife of Dr. William Crocker, Director of the Institute.

One of the hardest things to study is the carbon dioxide supply, but recent apparatus, which permits the investigator to control the supply of that gas makes it apparent that it, too, is often the factor that limits the rate of the amount of growth. Three-hundredths of a per cent of carbon dioxide gas is present in average air. If in the course of an experiment the carbon dioxide is kept at ten times the average amount or three-tenths of a per cent, and the other growth factors are kept at a favorable point, plants kept in these conditions show a great increase in rate of growth. If the plants are given not only more CO_2, but also a longer period of light, that is, if the normal day is supplanted by artificial light, the increased rate of growth is startling.

A room at Boyce-Thompson Institute, the winter of 1928, was equipped with powerful lights, so powerful that their light closely approached sunlight, both in intensity and quality. Temperature, humidity, and carbon dioxide supply were closely controlled. Beside this room was another exactly like it, except it was perfectly dark. A variety of plants were placed in these rooms, some of them staying in the light all the time and some being moved on a regular schedule between the light and dark rooms. By means of this experiment it has been determined how the length of the day influences plant growth.

Influence of Day Length

One thing comes out clearly, in many plants it is the *length of time* that they are *illuminated* each day and *not the temperature* that brings on flowering. There are short-day plants, long-day plants and indifferent plants. Our Fall-blooming flowers, Salvia, Cosmos, Dahlia, Chrysanthemum, and possibly Sunflower, are some of the many plants that flower on the short day. Salvia blooms, as a tiny seedling, in the cold frame in the Spring, but stops and forms no buds at all as the days grow longer. With more than twelve hours of sunlight the plants grow larger and larger, but form no buds until the days grow shorter in the Fall. When a twelve-hour, or shorter day arrives, bud formation begins and flowering continues until frost.

There are very few long-day plants among the greenhouse

plants. They have no flower on a short day to do well in usual greenhouse conditions. So, any plants that are normally grown in a greenhouse are either short-day plants or plants that are indifferent.

EFFECT OF CONTROLL OF LIGHT ON SALVIA.

Lettuce Long Day Plants

A plant that needs a long day for flowering is Lettuce. One commonly hears, "The days are getting warmer, so the Lettuce will shoot," but it has been determined that unless the *length* of *day* is more than twelve hours, the same Lettuce cannot be kept from blossoming, even at a much lower temperature.

Short Day Plants

In both Lettuce and Salvia, usefulness is increased by a short day, because in one case we want the plant to bloom and in the other we want it not to. By planting Salvia close to the east side of a building, the heavy shading the plants get in the afternoon will shorten their day length and hasten their flowering somewhat. Salvia grows well but will not flower when it receives more than sixteen hours of daylight —remaining vegetative when receiving seventeen hours or greater, yet when receiving as few as five hours will come into flower, though imperfectly. Chrysanthemums may be brought into flower much earlier by the exclusion of the sunlight for several hours of each day. It has been suggested that paper cups may be used for this purpose or other protective shade.

Asters will flower on a short day, but on a funny, shortened stem, so the whole plant looks like a blossoming Hyacinth. Petunias, Nasturtiums and Sweet Peas will bloom very sparingly on a short day, but reserve their greatest efforts for the long ones.

Certain plants pay no attention to day length. Marigolds, Snapdragons, Roses and Calendulas are notable examples in the garden. In these plants blossoming begins as soon as the plants grow big enough and continues until cut off by cold weather. In the tropics many plants have the characteristic of flowering continuously.

Since the length of day varies according to the latitude, from the twelve-hour day at the equator to the twenty-four hour midsummer day at the poles, it is evident that plants with definite requirements in day length will vary greatly in their time of flowering, depending on *where* they are being grown. In general, the plants of the very cold regions have to be those that respond to the very long days by rushing through their life history at a rate unheard of in the regions nearer the tropics. Short-day plants have no place in these conditions because cold becomes a limiting factor before short days arrive. Just the opposite is the case in the subtropics where the days follow one another with little change in temperature or day-length and there the plants wander through their life history, growing to a great size, it is true, on account of favorable conditions, but not rushing from one thing to another as a successful plant must in arctic conditions.

IX. HOW TO PLANT

Plants and seed, Sir Wm. Hooker discovered by trial, thrive best and are most vigorous when imported from North to South . . . even from North to South America. From South America those most adapted to North American temperate zone are from the heights of the Andes, not the lowlands, nor from the same temperature and climatic range.

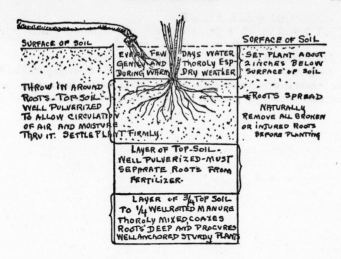

SURFACE OF SOIL

SURFACE OF SOIL

EVERY FEW DAYS WATER GENTLY AND THOROLY ESP DURING WARM DRY WEATHER

SET PLANT ABOUT 2 INCHES BELOW SURFACE OF SOIL

THROW IN AROUND ROOTS - TOP SOIL WELL PULVERIZED TO ALLOW CIRCULATION OF AIR AND MOISTURE THRU IT. SETTLE PLANT FIRMLY.

ROOTS SPREAD NATURALLY REMOVE ALL BROKEN OR INJURED ROOTS BEFORE PLANTING

LAYER OF TOP-SOIL. WELL PULVERIZED-MUST SEPARATE ROOTS FROM FERTILIZER.

LAYER OF 3/4 TOP SOIL TO 1/4 WELL ROTTED MANURE THOROLY MIXED COAXES ROOTS DEEP AND PROCURES WELL ANCHORED STURDY PLANTS

PROPAGATION QUICKENERS

(1) All seed planted in flats or out of doors: use disinfectant (see page 127).

(2) Bulbs—especially gladioli. Dip in solution of *corrosive sublimate* (see Bug article).

As preventative for lilies sprinkle *sulphur* (see Bug article).

All bulbs may be dipped quickly in and out of hot water; or into a 2% *lime sulphur* solution for half an hour—dry thoroughly.

(3) Hard-coat seeds. (Broom, Lupine, Redbud, Peas, etc.) (see page 125).

(4) Cuttings set in sand or soil:

a. Soft—(Chrysanthemums, Hardy Phlox, etc.)

Use white vinegar (*acetic acid*), 3 teaspoons to 1 gallon water. Soak 24 hours; *Potassium Permanganate*, 1 ounce to 5 gals. water; also

b. Hard—(woody plants, shrubs, etc.) Use as above except after cuttings are set in soil water with solution at first, then clear water as soon as foliage appears. (p. 63, 134).

c. Carnation cuttings in sand. Water with *Permanganate of Potash* (taking only side shoots from center of stem). Teaspoon to 2½ quarts water.

d. See "Textbook of Botany" by Prof. Small of Belfast, for additional specific information.

(5) Bluebonnet seed: Soak in *Sulphuric Acid* 10 to 20 minutes. Wash thoroughly and plant. Will germinate quickly and readily. They are especially adaptable plants for hillsides.

TO AVOID WEAK STEMS:

Soil devoid of *silica* produces weak soft-stemmed plants. Also too much *nitrogen* causes weak, lush growth.

TO PRODUCE LONGER STEMS:

To produce long stems, especially on early flowering bulbs, if the season is dry, water until tops of leaves appear. Semi-shade and moisture encourage growth, heat combined with dryness dwarf it.

Spring-Flowering Bulbs

OMEONE HAS compared the Bulb season to a The Bulb Season many-coursed meal. The blossoms of the tiny, early Spring Bulbs are the appetizer or relish. What greater whet to one's appetite for beauty could be found? Then come the substantial things—Daffodils, Hyacinths, Tulips, and Gladioli. These are followed by an entree of Lilies, Dahlias and Montbretias, with Autumn Crocus for dessert.

A thrill of joy is experienced on discovering these dainty The Earliest Bloom little flowers, many of the first of which are so tiny they elude the eye, and only reward one after diligent search. All of these early Spring Bulbs may be used for naturalizing under the trees or where grass is difficult, or they may be planted in shoals in the perennial border. They may be planted fairly deep and do not require transplanting (or thinning) for several years.

SMALL BULBS

Glory of the Snow (*Chionodoxa*) has flowers of white, blue and rose. It is one of the first Spring Bulbs to bloom. Mass-planting forms a sumptuous display. It multiplies rapidly in loose soil and can be propagated easily from seed.

Scilla (Squill, in variety) is one of the best Bulbs for naturalizing and will succeed well in the shade, under cedars, and in moist places. Among the *campanulata* types there are *cærula* (blue); *rosea* (pink), and *alba* (white). They bear spikes about fifteen inches high. It is difficult in calcareous soil.

Anemones are considered half-hardy, so should have protection in coldest weather. *St. Brigid* is a fine strain, and shows many lovely shades. There are native varieties, known as "Woodland Violets," indigenous to the oakwood and limestone rocks of East Texas.

Montbretias are among the most colorful of the Summer-flowering Bulbs. They are very like Gladioli and make a brilliant display in June and July. The blooms are produced in many flowered sprays on long stalks, and are fine for cutting. They are easy to grow, but should be planted in the Fall, three to four inches deep, and three to six inches or more apart.

Ranunculas are quite tender, and must have protection. They have beautiful double flowers of many colors on strong straight stems, eight to twelve inches long. Treat them as annuals.

Crocus come in several named varieties and are all beautiful. They are not dependable. In many sections should be treated as an annual. They apparently do not like heavy soil. They relish melting snow and ice, so water through the winter.

Galanthus (Snow Drops) are very effective under hedges and cedar trees. They multiply well, but resent being disturbed.

Erythronium (Dog-toothed Violet) is hardy and very early. There are several native varieties. The most generally known is light lavender, yet white, pink and yellow varieties may be obtained. All are very lovely for Rock Gardens, but prefer semi-shady places. They should be planted about five inches deep.

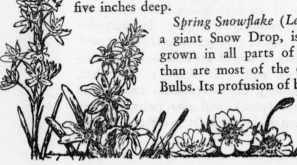

Spring Snowflake (*Leucojum vernum*), like a giant Snow Drop, is perhaps more easily grown in all parts of the South and West than are most of the early Spring-flowering Bulbs. Its profusion of bell-shaped, pure white flowers, tipped with bright green, are so lovely that its failure to have a pleasing perfume is a real disappointment. They are very charming in large clumps where it is wise to let remain undisturbed for several years, under trees, or among other plants. *Leucojum Autumnale* blooms in Fall and has red instead of green tips on its white bells.

Triteleias, lovely pale blue-lavender *Brodiaea,* prefer rather dry locations, well-drained, loose and not too rich soil. Under Spanish oaks and pecan trees they seem to thrive in the semi-protection and semi-shade. Some varieties require moist conditions. All grow readily from seed.

Muscari (Grape Hyacinths) are especially effective in mass-planting. They are bright blue and make a brilliant spot of color under trees. They like a *loose, sandy soil,* just *as all Bulbs prefer,* that they may multiply more readily.

Hyacinths are suitable for bedding purposes. Their colors of yellow, pink, red, blue, lavender, purple and white, with their rich, green foliage, form a lovely picture, besides filling the air with fragrance. The Dutch and French single varieties are dainty and lovely. These may be used in naturalizing and are most advisable out of doors, and will multiply if not given too much water.

HYACINTHS

SHORTLY AFTER World War I a quarantine preventing the importation of Narcissus bulbs was put into effect, in the effort to control introduction of those insects and diseases which had attacked this bulb in other countries. No Narcissi of any kind were admitted, except under special permit, and then only in limited quantities for commercial propagation. American growers, as an inevitable result of this quarantine, started a new industry as soon as it was definitely proved the Narcissus could be successfully grown in this country on a commercial basis. Several Dutch firms transferred their stocks, worth hundreds of thousands of dollars, to this side of the Atlantic. The Pacific Northwest and Virginia have taken the lead in bulb-growing and a great number of varieties have already been introduced. However, America has just begun to know the joy of growing Daffodils.

MODERN DAFFODILS

The Narcissi are divided into many very definite groups. It would be most difficult to name all of the types. From the gorgeous array offered by the catalogues it is most bewildering to make a choice until one realizes that the several types follow each other in their time of bloom. Also, the individual varieties under each type offer many possibilities of having early, intermediate, and late flowering.

It would be impossible to give an adequate description of the modern Daffodils. They beggar description. Not only in size, but in texture, color-harmony, types and heights, they are marvelous.

The following outline may be of assistance to the amateur in choosing a representative collection.

NARCISSI CLASSIFICATIONS

The Giant Trumpets: Best known of the Narcissi, perhaps, are the Giant Trumpets, which are distinguished by their very long cups. The blossoms are of tremendous size; many are all yellow; a few all white; and some, white and yellow.

The Yellow Trumpets are valuable because of their early appearance and for their rich color, among them *King Alfred*, with his court of long Trumpeters, has long asserted supremacy through unusual adaptability to this region, literally thousands being grown in our sandy lands for commercial purposes.

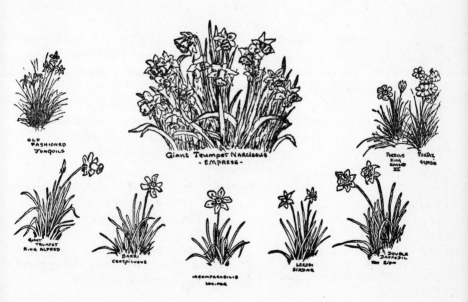

Soon after *King Alfred* begins to bloom *Treserve* appears. This in turn, is followed several days later by *Robert Snydenham*. The individual blossoms of each have such amazing durability that a wealth of bloom may be secured from a limited number of bulbs of these three varieties alone. Should one desire varieties of the earlier blooming Trumpets, *Treserve* and *Robert Snydenham, Olympia, Weardale's Perfection* and *Van Waverings' Giant* are the nearest to follow *King Alfred. Emperor* and *Empress* prolong the season, blooming about the time of *Robert Snydenham*.

Mme. de Graaff has long been considered the best all-white, but she is fast being supplanted by *Mrs. E. H. Krelage. Weardale's Perfection* and *Empress* are very popular among the striking bi-color trumpets.

The Incomparabilis: Incomparabilis are among the most beautiful of the Narcissi, with their large cups that are shorter, or equal, in length with the perianth (or surrounding circle of petals). The several types are all yellow, yellow perianth with white cups, and yellow perianth with red and orange cups. Try *Sir Watkin* and *Will Scarlet.*

Incomparabilis Sir Watkin begins to flower before the Long Trumpets have gone, while later blooming varieties of the *Incomparabilis* group overlap, again, the *Leedsis*, the *Barris* and the *Poeticus.*

The Leedsii: These are the nymphs of the Daffodils. They have both large and small cups, in whicn the perianth segments are white, and the cups white cream, or lemon.

White Lady, Queen of the North, Evangeline and *Sirdar* have all proved satisfactory.

The Barrii: The cups of the *Barrii* are about one-third the length of the petals.

The most outstanding of this class is *Conspicuous*, while other varieties are *Albatross, Lady Godiva*, and *Bath's Flame.* All of these have proved satisfactory.

The Poeticus: The chief characteristic of the *Poeticus* group is the white Perianth that surrounds the short, wide-mouthed cup. The *Poeticus,* or *Pheasant's Eye* has been named "The Poet's Narcissus."

Poeticus Horace and *Poeticus Recurvus* are both lovely.

The Poetaz: No collection should be complete without a few of the late blooming *Poetaz,* for their unusual habit of blooming in clusters makes them very distinct and desirable.

The Double Daffodils: The Double Daffodils are not generally satisfactory, often green and do not open well. *Von Sion* is considered the best of this group for the Southwest, although it has many newer rivals.

BULB CULTURE

Daffodils require much the same culture as other bulbs. Fork the ground deep; and, if the soil is heavy, lighten with some sand. Add bonemeal and mix thoroughly. Remember that good drainage is very essential. Always select the largest, firmest bulbs possible when buying, for these are usually the double-nosed, or "mother" bulbs, that will split into three or more the next season.

Plant four to six inches deep, preferably in August or September, if they can be secured at that time. Narcissi may be left where they are planted for several years, or until the clumps need dividing; or, after foliage has died down, they may be dug and replanted.

Never cut the foliage off while green, for this year's foliage makes next year's blossoms. A good plan is to tie it up to a stake until mature, or browned, to keep it from sprawling untidily.

TULIPS

As far back as 1554 we know that the Saracens saw Tulips in the gardens of Egypt. They were later carried into Western Europe and were seen in the beautiful gardens of Spain at an early date. From Spain the Dutch carried Tulip bulbs to their gardens, and soon their culture became an important industry in Holland.

In the early part of the seventeenth century this cultivation of Tulips developed very rapidly. Everybody wanted Tulips. It was a fine hobby, but alas! it degenerated into gambling. A Tulip-mania struck the land, and soon the Dutch were gambling with bulbs as Americans do with cotton, oil and stocks of all kinds. This gambling lasted from 1634 to 1637. All kinds of auctions were held, and enormous sums of money changed hands. People of every walk of life tried to make a fortune. In 1637 the States of Holland decided to put a stop to this gambling, and issued a proclamation to that effect. The gambling mania was finally curbed, yet the fever for perfection of bulbs has never died out; so the present high standard has gradually evolved.

The different groups come into bloom in this order: single and double-flowering Darwins; the Breeder; and, lastly, the Cottage Tulips. There are varieties of each of such outstanding merit that they retain their popularity year after year.

Darwins are distinguished by their bright colors and tall stems.

In Breeder Tulips one finds the blends and the pastel shades. They are somewhat taller than the Darwins.

In Cottage Tulips you find every shade and color. Yellow is found in this, and, until recently, was not to be had in the Darwins or Breeders.

Tulips are best in herbaceous borders in groups, planted generally about five inches below the surface, sometimes a bit deeper.

SOME NATIVE BULBS AND TUBERS

Allium *Helleri* and **Allium** *mutabile*—Loose umbel of white and pink florets. Grassy foliage.

Anemone (*Decapetala*) (Wood Violets)—Pale blue; grow under oaks and elms. Found in pockets of limestone rocks; good for rock gardens.

Androstephium (*Caeruleum*) (Wild Hyacinth)—Light blue, sometimes pale violet like Camassias. A low plant; good for rock gardens.

Betony (*Pedicularis*)—Purplish-bronze flowers; delicate, fern-like foliage. Early spring blooming; excellent hillside plant.

Blue-Eyed Grass (*Sisyrinchium varians*)—Violet-blue flowers. Central Texas variety.

Blue-Eyed Grass (*Sisyrinchium pruinosum*)—North Texas variety. Good for rock gardens.

ANEMONE DECAPETALA

Blue-Eyed Grass (*Sisyrinchium exile*)—Gulf variety. Sandy soil.

Blue-Eyed Grass (*Sisyrinchium colubriferum*)—East Texas variety. Sandy prairies.

Blue-Eyed Grass (*Sisyrinchium longipedunculatum*)—West Texas and Mountain variety.

Blue-Eyed Grass (*Sisyrinchium minus*) (Dwarf)—East Texas variety. Moist prairies.

Celestials (*Nemastylis acuta*)—Grass-like leaves, pale blue flowers, six to twelve inches.

Celestials (*Nemastylis coelestina*)—Grass-like leaves, pale blue flowers, denizens of both the prairies and woods.

Callirhoe (*pedata*) (Poppy Mallow)—Cherry red or deep wine; poppy-like flowers; gay on hillsides. Prefers sunny location.

Callirhoe (*Linearibola*)—Pinkish Lilac, or white. Trailing; withstands drought.

Camassia (*Fraseri*) (False Hyacinth)—Pale violet or blue flowers; lovely in clumps. Found on well-drained slopes.

Camassia (*hyacinthiana*)—Sky blue flowers.

Claytonia (*virginica*) (Spring Beauty)—Flowers in pink racemes. Found thriving where the Dogwood grows.

Dodecatheon (*Meadia*) (Shooting Star)—Rose white flowers. Grows with Spring Beauties. "American Cyclamen."

Dodecatheon (*Albesceus*)—Lavender and rose flowers.

Erythronium (*americanum*) (Dogtoothed Violet)—Yellow and lavender.

Erythronium (*albidum*)—White. Grows in shade.

Erythronium (*Coloratum*)—Rose-colored. Grows in shade.

Liatris (*Punctata*) (Blazing Star or Gay Feather)—Purple plumes on upright, tall spikes. Grows well in dry, poor locations, in sun.

Viola (*Missouriensis*)—Tufted, large, pale blue. Prefers semi shade.

Viola (*Rafinesque*) (Heartsease)—Tufted, darker, pansy-like, blue flowers.

The Lily, The Iris, The Rose

THROUGH song and story, down the ages innumerable, has come the fame of the Lily, the Iris, and the Rose. This immortal trio continues to hold chief place in the hearts and minds of men.

Lilies are the Aristocrats of the Garden, and so they should be treated. The exquisite beauty of a single stalk, against soft green (the most complimentary of backgrounds for a Lily's delicacy) gives one that thrill of subtle pleasure which is never attained through mass-effect.

Symbols that antedate written history picture the Lily in intimate association with Royalty, a silent testimony to the fact that these early rulers of men were capable of appreciation of the most exquisite of all of Nature's offerings; and, appropriating it for their individual use, expressed to the world their haughty belief in their own and Nature's attainment to perfection.

The majesty of the Iris has long been immortalized, and its pictorial images have been used as symbols of man's religion and emotions. To the people of France, their *Fleur de Lis* symbolizes the Christian religion, and under that conventionalized form, Iris was chosen the royal emblem of the ancient monarch of the realm.

Named for the Greek Goddess of the Rainbow, the Iris reigns in the hearts of the Southern and Gaelic peoples. Its exquisite, classic beauty is closely allied with that of the Lily, whose chaste purity is unexcelled—a true symbol of perfection arising out of and above the mire, untouched by its contaminating nearness!

For many centuries in company with the Lotus of the Egyptian Pharaohs (the Lily of the Nile) and the *Fleur de Lis* of France, the Rose of England has been used extensively for ornamentation and in heraldry. With them it has shared the love and admiration of countless thousands. Its warm beauty nestles close to the hearts of men, and glows in the full bloom of their affections.

The Rose is the Queen of the North! During the fifteenth century in England, the contestants for the throne chose as their emblem the Rose—the House of York wearing the White Rose, and the House of Lancaster the Red Rose. As both York and Lancaster were descendants of Owen Tudor and Queen Catherine, the succeeding monarchs combined the two roses in heraldic design into one that is known as the Tudor Rose.

Based on the ancient fable that the heart of a Rose is never disclosed, from time immemorial at Council meetings the emblem hung on the walls was a Rose—a symbol that meant that secrecy would be asked of those gathered "under the Rose."

Lilies

ESS THAN A generation ago it was the general belief that few Lilies could be grown in heavy lime soil (of the Southwest) yet, today, a number of varieties are being cultivated most successfully. The reason for this is that the information which has been so generously published by the horticulturists who have been studying the best growing conditions for plants has enabled the selection of those types best suited or adaptable to climate and soil.

Scientists have divided the members of the Lily family into three groups: (1) those that abhor lime, (2) those that tolerate it, and (3) those that seem to thrive under any soil condition. The type of soil required by each variety of Lily is often stated in the catalogues of the commercial growers who specialize in their cultivation.

Comparatively little experimental work has been done by amateur gardeners with Lilies. Interest in them, however, particularly in the hardy varieties, has tremendously increased in recent years. It can be safely stated that they are becoming the most popular of hardy bulbs. Not a little of this popularity has come from the lovely *Lily regale*, brought from Western China to this country by the revered Ernest H. Wilson.

The Lily has been prominent in literature for thousands of years. Biblical writers of both the Old and New Testaments extol its beauty. It is probable that "The Lily of the Field" in Holy Scriptures was the true *Lilium candidum*, the *Madonna Lily*, this being a native of parts of the Holy Land.

Lilies are natives of the Northern Hemisphere; and extend around the world. China and Japan have furnished us with the greatest number of varieties, but Europe and North America have quite a number to their credit.

We are indebted to South Africa for a number of most interesting bulbs and lilies . . . among them, Amaryllis, Clivia, Nerine, Freesias, Gladioli (best known), Tritonia, Montbretias (easily grown), Ixia, Morea, Watsonia and a host of lesser known bulbs that bid fair to become very popular now that they may be secured readily. The testing of these to develop their hardiness and garden value presents a challenge to the venturesome gardener.

Fritillaria imperialis (Crown Imperial) is also being more generally planted. It is the showiest of its specie.

Oxalis and *Cooperi* are native and hardy—excellent in borders.

The Shell-flowers of Mexico—the *Tigridias*—bloom from July to frost. They require a sunny location, and are very effective.

Lilium longifolium (Out-of-door Easter Lily) is hardy and fragrant.

Lilium philippinense formosanum is fragrant, hardy, and grows from two to three feet—is white marked with reddish-brown—and has proved resistant to winds and weather.

Lilium auratum—the Goldband Lily of Japan—is possibly the loveliest of all garden flowers. It blooms in midsummer; and *demands* acid soil.

I. LILY CULTURE

Lilies like their bloom-stalks in the sun, but their feet cool, so plant them among low-growing Annuals or Perennials, or near shrubs.

There are many Lilies that will grow where the Dogwood is to be found that will not live elsewhere.

SOIL

Pearl Van Horn Stuart has said:

"There seems to be no general agreement as to what constitutes ideal soil for Lilies. However, if the beds are pre-

pared properly, the Lily will be grateful. My experience has
been in sandy soil. Yet, I dig out my bed eighteen inches
deep, put in about three inches of well-decayed compost of
leaf-mold, cover this about six inches with natural (sandy)
soil. The trench is then nine inches deep.

"To plant large bulbs, cover the bulb with three inches of
same soil, then three inches of well-decayed cow manure, the
remaining three inches cover with same mixture as first. This
may apply in tight black or clay soil, but the bulbs should be
planted seven inches instead of nine inches deep. (*With all
Lilies, be SURE to PRESS the bulbs FIRMLY into the sand,
so that there are no air-pockets left under them. Root-
growth will begin quicker and be more satisfactory.*) Mix
the covering soil with fifty per cent sand or peat-moss.

"All Lily beds should be slightly above the level of the
ground to give the proper drainage.

"In planting, distinction must be made between what is
known as stem-rooting and those which only send their roots
from the base of the bulb. Some of the better known varieties which send no roots from the
stem are *Madonna, Superbum,
Martigon,* and others. These bulbs
should not be covered with more
than two inches in stiff soil, and
three inches in sand or loam. The
*Regale, Superbum, Auratum, Specio-
sum* and others which root both at
base of bulb and stem above the bulb
should be covered seven to eight
inches in stiff soil, and nine to twelve
in sand. It is well, before planting, to
sprinkle sulphur generously over all
Lilies whose bulbs consist of loose
scales, as a precaution against disease

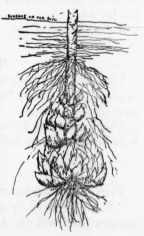

(*Candium* being an example of this type). These bulbs should be slightly tilted to one side, and entirely surrounded with sand, to give them the correct drainage.

PROPAGATION

"I have had some experience in growing the *Regale Lily*. When the stalks are about dead, remove the dirt carefully and you will find an inch below the surface, down at the mother-bulb, bulblets, one-eighth to one-half inch in diameter, which you may remove. Grade these to size; plant immediately, and cover about three inches.

Bulblets of Regale Lily

"Next year they will not bloom, but as soon as stalks become dry, dig and plant at once, about five inches deep.

"The following season these bulbs will produce from one to two blooms.

"The next year plant full depth, in their permanent home, and let them remain without disturbing for a number of years. I have some of these, three years old, which have had as many as fourteen blooms.

"This Lily also has the habit of making the mother-bulb split. In lifting them after three or four years one may find several large, well-formed bulbs.

Splitting Seed

"I have never grown this Lily from seed, which I understand is easily done. I prefer getting them from the stem, as previously described.

"I have grown several thousand *Lilium tigrinum* from bulblets which form in the axil of each leaf. Gather these while the plants are blooming. Plant immediately in flats, cold frames, or open ground. Cover two inches deep, and keep moist by mulching. After a year's growth, plant five inches deep, and the following year, regular depth of eight or ten inches. I understand quite a few other varieties of Lilies are propagated in this way. Still others are grown from scales, and must have expert attention.

Bulblets of Lilium Tigrinum

"Lilies can be grown from seed, but seeds of different varieties should not be planted together, because some kinds germinate within two weeks, while others require six months

Lily Seed

Separate Varieties in Planting

or more. Continued moisture is needed to create germination. This is injurious to young plants. If the slow-growing kind are kept moist enough, it would naturally dampen off those young plants that have begun to grow. Therefore, it is best to plant each variety in separate flats.

When and How to Plant Lily Seed

"Lily seeds should be planted in cold frames or flats in February or March; but later in open ground. Cover the frames with glass or canvas. Barely cover seed in planting. Gunny sacks, kept moist, placed over the bed, quicken germination. Watch closely and lift the sacks as soon as the seedlings appear. Seedlings should remain in flats or cold frames until the following Spring. Prick them out and plant shallow, about two or three inches. The following year they may be planted in full depth, provided the bulbs are one-half inch or more *in diameter*. I mention diameter because most catalogues describe bulbs as to size in circumference, which is very deceptive and disappointing to the average buyer.

Time of Planting

"Hardy Lily bulbs can be planted any month in the year by carefully lifting and planting. If possible, try to secure domestic bulbs. Imported bulbs are often out of the ground so long that they do not make a good root-system the first year. These directions apply particularly to these Lilies whose bulbs are composed of scales or slabs.

Smooth Bulbs

"A number of varieties that have a smooth, onion-like bulb have proved quite successful in the Southwest, as there are several that are native to this section."

VALLEY NOTE (SEMI-TROPICAL)

The following bulbs, tubers and rhizomes are grown easily in the Valley:

Agapanthus (Blue Lily of the Nile), Amaryllis, Canna, Calla, Crinum, Dahlia, Hemerocallis (Day Lily), Madonna or Easter Lily, Waterlilies, Tuberose, Gladiolus* and Narcissus.

---

*Set in January.

II. LILIES NATIVE TO SOUTHWEST

Atamosco (*Copper Lily*)
Dainty, single blossom on one stem. Should be planted in colonies, two or three inches deep.

Allium *palmeri*
Rose-colored flowers.

Allium *cernuum*
"Fairy pearls," white.

Allium *Deserticola*
White with purple midrib. Chooses open places, often poor rocky soil.

Cooperia drummondi
Similar to *peduculata*. Blossoms later in the fall and habitually after rains.

***Cooperia peduculata* (*Rain Lily*) or Fairy Lily**
White flowers on stems from six to twelve inches.

***Cooperia prairia* or Field Lily**
Multiplies both by seed and bulbs.

Nelumbo lutea
Only native Lotus of the western hemisphere. Has strange, leathery-waxy textured, cream to pale yellow, fragrant blossoms, borne high on long, firm stalks rising directly out of the mud.

Nymphaea microcarpa
Yellow Pond Lily.

White Lily *Zygadenus Nuttallii* or *Toxicoscordion Nuttallii*)
Grows from one to two feet high with numerous small white blossoms on branched stem. Prefers well drained hillsides, often rocky.

ERYTHRONIUM ALBIDUM.
DOG-TOOTHED VIOLET

Umbellatum—The *Umbellatum Lilies* are a brilliant addition to the garden. They are perfectly hardy and multiply surprisingly well in heavy soil. This variety does not seem to be very choosey

about soil, as it is thriving in several locations where conditions vary greatly. Its
blossom-time follows the Jonquils, and
because it does not grow as tall
as many other Lilies its garden
value lies in mass planting or
clumps where a strong splash of
color is desired. The shape of the
flower, which clusters at the top
of the bloom-stalk, is quite individual, while its color ranges
from yellow and orange to a
brick-dusty red. Named varieties are usually more to be desired than a varied collection, for
one may thus select both color
and height of stem. Orange and
yellow Zinnias and Marigolds may be
planted among them, to follow them
(where the same vivid note is needed
until frost).

Madonna (*Lilium candidum*)—Madonna
Lilies, like the Umbellatum, may be
grown in groups, yet care must be
taken that they never have a "hard"
background, but must be protected
by plants or shrubs having delicate
blossoms and foliage (always remembering they should be planted in August).
Plant shallow—not more than two inches
deep.

Tiger Lilies (*tigrinum*)—The old Tiger Lily,
that is so common in many sections, has been
greatly improved by cultivation, and the new
Tigrinum splendens is of such height and
beauty that it takes its place among the
Aristocrats when placed in the proper setting.
In early Spring it may be planted in sand, nine
inches deep, singly or in small groups. It requires less water than most Lilies or Bulbs.
The bulbels that form in the axils of the
leaves may be gathered, or planted by bend-
ing the leaves over and covering them with
sand. These bulbels will grow and flower
in three years. (See page 161.)

Speciosum Lilies (*Rubrum and Melpomene*)—The most beautiful of all the Lilies are *Rubrum*, and *Melpomene* of the Speciosum group. The blossoms, whose segments curl back are not unlike the well-known *Tiger Lily*, "white, shaded rose and spotted crimson." In coloring *Melpomene* differs from *Rubrum* only by its deeper tones. The bulbs of these Lilies should be planted from eight to twelve inches deep, for they are stem-rooting, and bulblets form between the main bulb and the surface of the soil. It is preferable to plant them in the Fall, although, as with most Lilies, they *may* be planted in the Spring. Unfortunately they do not flower until after the Spring pageantry of blossoms has passed, and those who are away during midsummer fail to see the tall graceful bloom-stalks whose blossoms range up and down, making a joyous pyramid of daintiness.

Lilium Henryi—Sometimes called the "Yellow *Speciosum*", gives promise to prove one of the most reliable and dependable garden lilies.

Amaryllis—Among the most gorgeous of all the bulbous plants which are grown extensively in the Southwest are the Amaryllis. They are especially noted for their clear, beautiful tones of

AMARYLLIS WITH BULBLETS.

red. Some have solid color with a whitish star in the throat (*Hippeastrum Reginae*). Others have a white stripe down the center of each petal (*Johnsonii*), while still others have every conceivable combination of red on white, which are seen in the so-called Hybrids, the markings of many of which are more pink than red. These latter may be grown from seed and, as they cannot be relied on as a parent stock, it is impossible to know the exact markings to be expected. However, all of them are interesting and striking. Amaryllis is one of the most adaptable of the bulb family, for it may be used as a window or indoor plant, or for bedding purposes (in a spot where they should not be disturbed for a number of years).

Lily of the Nile (*Agapanthus*) (Blue), "Amazon Lily" (*Eucharis*) (White)—These showy, fragrant Lilies are only semi-hardy, requiring to be brought indoors during the Winter months. Both are most attractive used in tubs or pots (so necessary to create a Spanish atmosphere in that type garden).

Crinum—The various showy Crinums grow well in many sections. The well-known "Milk and Wine" blooms from August to frost. The "Snow-White Angel" with its crown of gorgeous white bells, begins blooming in May and June, and has been known to have as many as twenty-two flowers on one stalk. A mature bulb will sometimes produce five or six stalks. "Lily of the Dawn," a lovely blush-pink, flowers from July to frost. The "Deep Sea Lily" flowers all season, beginning in June. It is a free bloomer. The flower is of good texture and is very valuable for cutting. Many people hesitate to grow crinum because of the amount of room their wide, light-green drooping leaves require. Gladioli may be planted rather near them, and Petunias thoroughly enjoy using their leaves to climb up on as a sort of natural trellis. They seem to like a sandy soil, and do better when the heavier soil has sand mixed in it, yet they will grow fairly well without the sand. [*Crinum are planted, or divided, in the Spring at the same time that Tuberoses (see page 172) are planted.* Place the long, large bulbs so that the top is on the level *of the ground*. With *Crinum*, it is *never* wise to *let fertilizer touch the bulb*. This is true of all Lilies. Yet they need the additional nourishment, or feeding, gained by placing it in the ground surrounding the plant. This extra nourishment will always be received by the bulbs much quicker if the ground is scratched or loosened well an inch or two in depth before scattering the fertilizer. It is appreciated especially when the bloomstalks are forming. They bloom more profusely if watered frequently.]

Hemerocallis—The Lemon Lily or Day Lily, as the various varieties of Hemerocallis are known, has its place in every garden. There are many varieties, growing from one to six feet in height, having a blooming period from early Spring to late Summer. The hybrids, whose color-range shades from palest yellow to deep orange and tones of red with many having characteristic markings of dark on light, far exceed in size and beauty the more commonly grown types *Kwanso* (Double Orange, five feet in height) handsome and brighter in tone than the single *Fulva* (Tawny Lily) both being much deeper in tone than the light yellow *Flava*.

Liriope (Lily Turf) (*Liriope graminifolia*)—With its grass-like leaves, is valuable as a ground-cover. It seems to grow in any soil. Its spikes of lilac to deep purple flowers are not produced freely in the shade, and resemble a large *fall-blooming* Grape Hyacinth.

Ophiopogon (*Japonica*)—Belongs to the Lily family, and is excellent as a border plant, in flower boxes or as a ground-cover. (See page 239). It is surprisingly vigorous under trying conditions. It resembles the *Liriope*.

Bleeding Heart (*Dicentra spectabilis*) & (*Dicentra formosa*)— Wild variety Bleeding-Heart, which is usually classed among the bulbs, has lovely, pendant, heart-shaped blossoms that appear in the early Spring. Its foliage is unusually attractive, but has the habit of disappearing before summer is well advanced. This plant is especially fine in a rockery, for its racemes of drooping, pink flowers lend contrast to those plants generally selected for the hillside. It must be placed in a location that is protected from mid-day and afternoon sun.

Spider or Guernsey Lily (*Lycoris radiata*)—The Guernsey (Spider, Resurrection or Coral) Lily is of wonderful texture and construction, valuable for cutting and perfectly hardy. They become dormant in late spring; and the bulbs, therefore, should be planted during June and July. Early in September bloom-stalks appear and make a striking effect with their odd, unusual-colored flowers clustered at the top of the stalk. After blooming, the foliage starts and remains green all winter. The strange habits and unusual season of blooming of the Spider Lily (or Guernsey) and the *Habranthus* suggest unusual combinations. They are especially effective if used in masses, or bordering shrubbery. These Lilies may be divided or transplanted when the leaves die. *Lycoris squamigera* (pink) and *Lycoris aurea* (golden yellow) have similar habits.

Habranthus—*Habranthus* just precedes the "Guernsey" (Spider) Lily, and has the same strange habit of blooming before the leaves appear. The flowers are a brilliant crimson. It gives excellent results planted either in shade or in sun and covets neither rich soil nor cultivation.

Zephranthes ("Rain Lilies")—Give an element of surprise and delight when they appear as if by magic after a rain. They multiply rapidly and are one of the few small bulbs that can be used successfully to outline borders. *Z . . candida* has large white cups and is very hardy. *Z . . rosea* (rose-color) has larger flowers but is less hardy. *Z . . texanum,* one of the several varieties native to Texas is a lovely yellow that requires loose, sandy soil. There are several varieties indigenous to Florida and other states.

Hymenocallis—"White Spider Lily"—one of the largest of the native bulbs of the South. Is readily adaptable to ordinary garden treatment, although its habitat is low, swampy lands and ditches its blossoms are *quite* distinctive!

Ismene Calathina or **Peruvian Daffodil** (Of the Hymenocallis family)—The *Great Ismene* is a beautiful addition to the list of bulbous plants which live in a mild climate although it is not hardy in all sections. Its large, pure white, amaryllis-like blossoms are fragrant and bring a distinct charm to the Summer garden. "For such beauty in an unusual flower, its requirements are not too exacting, although they must be met."

Gladioli—As the Zinnia is by far the outstanding annual, so the Gladiolus is the most adaptable of the family of bulbs. It can be planted at intervals during the entire season, to blossom at any desired time in order to supply a special splash of color at a certain spot in the garden. It will rarely fail to produce its flower-spikes at the end of six weeks after planting. Its color range is almost unlimited, so that one may form exquisite combinations with other plants. Nothing could be more beautiful than the tall hemerocallis "Golden Bell," and a group of salmon-pink gladioli. This tiny little bulb that produces but one flower-stalk a season boasts a society formed of its admirers whose hundreds of members are interested in its culture. Gladioli are most effective when planted some five or more in a circle, with a supporting stake in the center. They should not be planted less than five inches deep. They may be left in the ground, for they are hardy in the Southwest, but will often disappear after the third or fourth year. However, they may be dug each year, dried in shallow baskets, and kept in a dry, moderately cool place, through the Winter. Planted fairly deep, gladioli resist high winds and dry weather.

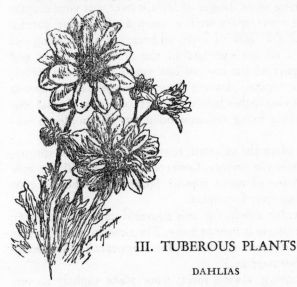

III. TUBEROUS PLANTS

DAHLIAS

Among the distinct types of dahlias, that have been arbitrarily named (usually for convenience in identification of character of blossom), the principal groupings are classified under Decorative, Anemone, Cactus, Pompon, Peony-flowered, Single and Miniature.

To store dahlias, for the winter, cut the stalks to within a few inches of the ground (in the fall after the first frost) and leave for about ten days. Then dig the clumps very carefully. Place them in the open, where it is dry, for a few days.

Then place the entire clump in dry sand (in a dry basement, neither too warm nor too cool) and leave until spring. For feeding Dahlias, see p. 22.

With Dahlias, as with all other plants, to have large beautiful blooms and healthy growth, the soil must be properly prepared. Cow manure or a well-balanced commercial fertilizer should be thoroughly worked into the soil a month or more before planting. Then respade the bed and plant. Be sure that you have good drainage. Dahlias may be grown from seed (page 139).

In the spring when danger of frost is over, cut your clumps of tuberous roots apart with a sharp knife (being careful not to break the neck of each, and leaving a sprouting eye to each . . . all the eyes are in the crown or upper end which is a part of the base of last year's growth on stem). Plant these separately, leaving the topmost part of the sprout from one to two inches below the surface of the ground, the deeper planting being recommended for the northern sections.

To plant, place the tuberous root slanting with the sprouting end nearest the surface. Cover with sand and fill the hole with two inches of moist topsoil. Space each tuberous root about three or four feet apart.

Do not water much, for this causes decay, but cultivate the soil slightly, so it cannot bake. The time to water or fertilize freely is when the flower-buds appear. Dahlias relish sunshine! (See page 23.)

When planting, always insert your *stake* slightly to one side, because a dahlia stalk should be tied *as it grows* to protect it against winds. When the tuberous root has sent up several sprouts, cut away all but one stalk, forcing the strength of the plant into the one development.

In order to produce large blooms, disbudding is advised. This consists of the removal of the two side-buds in each group of three. If commercial fertilizer is used, place it six or eight inches away from the stalk and water it in. This will force maturity. (See page 20.)

PEONIES

The Peony, after once planted in the right location, in a thoroughly prepared bed, asks to be undisturbed (except for a little fertilizer added now and then) for years. Plant where it will be shaded from the hot afternoon sun. Always plant peonies in the early fall.

Dig a hole about one and one-half to two feet deep. Mix sand and leafloam with soil. If one prefers using stable manure, place it at the *very bottom* of the hole. Cover the manure with some of the topsoil, so that it does not touch the large root of the plant. Set the root with the eyes upward. Fill in dirt around the root and tamp it firmly. Water thoroughly before the hole is filled, and again after it is filled.

If peonies are planted too deeply, they will form large bushes but will never bloom. Another failure to produce bloom is *botrytis* (brown spots on the leaves) for which spray with nicotine solutions once a week. Set them so that the dormant buds are covered with earth only to a depth of from one-half to one inch, the eyes just below the surface of the ground. This insures freezing of the roots in the winter time, a very essential requirement of the peony.

During the winter, water the beds well about once a month. This moisture takes the place of the winter snows. Every fall and spring fertilize with bonemeal, worked into the soil with a little trowel, not too close to the plant. Once or twice a year sprinkle a little lime on the soil around each plant, and water it in.

A quarter of a century ago there were three favorites in the Southwestern gardens that have been pushed aside for newer, more popular plants—the Tuberose, the Canna, and the Caladium.

TUBEROSE

The Tuberose is the only one of the three whose blossoms are treasured for their extremely heavy sweetness, although their tall spikes of milk-white flowers have a beauty all their own. These come later than most Lilies (late August and early September), and are perfectly hardy. There can be secured today an improved variety, much larger and taller, known as the *Mexican Tuberose*. Tuberoses should be planted in Spring, with not more than an inch of earth covering the top of the bulb, unless there is an earth-stain on the bulb-stalk which indicates the depth the plant had been covered. This is true, also, of other bulbs and tubers.

CANNA

The newer varieties of Canna demonstrate the fact that they, too, have received recognition and have profited by the cultivation and attention given them by plant experts.

They vary in stature from two and one-half feet to those that tower above one's head. Their colors, that once startled one with their brilliancy, have become subdued and softened, and are in better accord with other flowers. The blossoms are large and range in color from white through yellow to deep maroon.

Because of the fact that cannas are rather coarse, with their large tropical leaves, they do not combine well with most other plants and shrubs. A more pleasing effect is gained by planting them in clumps wherever one wishes to give a definitely tropical effect.

Cannas multiply very rapidly and their roots spread in every direction. If planted near perennials or shrubs, they crowd out the other plants.

Some varieties of cannas are perfectly hardy, but many should have protection.

They have been used extensively as quick-growing hedges or screens, although the fact that they die down at the first frost makes them questionable for this purpose.

CALADIUM

("ELEPHANT EARS")

Another bulbous plant that has always been associated with the canna is the caladium (or "Elephant Ears"). These, like the cannas, are semi-hardy, for they only weather the mild Winters. They, too, should be taken up after the leaves die down in the Fall, planted again in the Spring, with only a light covering of earth on top of the crown of the bulb.

Caladiums are grown for the decorative qualities of their tremendous leaves that so distinctly resemble huge Elephant's Ears. These leaves reach unbelievable proportions, if the bulbs are planted in sandy, rather moist, soil. The Lily-like, odd blossom is completely hidden. They require a great deal of water.

Iris

THE IRIS is revered for its stately beauty; it is beloved for its dainty perfection. It can be found flourishing in marshy places and blooming cheerfully on mud and thatched roofs, proclaiming to all its adaptability to every condition. It is at home in many parts of the world, yet each section produces a plant having distinct and individual characteristics.

This old, yet ever new flower, is creating the greatest interest in the flower-loving world; in fact its popularity all but rivals the Tulip craze that swept through Europe some years ago.

To appreciate a bit of its fascination, one need only possess a small collection of the various types with their alluring tones and shades.

Classification

Horticulturalists have classified the Iris into three general groups—Bearded Iris, Beardless Iris, and Bulbous Iris.

Bearded Iris

The Bearded Iris has been so classed because of the line of tiny hair-like fuzz that is to be found on the three lower petals, or *falls*, at the curve of their upper surface. This so-called "beard" is one of the distinguishing features of this class.

Characteristics

The root-growth is another item of unusual interest. This is composed of a thick, bulb-like root-stock that grows horizontally along the surface of the ground. From these "rhizomes" the feeder-roots extend down into the soil. The size of this root-stock does not typify the size of the blossoms, however, for some of the varieties having large flowers have notably small *rhizomes*.

Location

Bearded Iris, like roses, do not like wet feet. The chief requirement in the selection of a location is good drainage and plenty of sunlight. Experience has proved, however, that they do not need as much sunlight in the South as they do in the North, but will bloom very satisfactorily in partial shade. The lighter shades are more delicate if they are not subjected to the rays of the sun all day, and hold their color better.

Culture

The correct way to plant Iris has caused much discussion, and many articles have been written on the subject. Possibly a different method is required in each part of the country. In the South and West the ground should be carefully prepared by taking off the topsoil, then spading deep, mixing a good fertilizer well into this lower soil to nourish the long feeder-roots and induce them to grow deeply downward that the plant may withstand the rigors of the winds more easily. Next surround the rhizomes with the topsoil, taking care that no fertilizer touches them, for it may cause the dreaded root-rot.

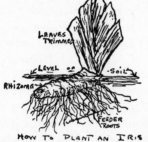

HOW TO PLANT AN IRIS

When to Plant

The experience of growers has been that only the strongest plants can survive if planted after the ground is thoroughly heated; yet should it become necessary to plant them during July and August, cover the rhizomes well with soil, provided no water stands around them, and they keep quite dry.

Planted in June they will become established before the very hot weather, but a small amount of soil should be kept over them during the summer. Plants secured near by, or subdivided in one's own garden, if the roots are not allowed to become dry, can be safely planted at any time.

Clumps

September seems to be the ideal time for planting if purchased from distant growers. Planted at that time, the top of the rhizomes should be set just below the level of the ground.

These directions apply to single divisions, for clumps of Iris can be transplanted at any time during the year if well watered. Feeding note, see p. 22.

Mass Effect

Iris require several years to become established if planted as single rhizomes; therefore, to get a mass effect, it is advisable to plant several of a kind in a group about six inches apart with the fans pointing in different directions in order that the effect will be of a large clump when blooming.

Dividing

Iris should not be divided until they have become matted and crowded. Those varieties that multiply rapidly should be separated in two years, while others may remain untouched for several years.

Iris Need Not Be Expensive

It is a mistake to think that one cannot have a desirable collection of Iris without undue expense, for the price is entirely determined by the abundance of the supply on the market. Some varieties multiply very slowly and continue high priced, while the new varieties that receive high rating and special awards are very expensive for a time.

Season of Bloom

Bearded Iris have been subdivided into three classes that follow each other *as to time of blooming,* prolonging the season for many months.

Dwarf Iris

The Iris season opens early in the new year with the Dwarfs that can be found in yellow, blue and purple. The Dwarf Iris are so called because of shortness of stem (seldom growing more than nine inches) rather than size of blossom. The earliest varieties have very short stems, but as the season advances, the height increases. This class includes *Iris pumila,* the *pseudo-pumila* and *chamaeiris,* all of whom grow from creeping rhizomes.

Flags

These early varieties are followed in March by the well-known "Blue, and White Flags" of our Grandmothers' gardens. These have been little valued, possibly because they demand so little care, though more probably because they bloom so early in the season that the prevailing spring winds often mar their delicate beauty. This variety is more fragile than some of the later ones, and they are easily bruised. Yet nothing can be more beautiful than a large clump of the lovely "Blue," whose name is listed as *"germanica,"* growing in well-drained, rich garden soil, especially if jonquils or light *Blue germanica* yellow wall-flowers nestle at their feet. Its companion, the "White Flag," or *florentina,* has long been identified with the Mohammedans, who have carried it with them wherever they have journeyed, to be used for the ornamentation of their burial places. This custom has made it impossible to determine its place of origin. For many centuries this delicate, *White florentina* white *"florentina"* has been loved for its beauty of blossom and greatly valued for the perfume derived from powdering the dried roots. This, "Orris-root," has been, until quite recently, the best artificial violet scent.

"Kochii," a native of Italy, a very lovely dark purple, *Intermediates* blooms about the same time. This Iris has an added value in that it often blooms a second time, at the end of the Iris season. *"Kochii"* is the forerunner of a large group of what are known as *Intermediates.* Until the last few years not many *Intermediates* were introduced because the breeders of Iris were directing their attention toward creating Tall-Bearded varieties. *"Nymph"* (a deep yellow), *"Zua,"* whose exquisite fragrance and crinkle-paper-appearance make it most unique, and *"Zwanenburg,"* with its unusual, mottled coloring (very odd-looking), are most desirable.

I. TALL BEARDED IRIS

April is the height of the Iris season in the Southwest. A *Time of Bloom* great adventure is in store for those gardeners who have yet to learn the value of the newer Tall Bearded Iris.

Since the beginning of the twentieth century a host of *Great Range of Choice* varieties, some most brilliant, others delicate and exquisite as the beloved Orchid, have been developed. This has been done with several ideals in view. One group of scientists have striven for color, or the combination of colors, while another has been occupied with the effort to combine size and durability of blossom with beauty of form. Therefore, one finds difficulty in making a selection, even from the multitude of desirable old ones that have continued to hold their place with the newer creations, which are introduced each year, each boasting some alluring feature.

The Best White Varieties

Among the lighter-toned varieties that give the effect of white, what could be lovelier than *"Los Angeles"* with its pencilings of blue? Yet, *"San Francisco,"* similar in coloring, is much more beautiful. *"Purissima"* is a fine pure white, sharing honors with several others equally popular, many of which are more creamy in tone.

Blue and Lavender Varieties

It would be impossible to give even a partial list of the desirable light blue and lavender Iris. Many are so-called "True Selfs", that is having standards and falls the same—while with others the falls are a little different from their standards. Among the selfs the large group of medium blues and lavenders present a wealth of choice while the dark blues and purples are glowingly rich and regally outstanding in any garden.

Pink Varieties

There are a host of pinks which appear pink to some and decidedly lavender to others, charming under either name. These vary in tone from the lavender-pink to the yellow-pink, giving one the opportunity to complete any specific type of garden picture desired.

Red Varieties

The so-called red Iris, if planted in semi-shade, appear more vivid. Some are extremely vigorous, very adaptable, tall, velvety, handsome and attractive.

Among the many creations known as bronzes few have **Bronze**
been accorded the popularity enjoyed by *"Mrs. Valeri West,"* **Varieties**
a most gorgeous dark iris. This iris was considered by its
originator, the late Mr. A. J. Bliss, as the culmination of his
efforts at iris breeding. The marvelous velvety texture of its
falls proclaims it a descendant of his great creation, *"Do-
minion,"* whose advent in the iris world was the forerunner
of a new race much more magnificent than any that had
preceded it. Unfortunately it has all but disappeared in many
sections because of its susceptibility to root rot.

The most striking of the whole family are the Bicolors that **Bi-colors**
have yellow standards, and reddish or purplish falls.

The hybridizers have vied with each other for years to **Yellow**
produce a yellow that had all the qualities of the darker- **Varieties**
toned iris. As a result there are a number from which a selection may be made. *"Shekinah"* (Sturdevant) was the first
good yellow produced. Here again one has the opportunity
of wide selection for one may obtain yellows ranging from
the palest tints to the deepest gold.

While it is a question if the real, great yellow has been de- **Blends**
veloped, yet there is no debating the fact that through their
endeavors a splendid group of blends have appeared, magnificent in their strength and beauty. All these have a varying amount of yellow that blends with lavender and purple
and blue in every conceivable manner. This class has been
divided into two groups, the light and dark blends.

The dark blends with their deep, glowing colors, are par- **Dark**
ticularly attractive. There are a number of very beautiful **Blends**
ones, varying in price.

IRIS IN ARID SECTIONS

It has been claimed that there can be found a variety of **Suggested**
iris for every climatic condition. So where high winds pre- **Types and**
vail, it is suggested that the strongest, and those listed as **Treatment**
having stems of medium height, be selected. The catalogues
usually state the length of the stem and the quality of both
stem and blossom. By using shrubs as windbreaks or planting
them where they will be protected, better results will be

secured, for iris will bloom very satisfactorily even in partial shade.

The yellows and delicate blends seem to have the most fragile blossoms. The darker-toned have proved more sturdy, wind-resistant and adaptable to all conditions.

Monsignor   "*Monsignor*" was quite a favorite some years ago, but it has been discarded by many for more desirable varieties. It has, however, the qualifications of being able to thrive under most adverse conditions.

NATIVE IRIS

Iris (*Fulva*)—Found in East Texas. Reddish brown flowers, variegated blue or green.

Iris (*Hexagona*)—Violet blue flowers variegated with purple, yellow and white.

Iris (*Pumila*)—An exotic.

II. BEARDLESS AND BULBOUS IRIS

Beardless   A number of interesting types of Iris have been grouped together and are known as Beardless Iris. These desire similar treatment which differs greatly from that usually considered best for Bearded Iris. They like moisture during the growing season and are supposed to object to lime, although many varieties have been grown very successfully in the heavy limestone section.

Location   Try to select a moist but sunny location, and plant in soil that contains a generous amount of well-rotted manure or peat-moss. The crowns (or top of root-growth) should be covered with about two inches of soil.

Ochroleuca   The Beardless Iris are not grown extensively in the Southwest, although the tall-growing *Ochroleuca* (see page 184) is probably the best known. Its long, narrow leaves are quite distinctive, while its wealth of white blossoms with a light yellow blotch near the center of the petals always suggest a flight of white butterflies. It will not tolerate water around its roots after blooming. The one objection to it is that the leaves often die down after the seed-pods have matured, leaving a large, bare spot (to provide for which, quick-growing annuals—Cleome, if height is desired, Marigolds, or low-growing Petunias—are suggested).

The so-called "Japanese Iris" has not proved dependable as *Kaempferi* a garden flower where lime prevails. It requires special care, and more often proves a disappointment than a pleasure. The blossoms are so exquisite that a strain adaptable to all

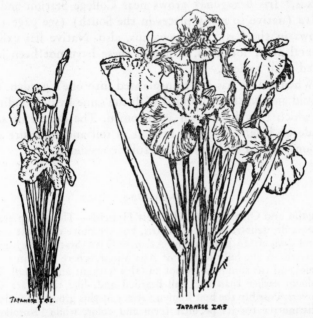

JAPANESE IRIS.

JAPANESE IRIS

climatic conditions would be most welcome. This desired strain will possibly be secured from seedlings scientifically developed. If in turn seeds can be secured from these seedlings, naturally or by hybridization, a race of acclimated plants should be the result. Japanese Iris seed will mature if planted in the spring but it is much more advisable to plant them in the fall.

The Siberican group are of special value because they will *Siberican* grow in partial shade.

The iris is native to the North Temperate Zone, the ma- *Specie* jority being found in the far Eastern Asiatic countries, although America contributes several varieties. All native iris in this country and abroad are classified as Species. The most brilliant and varicolored of the American Species are to be found in the swamps of Louisiana and the Southern States. (See pages 180, 184).

Those Native to the Southwest

There are several varieties indigenous to Texas. Among these iris *versicolor* is said to be quite abundant in East Texas,* Iris *hexagona*† grows near College Station and Iris *fulva* (native to many places in the South) (see page 184), grows in the East Texas swamps, also. Native iris exist in several other localities, although these have not been identified as to variety.

When native iris are transplanted into one's garden, they should and *must* be supplied with the same living conditions to which they have been accustomed. The degree of semi-shade or bright sunlight, as well as soil and moisture conditions, should all be most carefully considered.

NATIVE IRIS

Regelia and Oncocyclus and Their Hybrids—This group are the most drought-resistant of all Iris, but are quite the most erratic and difficult to grow in the Atlantic Coast States. They are all natives of the hilly regions of Asia Minor, where the winters are cool and the summers are hot and dry without any rainfall. They bloom earlier than the Tall-Bearded and, like them, are lime-lovers. Possibly the best known variety of this group is "Susiana," distinctive for its peculiar form and color, while "Korolkowi" and "Hoogiana," both natives of Turkestan, are also most interesting examples.

Pogocyclus—A group called Pogocyclus that are the result of crossing the Oncocyclus and the Tall-Bearded, may prove to be of special interest to gardeners of the arid sections, for they do not demand the dormant period that the Oncocyclus require, yet will endure drier conditions than the Tall-Bearded. A good collection of Pogocyclus include "Psyche," "Shiraz," "Zwanenburg," "Nazarin" and "Ib-Pall."

Evansia—Another small but distinct class is known as Evansia, whose chief characteristic is the ragged crest which replaces the well-known "beard" of our familiar varieties.

*Foster, Texas.
†Yarnell, Texas.

Bulbous—The Spanish, Dutch and English compose the Bulbous *Spanish,* Iris group (see page 186). They are very showy and are of value *English* if used singly, or in groups as points of accent in the border. *and Dutch* The colors of the Spanish are white, yellow, brown and blue, while the English include the lavender, deep mauve, and violet tones. The Dutch are usually white and shades of blue, the most outstanding being "Wedgewood." This must not be confused with the Tall-Bearded of the same name. These blossom with the Tall-Bearded and do not prolong the season of bloom in the Southwest. The Spanish and Dutch Iris require a dry situation, multiply well and are exceedingly desirable; while the English prefer partial shade and moist, rich soil—they do not seem to succeed in many sections. Bulbous Iris should be planted in the fall, just as one plants tulips. If they should dwindle and disappear, they are not too expensive to repurchase, for they contribute an indescribable charm.

III. IRIS FOR TRIAL†

"The Temperate Zone is so large and has so many different *in Succes-* climates, soil, and moisture conditions that what will succeed *sion of* in one part will not grow in another. There are many places *Bloom* where various species of Iris can undoubtedly be well grown, where they have not been attempted.

"Bearded Iris like sunshine, heat, and dryness; and there are many situations on high, drained land where they succeed well. A long season can be had by having Dwarf-Bearded Iris, Intermediate Iris, Germanica types and Oncocyclus-hybrid, ending with the Tall Bearded Hybrids. The progress that breeders have made in these varieties in the last few years is astonishing!

†The writer of this article, John C. Wister, is an authority on Iris and other bulbous plants. He has written many valuable articles for various publications, and has published several books on these subjects.

"There are many Beardless which are worthy of a trial. Some of these will undoubtedly succeed in many parts of the South and West. Others may succeed only in a few parts and only under special attention.

Siberican Iris

"The Siberica Section is one of the largest and one of the easiest to grow. Many of these, undoubtedly, will do well, if given a situation where they can have a little extra moisture in the spring months.

"The best known are the varieties of the species Siberica *orientalis* and their hybrids. Of these 'Emperor,' 'Perry's Blue,' 'Lactea,' and 'Snow Queen' are some of the best known, but there are many new varieties being introduced from Europe and also from one or more American breeders. The best varieties usually combine the height of Siberica with the flower of *orientalis* but the color range is not large, running through the whites, blues and purples mainly, although reddish-purples are often seen.

Spuria Iris

"An important group which deserves a thorough trial is the Spuria group. Some of its species (from which the group receives its name) ought to grow in many sections. Others are a little bit finicky as to moisture and soil conditions, but are very well worth extra effort. The first of these to be considered is *Ochroleuca,* which, under good conditions, sometimes grows five feet high. Smaller than *Ochroleuca* but a very fine flower of clear golden yellow is *Aurea* (not to be confused with a Bearded Iris of the same name).

Wild Iris Foliosa Fulva

"A group which certainly needs much closer attention from all gardeners is the group that comprises the wild Iris *foliosa* and *fulva* as they grow in our Southern states. Plants under this name have been in cultivation for many years in the North and have been more or less unsatisfactory on account of shy bloom. But they seem to be perfectly hardy as far north as Boston and sometimes even in Canada. The hybrids *fulva* and *fulvaea* and *violacea* as grown by Dykes, and 'Dorothy K. Williamson,' as grown by Williamson, have been better known in gardens than their parent species, and do well apparently over greater climatic range.

"The *fulva* types, particularly, run from the usual red

color to a deeper crimson on one side, and yellowish colors on the other.

"Yet the beautiful species *fulva* is rather sparse blooming under most garden conditions. It is, however, well worthy of a place in any garden, no matter how small, because it is so absolutely unique in its color, its terra-cotta red being very seldom seen in any out-door flowers.

"It looks as if we were just beginning to understand what valuable wild species we have in this country, and to make

use of them for plant breeding. Some of these types undoubtedly grow as far west as Texas, but if they are not found wild in certain sections, they should at least be tried there in gardens.

"There are many native American Beardless Iris. The California group and Iris *versicolor* would probably prove difficult.

Crested Iris

"Closely related to *versicolor* is the Iris of Europe—*pseudacorus*—the species from which the 'Fleur de Lys' has been taken as a patriotic emblem. Its color is a splendid clear yellow, and it thrives best under moist conditions.

"Distinct from the beardless group, but for convenience treated with them, is the small-crested Iris group consisting of one American species, *cristata*, and two Japanese species,

tectorum, and *gracilipes.* The group gets its name from the
golden crest down the center line of the lower petal. All the
plants are small and suited best to half-shady, rock gardens.
Cristata is but a few inches high, blooming in April or early
May—in the north—delightfully fragrant and of great value
to gardens, and yet but seldom seen! Any good (neutral or
acid) garden soil with humus in it should suit it, and half-
shade is welcomed by it; the members of this group are the
only important Irises which do not demand full sun.

"Iris *tectorum* (called 'Japanese Roof-Iris') is slightly
larger, standing perhaps a foot in height, and is easily grown
from seed. Its white form is particularly desirable. It needs
replanting oftener than most Irises, and when it becomes
crowded is apt to die out. I believe it can best be handled by
saving seed yearly and keeping some young plants coming
along. Iris *gracilipes* is the scarcest and perhaps the loveliest
of the three, a tiny flower held on eight- or ten-inch stems—
a gem for any rock garden.

*Bulbous
Iris*

"The Bulbous Iris group is another great group. Its head-
quarters are around the Mediterranean, or in Asia Minor.
Most readily available of the bulbous types are the varieties

*Spanish
Iris*

of the Spanish Iris group. These are hybrids of Iris *Xiphium.*
Try also, *Iris Reticulata!*

IRIS CRISTATA.

"The English Irises are later blooming and much more exacting as to cultural requirements. They do not seem to succeed in as many sections, and are most difficult of all.

"These are but a few of the many types of Iris which might well be tried, for Iris-growing is still in its pioneer stage everywhere in America. It is evident that there are no states in the Union where some types will not succeed admirably, but many years of careful experimentation are needed before we know how many different kinds will succeed in each different climatic section of the country."

A Garden of Bulbs

I T IS QUITE an interesting experiment to determine how nearly a garden of continuous bloom may be secured from Bulbs and Tubers, framed and softened by a few congenial Annuals and Perennials.

In some parts of the country the opening of the tiny cups of the Snowdrops and Crocus may be relied on to welcome the Spring, but the first flowers in the Southwest are usually the colorful Dwarf Iris, whose time of blossom can never be fixed, as they appear all through the winter after every short period of mild weather.

The old-fashioned yellow Jonquil ventures almost as early. These have long been favorites because of the delicious fragrance of their clusters of golden-yellow blossoms on rush-like stems, amidst a multitude of fine, narrow leaves. There are a number of types of small bulbs of this family (Daffodils)—the *Triandrus* hybrids; the *Jonquillas* (single and double); the *Bulbocodium* ("Hoop petticoats").

The species Tulips (*Tulipas*) and Crocus—tiny, early-flowering varieties, also are of great interest to the connoisseur or collector.

By careful selection the Bulb garden may be filled with blossoms for many weeks. Their dainty beauty is so alluring and enticing that one cannot resist trying to possess them (often with marked success).

As the Iris and Narcissus are *the* dependable Bulbs, it is very fortunate that each has many types, blossoming at various times.

The Iris pageant often runs parallel with the Daffodils (see page 150), but extends far beyond their time of bloom. These, in turn, have had as their companions the early Hemerocallis (Lemon Lilies) and Umbellatum Lilies, Gladioli, and various smaller bulbs.

The later Spring brings the Madonna Lilies, the *Regale*, the *Lilies* Tiger, and the *Speciosum*, with the Cannas doing their part during the extreme hot weather. The Guernsey (Spider Lily) and Habranthus (see page 168), are always a surprise with their interesting blossoms, the very first weeks of Fall; while the Crinum (some variety of which has been in flower constantly since June) help with Cannas and Dahlias to make a Bulb garden glorious until the first frost.

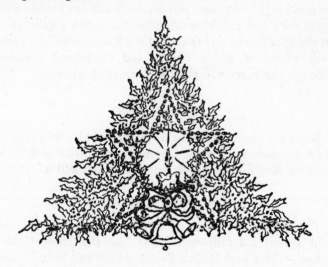

Roses

W HAT A host of lovely images the word Rose recalls! Such happy associations and charming memories should make rose-growing the most delightful of occupations. But if it to be so, in this modern multiplicity, we must pick and choose our methods and our bushes with as much care and experienced judgment as we usually bestow on the selection of our friends, for a Rose can be like a friend with whom, if wisely chosen and cultivated, association through the years will yield an increasing pleasure.

Types of Roses

Roses are among the most diversified of plants in type. The main divisions are Shrubs, Climbers, Polyanthas and Bush or Bedding Roses. Each has its particular uses and adaptations.

I. SHRUB ROSES

Types of Shrub Roses

The Shrubs are made up largely of Rugosas; Species or wild types; old-fashioned kinds like the Moss, Cabbage, Bengal, China and Gallica Roses; dwarf and ever-blooming Climbers; Briers and the hybrids of all of them. These all make good specimen plants, sometimes may be used as hedges, but are not suitable for beds or for planting in a small garden.

RUGOSAS

Chief Characteristics

The first of the shrub class, the Rugosas, are not adapted for cultivation in all climates. They are ruggedly hardy, thorny plants that can stand any amount of cold, but will not bloom well in prolonged heat. The flowers are coarse at best, and often wither and turn yellow without opening, and the hybrids show a strong tendency to mildew. Of these are the red and pink "*F. J. Grootendorst*," "*Conrad Ferdinand Meyer*," "*Rugosa Rubra*," "*Rosea Parfum de l'Hay*" and "*Amelie Gravereaux*," the latter two having the unpleasant characteristic common to the class, of turning from red to a sickly purple.

SPECIES

The Species, or wild types, furnish some of the loveliest of the Spring-blooming shrubs. *Hugonis*, the wild rose of China, with its sweetly-scented, golden-yellow flowers in April, is a great favorite, by far the most beautiful of the Spring-flowering shrubs—needing plenty of room—at least six feet square. *Moyesi*, very similar except in color, is a blood-red gem, if it can become safely established. The *Cherokee Roses* (or *Rosa laevigata*) have been naturalized in South Texas and make bewilderingly beautiful, fountain-like shrubs, with white, pink or red blossoms. But their large size and dreaded propensity to "sucker" make them rather difficult to handle in an average garden. They are better left to naturalistic treatment on a large scale, where their effect is tremendous.

Types of Species Roses

OLD-FASHIONED TYPES

Except for sentimental reasons, very few of the old-fashioned types (such as the Moss, Gallica and Cabbage Roses) seem to be generally grown, the only one often mentioned being *Blanche Moreau*, an old white *Moss*. But almost every garden has a plant or two of that fragrant, dark crimson Bengal, *Gruss an Teplitz*.

One of the China Roses still grown is *Hermosa*, with its lavender-pink clusters of small flowers on a bushy ever-blooming plant. But with the many Polyanthas so similar, having much more attractive coloring, it will not likely survive another generation, except in educational collections.

DWARF OR SEMI-CLIMBERS

Three Classes

The dwarf or semi-climbing Roses which make good shrubs are mainly of three classes: the Lambertina Roses or *multiflora* hybrids; the Pemberton Roses, *moschata* or musk hybrids, and Captain Thomas' Roses.

Lambertina

The Lambertina Roses have not been widely grown, but are suggested as possibly good subjects for trial.

Pemberton

The Pemberton Roses, or hybrid musks, have been grown with very good results. The varieties tried are *Penelope,* soft saffron; *Prosperity,* white; *Cornelia,* strawberry; and *Vanity,* rose-colored. They seem immune to mildew and leaf diseases, are practically ever-blooming, and certainly deserve a much wider distribution.

Captain Thomas' Varieties

Captain Thomas' ever-blooming dwarf climbers may be recognized by the prefix, *Bloomfield,* to their names. They have caused considerable interest, not only from the viewpoint of possibly desirable shrubs, but as good subjects for pillar treatment, to replace the rambler group which has caused more trouble in the garden by spreading mildew than any other one class. Captain Thomas' Roses are all heartily recommended for trial, as they seem immune to mildew and leaf diseases, and, when established, bloom more than once. Two are sufficiently vigorous to handle as ramblers. *Bloomfield Perfection,* creamy flesh, and *Bloomfield Courage,* dark red.

BRIERS

Briers in the Southwest

The Brier Roses, most of which bloom but once, have at least one native representative in the Southwest, a low, very thorny bush with small, golden yellow blossoms. The flower resembles somewhat that of *Hugonis,* but the latter makes a much larger and infinitely more attractive plant, which comment applies to practically all of the Brier group except the Austrian, which has furnished *Austrian Copper, Le Reve,*

Star of Persia, and the old *"Persian Yellow"*—all of *Rosa foetida* family.

Austrian Copper, one of the most outstanding shrubs offered in commerce today, has small single flowers, coppery-red on the inside and bright yellow on the outside. The foliage is very beautiful, but the startling color of the blossoms makes the plant a little difficult to place in a garden except with an evergreen background.

Austrian Copper

Le Reve and *Star of Persia* are usually listed as Hardy Climbers, but are really tall, stiff shrubs, needing some support. They are immune to mildew, but are a prey to the most devastating blackspot and possess a distinctly disagreeable odor. To offset these disadvantages, the beauty of their large, pure yellow blossoms is most compelling to those who are addicted to yellow Roses.

Harrison's Yellow is another member of this class.

* * * * *

The great majority of us, when we say "Roses," do not think of them as shrubs, but a vast number of Rose plants can be used as shrubs in our gardens whether they are Rose gardens or not. A few points to bear in mind concerning Rose shrubs are: first, learn the probable height and habit of growth of each in order to place it to advantage; second, it is better not to prune at all than too much. Be content with cutting out dead or very old wood *at the base* of the plant; third, plant them in good soil, but do not pile fertilizer around them. They usually prefer a little bonemeal and an occasional dressing of wood-ashes to anything else in the way of nourishment.

Pruning

Planting

Fertilization

II. CLIMBING ROSES

Climbing
Rose Types

The correct classification of climbing Roses is one of the most difficult things the amateur Rose-grower encounters. Only by classifying them properly can he learn to care for them, because each class demands a different treatment for best results. There are four main types of so-called climbing Roses—*Climbers, Ramblers, Pillars* and *Ground-covers.*

CLIMBERS

Character-
istics of
Climbers

The Climbers are the Roses which grow taller each year, new shoots springing from the ends of the old canes. They should be pruned very little, as they bloom best on mature wood. All that is necessary is to cut out dead, diseased or very old wood, and shorten branches which are too long for the space allotted to them. True Climbers should be grown on a tall fence, a pergola, over an archway or against the wall of a house, any place where there is sufficient height and width for them to spread out. They should never be planted as a pillar, since the canes are too long, too abundant, and usually too stiff and heavy to twist or twine.

The Climbers are themselves subdivided into Hardy and Tender Climbers.

Hardy: The Hardy Climbers are those which are able to endure zero weather without protection. They generally bloom only in the Spring, but for a long period. The profusion of their flowers, together with their hardiness, make them very desirable.

Chief
Hardy
Climbers

Looking at its immaculate white or pale yellow loveliness, its originator gave one of the most charming names in the Rose world to *Mermaid.* The flowers are borne in clusters at the tips of long branches, on a half-climbing, shrub-like plant with beautiful, waxy foliage, immune to disease. It should *never be pruned,* but allowed to grow in a sunny, sheltered spot where it will produce its exquisite, fleeting blossoms continuously from early Spring till Fall.

Some of the most widely-grown Hardy Climbers are *American Pillar, Gardenia, Emily Gray, Silver Moon, Mme.*

Gregoire Staechelin, the pink Gold Medal Rose, and *New Dawn,* identical in flower with the old *Dr. Van Fleet* and is said to be ever-blooming.

Tender: The Tender Climbers compose a large class which will not endure zero weather without protection and are best left for Southern planting. They are made up of *Noisettes, Teas,* some Australian types, *Bourbons* and such types peculiar to Southern climates. Most of the Hybrid-Teas and Polyanthas which have developed climbing tendencies belong to this group also, although some are not of sufficient vigor to climb very high and should be treated as pillars or large shrubs. *Tender Climbers Identified*

Until the disastrous winter of 1929–1930 with its subzero temperature, many of the Tender Climbers grown in California and the true South, such as the *Gold of Ophir, William Allen Richardson, Bouquet d'Or,* the *Banksia Roses,* white and yellow, *Marechal Niel,* and even the newer *Belle of Portugal* were thriving in gardens throughout the Southwest. But that winter took its toll, and it has been noted with sadness since that many of these Roses have disappeared.

Hybrid-Tea and Polyantha Climbers are relatively hardier than the strictly Tender Climbers, since they are seldom killed outright by extreme cold. But if their canes are badly nipped back, a whole season or two of bloom is lost, according to the severity of the cold, since they flower on mature wood. *Polyantha Climbers*

There is another disadvantage to the climbing forms of the ranker-growing Hybrid-Teas. In the northern part of the Southwest, Spring is almost always a false season. Warm days come early and the Tender Climbers put out confidently. Climbing forms are usually several weeks ahead of the bushes of the same variety, and often a sudden freeze, or a killing frost, destroys the blossoms. Only once in about five years does a strong-growing Climbing Tea or Hybrid-Tea reach perfection. That one time ought to be considered worth waiting for, as the vision of a climbing *Columbia,* thirty feet in extent, with several hundred perfect Roses all open at one time, will surely testify. *Hybrid-Tea*

There is another class of Climbing Hybrid-Teas that has

no dwarf, bush-form; examples of which are *Souvenir de Wooten* and *Rene Marie Henriette*. The latter, except in the most favorable season, discolors, mildews and balls in most sections, but is still planted because it often gives scattering bloom in the Fall.

RAMBLERS

Ramblers Classified

Ramblers are those Climbers characterized by long, pliant canes, renewing themselves from the ground each year, and covered with sprays or clusters of small flowers. They are the worst snare awaiting the amateur Rose-grower. They are deceptively beautiful and healthy-looking at times, yet rarely prove immune to mildew. *Dorothy Perkins, White Dorothy, Excelsa, Coronation, Hiawatha, La Fiamma* and the countless other Ramblers are the only types of Climbers which can be used to really good advantage twined around a post or in festoons along a rope.

Suggested Locations

If you must have Ramblers, the best way to handle them is to plant them in the open full sunlight where they will have free circulation of air. Cut out at the ground all the previous season's growth each year, immediately after they have finished blooming. Spray as often as you have the strength, with any good fungicide or sulphur mixture. The results are apt to be the same, no matter what you do. In a dry season there will be very little mildew and in a wet one, plenty.

PILLAR ROSES

Treatment of Pillar Roses

The Pillar Roses are those which, not being of such tall, strong growth as the true Climbers, may be trained on a high post, or like a fan on a fence or trellis. This latter treatment is the more desirable as the canes are usually, when mature, too stiff to bend without breaking. This pillar group embraces the most desirable of all the climbing Roses since as a class they are healthier than the Ramblers and more easily

Pruning

handled than the tall Climbers. The only pruning they require is to take out all wood more than three years old, and cut back the blooming lateral stems to within two eyes, or leaf buds, of the main canes, immediately after blooming.

The Pillars may be divided into the Hardy sorts, and the ever-blooming or half-tender varieties.

Of the Hardy Pillars, *Pauls Scarlet* tops the list as the most *Hardy* outstandingly beautiful and generally satisfactory climbing *Pillars* Rose in existence. Its color is vivid and unfading, its fragrance delicious, and its length of flowering, and multitude of blossoms most generous. Beginning in early April it often continues through the first week of June, its huge lasting clusters of shining red coming in a long succession of unbroken bloom.

Next to *Pauls Scarlet* perhaps the loveliest of the Hardy Pillars is *Jacotte*, with orange-pink, semi-double profuse flowers and holly-like foliage. It should always be planted against a fence or trellis where its strong horizontal, lateral canes will not interfere with passage, and should never be placed at a gateway or on a post, as its canes will usually break if you attempt to bend them too soon.

Primrose is a lovely pillar Rose which likes a sunny location where it will grow to some fifteen feet and bear, over a long season, large clusters of pure yellow, very double flowers.

Tausendschon (or *Thousand Beauties*) and its darker twin, *Roserie,* are billowy masses of dainty blossoms and *Mary Wallace* is a pink dream. *Climbing American Beauty* fades so badly that it cannot be enthusiastically recommended, but it is a lovely thing for a few days.

All the Hardy Pillars bloom abundantly, although only *Almost* once, except *Mary Wallace* which sometimes has a few scat- *Ever-* tered blossoms in the fall. Perhaps no question is more often *blooming* asked than, "Do you know any good everblooming climbing *Climbers* Roses?" While not quite everblooming, there is a class of *Australian* Half-Tender Pillar Roses which bloom more than once. Many *Climbers* of them come from Australia.

Then there is the long list of the less rank-growing Hybrid- *Espalier* Tea Climbers which do well spread out fanwise against a fence or trellis. They develop blooming branches from those *Pruning* "eyes" or "buds" exposed to the sun, and should have their canes trained as nearly horizontal as possible. The only pruning they require is to cut off flower stems and any diseased or very old wood. Some of the best are *Climbing Herriot, Mrs. Aaron Ward, Souvenir de Claudius Denoyel, Lady Ashtown* (the hardiest and best pink), *Rose Marie, Los Angeles, Hoosier Beauty, Killarney, Irish Fireflame, Clara Bow, Kaiserin Auguste Viktoria, Gen. MacArthur* and *Hadley,* and two Climbing Teas, *Lady Hillington* and *Papa Gontier.*

To this group may be added also the climbing forms of two Polyanthas, *Auguste Kordes,* or *Climbing Lafayette,* and *Climbing Cecile Brunner.* They are mildew proof, a most singular advantage in a climbing Rose. *Cecile Brunner* is densely clothed with almost evergreen foliage and makes a good-looking vine. *Auguste Kordes* is most highly recommended for training on a pillar and for festoons. Its early bloom is abundant and after being established, it repeats in the fall. Its only fault is a none-too-fast color, the bright cherry red turning to a pink.

GROUND COVERS

Ground covers are those Roses which are suited to trail *Ground* along the ground or over embankments. They are very *Covers* artistic and attractive looking in a naturalistic garden. *Jacotte,* while classed as a Pillar Rose, may be used. But the type is most often represented by the *Wichuraiana group.* These have practically evergreen, shining foliage.

Some points to remember about Climbing Roses, taken as a whole, are:

Prune, immediately after they bloom in the Spring, and *Prune* fertilize heavily to induce strong, new growth from which will come next year's blossoms.

Learn the color, season of bloom, probable size and habit *Character-* of growth of the plant, *before planting,* so as to locate *istics* properly. Climbers do not take kindly to being carted about. Be more than generous in the width and depth of the hole *Planting* and the amount of fertilizer used when planting, remembering you will seldom be given a second chance to correct any initial deficiency.

Of the Tender Climbers, choose the yellow *Banksia,* the *Selection* pink *Zephrine Drouhin* and perhaps *Marechal Niel.*

Of the Hardy Climbers, the *New Dawn, Albertine, Silver Moon, Bess Lovett, Mme. Gregoire Staechelin, Emily Gray* and *Mermaid* are not likely to disappoint you.

Of the Ramblers, don't indulge! But try the Pillar Roses *Bloomfield Courage* and *Bloomfield Perfection, Auguste Kordes* and the Hybrid Musk, *Vanity,* old varieties but always good.

Among the Climbing Teas and Hybrid Teas, buy all you can afford or accommodate, but remember the added care and attention they demand.

Of the Hardy Pillars, never rest until you acquire a *Pauls Scarlet* or two, a *Roserie* or a *Thousand Beauties,* a *Mary Wallace,* a *Primrose,* and several of the *Bracteata.*   ·

III. POLYANTHA AND FLORIBUNDA

Polyanthas are hardy, everblooming, shrubby, little plants, flowering in immense clusters and suitable for massing in beds, low hedges, or borders. They are *the* Roses for the gardener who wants to spend the minimum of time and energy on his bushes and reap the maximum results. When once established they increase in strength and beauty from year to year but always retain their original neat habit of growth. They require little pruning except to remove very old, dead or diseased wood; and, if wisely chosen, planted in the sun, and not exposed to unhealthy plant neighbors, they will require neither dusting nor spraying to any extent. All they *will* require is to have the old blooms cut off, and a little feeding now and then to keep them energetic.

The Polyanthas vary considerably in height, size, and type of flower, and coloring so that it is a good plan to see a plant before ordering in large numbers for any special purpose.

They should be used as hedges, massed in beds, or in front of evergreens, and as a border for taller-growing shrubs.

For beds or edging, or for a gay border anywhere, there are Polyanthas which should be in every garden. They are practically immune to mildew, are indescribably beautiful in coloring, and create a stunning effect if planted in large masses in beds of one variety. In fact, no rose garden, formal or otherwise, can afford to be without them.

There is another type of Polyanthas which has been grown very widely, represented by the *Cecile Brunner* or *Sweetheart Rose*. The flowers, which come both singly and in clusters, are really miniature double Roses, very attractive when cut in the bud for bouquets. But the plants for garden decoration are valueless, as the blossoms open too rapidly with their petals flared back in an ugly way.

Another favorite, *Gruss an Aachen*, which is said to be really a Bengal Bourbon and not a Polyantha, has rather large flowers for the class, of an exquisite color when conditions are favorable.

The Floribunda are intermediary between the low Polyanthas and the tall Hybrid Teas, having been bred for mass-plantings or decorative use.

The plants are sturdy, hardy, very bushy and of medium height. The blossoms composing the cluster flower-heads are larger than Polyanthas—some single, some double-petalled—and have the same habit of continuous bloom, retaining their color and shape even in hot summer sun.

Some are classed as Hybrid Polyanthas; some listed under *Classes* the Hybrid Teas.

They are particularly adapted to landscape use.

IV. BUSH OR BEDDING ROSES

The Bush or Bedding type is the one we usually associate with the word "Rose." This class may be divided into Hybrid Perpetual, Tea, Hybrid Tea, Pernetiana, and Single Roses.

HYBRID PERPETUALS

Hybrid Perpetuals are the strong, tall-growing, winter-hardy, generally once-blooming-only Roses of our grand-mothers' gardens. They are one of the oldest types of bush Roses, originating in France where they are still very popular and have a wider range in variety than in the United States. Germany, too, is fond of them, and great advances are being made both abroad and here at home in their hybridization. *Hybrid Perpetuals Bush Roses*

Some of the favorite Hybrid Perpetuals are *Paul Neyron, General Jacqueminot, Ulrich Brunner, George Arnends, Frau Karl Druschki,* and the fast disappearing *American Beauty, John Russell* (a fine red of perfect form), and *Mme. Albert Barbier* (light salmon-flesh and apricot).

Since the Hybrid Perpetuals, however hardy and beautiful, bloom only in the Spring, a very few of their kind should be included in a small Rose garden. Hybrid Perpetuals grow tall unless they are kept sharply pruned.

In pruning them, all wood more than two years old should *Pruning* be taken out at the base of the plant and the remaining canes shortened according to the results you want to achieve. The taller they are left, the more flowers, and the shorter they are cut, the finer the blooms on longer stems.

*Suggested
Uses*   The Hybrid Perpetuals make fine tall Pillars or shrubs, especially *Frau Karl Druschki*, which should be in every garden, as it furnishes all the white Roses anyone could wish.

SINGLE ROSES

*Attention
Called to
Single
Roses*   The single Roses are a decorative group which are being given an increasing amount of attention by the amateur grower. They usually have only five petals and their color is apt to fade rapidly. But cut as buds for the house, they possess an artistic grace that will charm the most unenthusiastic observer.

The Single Roses come in a variety of colors. There is the pink *Dainty Bess*, and the white *Innocence*. But the finest of all is *Isobel*. Give it plenty of room and it will reward you with a multitude of long, carmine-orange buds which fade with age to a pretty pink.

TEAS

*Tea Roses
Identified*   The Teas are an old race of bushy, everblooming Roses, mostly in yellow tones, with disease-resistant foliage which is little troubled by mildew or black-spot. They are not winter-hardy in the North, but are seldom killed by the cold weather in most sections of the South and West. Their chief faults are a restricted range of color, and an inclination to

"ball", a term which, when applied to Roses (mostly the soft, heavy ones) means that they do not open properly. This is due generally to weather conditions, but is one of the most exasperating traits that a Rose may possess, for no one likes to have a whole crop of blooms "go bad", and most of the Teas bloom in crops.

One Tea which never balls is *Lady Hillington*. It is widely planted and ranks as the most popular yellow rose. An often weak "neck" (a characteristic of the Teas) and a tendency to fade badly in the heat, constitute its major faults, but it is one of three Teas that should be in all Rose gardens. *Suggested Varieties*

They are generally of but average height. They require only light pruning, as their chief value to a garden lies more in the number than in the size of their blossoms. They improve wonderfully when given frequent cultivation and heavy feeding. *Height Pruning*

The Teas are almost as little adapted to the Southwest as the Rugosas and should be left as largely to the true South as the Rugosas to the true North. Their strong tea-fragrance and lovely foliage cannot make up for the fact that only a few of their multitudinous flowers are worth gathering, except in those seasons most favorable to their proper development. *Chief Character-istics*

HYBRID TEAS

The Hybrid-Tea originated as a cross between a Hybrid-Perpetual and a Tea. It inherited most of the hardiness of the former and the everblooming tendency of the latter. Though Hybrid-Teas are of comparatively recent origin, *La France* being the oldest one in existence, their popularity is so widespread that they have displaced most of their original progenitors in the modern Rose garden. *Origin*

The work of hybridization continues unabated, such crossing and recrossing having been accomplished that it is small wonder that in the resultant race there is apparent a decline in hardiness.

No one Rose can be perfect from every point of view, but many of the Hybrid-Teas have each their good points *Suggested Collections* which make them desirable in any Rose collection. Heading the list of Hybrid-Teas is the *Radiance* group, the greatest of these is *Red Radiance!* They are considered the backbone of any successful Rosegarden.

Climatic Characteristics of the Southwest: The Southwest is the half-way meeting ground for the East and the far West in more ways than one. It is influenced by both and yet totally unlike either. It has the long growing-season and tropical summer of California, but its winters can remind one more often of New England. This makes all rules of either section not safe to apply here culturally. But, the Southwest has a greater leaning toward California than it has toward Pennsylvania, when it comes to a matter of plant-growth, Rose-plants more closely resembling those of California in size than those of the North.

Pruning

Pruning Hybrid-Teas: When we consider this, it must have its *direct bearing* on the pruning of Hybrid-Teas. Nature demands a balance. This greater top-growth has its correspondingly greater root-growth and by unduly limiting the former we necessarily in time will limit the latter.

Beware of "forcing"

When you are told that you can prune, either to have a fine bush or fine flowers, you have heard only half of it. The end of that sentence is—if you don't have a fine bush you won't have any flowers very long! The extremely-low pruning theory comes to us from the florists who prune their bushes sharply and feed heavily to produce fine blooms. But they usually neglect to say what they do with those bushes at the end of one year, two years, or at the most, three years. They throw them out! This whole process is known as "forcing" and the result is an exhausted bush at the age when it should be at the height of its glory.

Adapt Contour to Root System

When pruning Hybrid-Teas, first of all, be sure the pruning shears are sharp. A great deal of harm can be done by hacking a Rose with dull shears. The next step is to walk around the bush and take a good look at it before deciding what particular type its cut should be. A rule of "proportion" in pruning all but newly set-out bushes (which latter should be cut back to within six inches of the ground) is ⌖

Proportion

well-established plants cut one-half. That is, *cut back one-half* the *new strong growth* of a *bush Rose*. All the old, diseased or weak wood should be cut away entirely. Try to create a well-balanced and symmetrical appearance.

PERNETIANAS

The Pernetianas are the newest of the bush creations. And they demand to be treated like the spoiled youngster of any large family. *Pernet Varieties*

Monsieur Pernet might be considered in the light of a modern Pandora, for when he crossed the Austrian Brier with a Hybrid-Perpetual and produced the Pernetiana race, he loosed upon the Rose world a host of hitherto unimagined evils. Black-spot, canker, die-back and defoliation all appear as if by magic to confound the Rose-grower.

But, if unknown evils accompanied the advent of the Pernetianas, it was marked by a great glory as well, for they possessed a beauty of color and a grace of form undreamed of, until then. The Austrian Brier strain infuses all of them with that dark golden or bright Primrose glow that makes them stand out in any garden like shining beacons.

There is a movement on foot among the commercial growers to combine the Hybrid-Teas and Pernetianas under the head of Hybrid-Tea. They claim that they have been so cross-bred with the Hybrid-Tea that only an arbitrary decision could say to which class they belonged. But let the growers by all means make such an arbitrary decision, for it ought not to be hard to say, if the foliage is faulty, "This is surely a Pernetiana". And it gives the amateur something to go by, for he knows then that it will demand special consideration. *Chief Character-istics*

Some of the Pernetianas are: *Talisman, President Hoover, Angele Pernet, Ville de Paris, Feu Joseph Looymans, Mrs. E. P. Thom* and that lovely witch, *Los Angeles; Cuba, Padre, Gwentha Jones, Margaret McGredy, Willomere* and *Georges Pernet*. Many of the newer introductions which have one or more of these as their progenitor unfortunately "inherit" their faults. *Suggested Collection*

Pruning

To sum up Pernetianas, the best way to treat them is to prune them slightly and plant them in beds to themselves where they can indulge in their idiosyncrasies, and give them the special treatment their beauty deserves without endangering the health of other Roses.

If you would escape their enchantment, never look at one, for once beholding their fleeting beauty, you are lost! They weave a spell that will rob you of all reason, for knowing they may wreck your whole garden, you will yet plant them and in time realize that your feeling for them is the same as the Greeks for Alcibiades—you "Love and hate, and cannot do without" them.

Planting Roses

*Time for
Planting*

November, after the first light freeze, is planting time for Roses in the Southwest. At this season the ground is relatively warmer than the air, which induces root-growth. If transplanting is postponed until February, one will discover, upon taking up the plants, a newly developed system of small, white roots which will be largely sacrificed when disturbed at this later time.

Exceptions

There are, however, two real exemptions from this Fall planting rule—pot-grown Roses and California-grown Roses. The former, being thoroughly active, if subjected to a sudden freeze will seldom survive. The latter, under the same conditions, not being acclimated, will receive a shock which often proves fatal. Spring is the best time to plant these two sorts in this section.

Rose beds may be any shape desired, but to arrive at a *Shape and* pleasing effect, they should have some definite plan. Not *Size of* more than two rows of bushes to a bed is advisable to make *Beds* cultivation and cutting easy. Avoid stepping in the bed, as it packs the ground, and injures the roots underneath. Average Rose-beds should be from three to four feet wide, with from two to three-foot paths in between. The distance apart of the bushes is determined by the size and habit of growth of the varieties chosen. *Radiance* bushes should be planted at least two feet apart in one direction and eighteen inches in the other; other bushes from sixteen to eighteen inches, depending upon their type of growth.

I. PREPARATION OF BEDS

If possible prepare beds some time before ready to plant. *Depth* Dig the ground to a depth of at least two feet and then *of Bed* thoroughly break up the "hard pan," if it has been reached. Only the top foot of soil taken out will be very fertile, and this should be mixed with an equal quantity of well-rotted manure or leaf-mold.

If the bushes have not been pruned, cut out all but the *Preparation* three strongest canes and cut these back to within three *of Bushes* "eyes" or leaf-buds from the ground. Trim off all broken *Planting* ends of roots; and then carry the bushes to the place of planting in a pail of water, exposing them (and especially the roots) *as little as possible to the sun and wind*.

If making an entire *new* bed, plant a row at a time by the *Trenching* trenching system. Dig a long trench down one side of the *System* bed to the proper depth, piling the earth taken out on the other side of the bed. (See page 15.)

Place the bushes the proper distance apart in this trench *How to* with their roots spread out, mounding the earth to the center *Place a* to fit the rounded contour of the Rose's root-system, leaving *Bush* the bush naturally placed, and not in a depressed condition. Set the plants so that the "bud" (or point of union of the plant and the understock) will be just beneath the surface of the ground. Draw the soil that was put aside around each bush in turn, taking care to keep the roots in a natural position, and pointing down.

Soil Preparation

In the first layer, incorporate five cups of bonemeal for each bush, being careful to thoroughly mix it with the soil; and, if soil is black and heavy, about one-third sand would be a good addition. Don't attempt to make your earth too light—heavy soil helps to anchor the Rose against the strong winds prevalent in the Southwest.

Water

When the entire bed has been filled within two inches of the top, firm the ground well, and then water until thoroughly saturated. Any air pockets left are easily detected, and may be filled with sand. When no holes appear, fill in the remaining two inches with loose soil. On top scatter some well-rotted manure, which will supply humus and retain moisture for the soil, and also act as the only Winter protection usually needed for Roses in this section.

Top Cover

FERTILIZATION

Avoid Over-Stimulation

There is a difference between feeding a plant and stimulating it. Too much stimulation, through the application of chemicals, may result in a "nervous wreck" of a plant. But it is a safe guess that more Roses die of starvation than of indigestion induced by too much feeding.

Essential

A well-balanced diet has been called an essential to Rose health.

Food

Well-rotted manure will release the necessary nitrogen and provide the necessary humus. Leaf mold in large quantities will work wonders. Two cupsful of *super-phosphate* to each plant—November, February, and July—will insure its phosphorus and potash. A light layer of *hardwood* ashes also furnishes a reasonable amount of potash. Tobacco stems fertilize and disinfect to a degree, but are apt to harbor insects.

Demands

Since roses prefer soil that is nearly neutral, where lime predominates an application of epsom salts usually once or twice a year will help correct the condition.

Roses also prefer their roots shaded, therefore light, shallow-rooting, ground-cover plants are suggested (Phlox, Petunias, California Poppies, etc., kept from becoming rank in growth often will protect from weather inclemencies).

If rose leaves turn yellow, it may be *chlorosin*. To correct this, work humus (well rotted manure) into the soil and *sulphur, zinc-sulphate,* or *iron-sulphate*. Cottonseed hulls, or one part cottonseed meal, to two parts bonemeal, *as a fertilizer* may be needed. Plain sulphur scratched into the soil, or a teaspoonful of iron-sulphate once a month is particularly relished by the yellow roses. (See page 139.)

Stimulation after the last of August is unwise, since it will cause a late, tender growth, endangering the life of the plant if caught in an early freeze.

II. HOW TO RECOGNIZE A GOOD BUSH

A good bush for an amateur to buy is a "two-year-old" plant, with a well-developed root-system showing no disease, and having three or four strong canes showing no signs of having been dried out.

If quick results and abundant bloom are desired, choose a well-budded plant; but if longevity is preferred, stick to the own-root kind (if you can find a good nursery that deals in them any more, for from a commercial point of view there is no question about the greater desirability of the budded).

Strong-growing types—such as Shrubs, Climbers, Poly-anthas, *Radiances,* and the like—will prosper very well on their own roots. Some new varieties have been too inbred to make roots for themselves rapidly enough or sufficiently sturdy to support the plant against wind and weather.

The list of Rose varieties contained in the accompanying garden sketch is by no means to be considered as including all the varieties that should, or might, be grown. It is designed for the sole purpose of offering some slight help to the amateur who, in the maze of vast and varied material the modern Rose world presents, may feel lost without a chart of some tried and true Rose friends he may count on to see him safely through.

LIST OF ROSES IN GARDEN SKETCH

CLIMBERS
Hardy Climbers

4	Auguste Kordes or Climbing La-fayette	Red
2	Pauls Scarlet	Red
2	Bloomfield Cour-age	Red
2	Roserie	Rose
2	Primrose	Yellow
2	Emily Gray	Yellow
2	Mary Wallace	Pink
2	Mme. Gregoire Staechelin	Pink
2	Silver Moon	White
2	New Dawn or Ever-Blooming Dr. Van Fleet	Flesh
2	Yellow Banksia	Yellow
1	Albertine	Orange
2	Jacotte	Orange
1	Chaplin's Pink	Pink
1	Zephrine Drouhin	Pink
1	Bess Lovett	Red

Climbing Hybrid Teas

1	Columbia	Pink
1	Mrs. Aaron Ward	Yellow
1	Rose Marie	Pink

18	Ideal	Dark Red
3	Katherine Zeimet	White
6	Golden Salmon	Orange
6	Gloria Mundi	Orange
6	Coral Cluster	Pink
12	Chatillon	Pink
18	Le Marne	Pink

Large Flowered

8	Lafayette	Rose Red
6	Else Poulsen	Pink
6	Salmon Spray	Pink
6	Kirsten Poulsen	Red
1	Gruss an Aachen	Flesh

BUSH VARIETIES IN BEDS
Pinks

18	Pink Radiance
6	Shell Pink or Mrs. Charles Bell
6	Los Angeles
6	Wilhelm Kordes
6	Betty Uprichard
6	Countess Ilchester
6	Columbia
6	Madame Butterfly
6	Georges Pernet

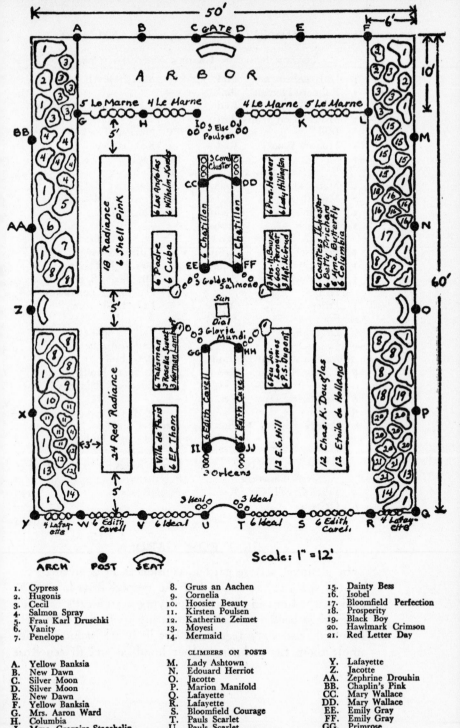

Scale: 1" = 12'

ARCH   POST   SEAT

1. Cypress	8. Gruss an Aachen	15. Dainty Bess
2. Hugonis	9. Cornelia	16. Isobel
3. Cecil	10. Hoosier Beauty	17. Bloomfield Perfection
4. Salmon Spray	11. Kirsten Poulsen	18. Prosperity
5. Frau Karl Druschki	12. Katherine Zeimet	19. Black Boy
6. Vanity	13. Moyesi	20. Hawlmark Crimson
7. Penelope	14. Mermaid	21. Red Letter Day

CLIMBERS ON POSTS

A. Yellow Banksia	M. Lady Ashtown	Y. Lafayette
B. New Dawn	N. Edouard Herriot	Z. Jacotte
C. Silver Moon	O. Jacotte	AA. Zephrine Drouhin
D. Silver Moon	P. Marion Manifold	BB. Chaplin's Pink
E. New Dawn	Q. Lafayette	CC. Mary Wallace
F. Yellow Banksia	R. Lafayette	DD. Mary Wallace
G. Mrs. Aaron Ward	S. Bloomfield Courage	EE. Emily Gray
H. Columbia	T. Pauls Scarlet	FF. Emily Gray
I. Mme. Gregoire Staechelin	U. Pauls Scarlet	GG. Primrose
J. Mme. Gregoire Staechelin	V. Bloomfield Courage	HH. Primrose
K. Rose Marie	W. Lafayette	II. Roserie
L. Albertine	X. Bess Lovett	JJ. Roserie

List of Roses in Garden Sketch—(Cont'd)

1	Lady Ashtown	Pink	3	Mrs. Henry Bowles	
1	Edouard Herriot	Pink	—		
1	Black Boy	Red		*Flame, Orange and Two*	
1	Miss Marion Manifold	Red		*Toned*	
			3	Norman Lambert	
1	Hoosier Beauty	Red	3	Rosella Sweet	
—			6	Padre	
	SHRUB ROSES		6	Cuba	
2	Mermaid	Yellow	3	Margaret McGredy	
2	Moyesi	Red	6	President Hoover	
2	Hugonis	Yellow	6	Talisman	
1	Cornelia	Strawberry	—		
1	Penelope	Cream		*Yellows*	
1	Vanity	Rose	6	Ville de Paris	
1	Bloomfield Perfection	Apricot	6	Mrs. E. P. Thom	
			6	Mrs. Pierre S. DuPont	
1	Prosperity	White	6	Feu Joseph Looymans	
1	Frau Karl Druschki	White	6	Lady Hillington	
—			—		
	SINGLE AND SEMI-DOUBLE			*Reds*	
			24	Red Radiance	
6	Hawlmark Crimson	Red	12	E. G. Hill	
			12	Etoile de Hollande	
6	Red Letter Day	Red	12	Charles K. Douglas	
6	Isobel	Flame	—		

6	Dainty Bess	Pink	GRAND TOTAL
12	Cecil	Yellow	Hardy Climbers 30
—			Hybrid-Tea Climbers 8
	POLYANTHAS		Shrub Roses 12
	Small Flowered		Single Roses 36
4	Edith Cavell	Red	Polyanthas 137
6	Orleans	Rose	Bush Roses 192
		Red	———
			Total 415

III. A ROSE GARDEN

In planning a Rose garden, consideration is given to the limited space at the disposal of the average Rose-lover. The plan worked out in the accompanying sketch calls for only an average back yard, accommodating itself to a plot fifty feet wide and sixty feet long. But in it are included, with ample room for each, some four hundred and fifteen Rose plants, representing most of the *types* in commerce in seventy-eight excellent varieties.

Directly opposite the gateway at the farther end of the garden is a long arbor or summer-house covered with climbing Roses and edged with Polyanthas. The remaining space in this garden is divided into four equal sections by two main intersecting walks. The main path from the gateway to the arbor is planted at ten-foot intervals with climbing Roses trained over arches and is bordered with Polyanthas. At either end of the intersecting main path is a seat and at intervals throughout the plan are placed accents in the form of tall cypress trees and small evergreens. Both main walks are of grass and meet in a large circular plot, in the center of which is a sundial.

The four main sections of the garden contain each three beds of bush Roses, one long outside bed for the taller growing varieties and two smaller ones for the lower growing sorts. The long beds are eighteen feet long and four feet wide and contain twenty-four bushes in two rows of twelve bushes each, planted eighteen inches apart one way and two feet the other. The two small beds in each section are eight feet long and three and one-half feet wide and contain twelve bushes in two rows of six each, planted sixteen inches apart.

The general color arrangement for the garden places the strong shades, such as reds, in the foreground and the lighter pinks, yellows and whites in the background. This lends an impression of greater distance to the perspective. The color arrangement for the beds groups Roses of the same or blending shades of one color in a bed; the four beds bordering on the central circular plot having shades of flame and orange Roses in those bushes closest to the showy brilliance of the orange Polyanthas, *Golden Salmon* and *Gloria Mundi*.

For the full length of two sides of the garden there is a six-foot border planted in shrub Roses, Polyanthas and the single varieties with a background of latticed fence supporting Climbers. This fence may extend across the back line of the garden also if the arbor is on the edge of the property.

Across the front of the garden are tall posts connected by

chains or rope-swags, over which the Climbing Roses planted at the posts are trained. At the base of these festoons there is a low border of Polyanthas, the whole of this front treatment being designed to give an unobstructed view of the garden.

The shrub border may be omitted where there is less space or may be planted in perennials and shrubs other than Rose . . . but its exclusion would mean a loss of many lovely varieties.

The summer-house also might be omitted, but it would be a pity, for it is with a probable sigh of relief from all concerned that after such a pilgrimage through countless Roses we should come at last to a place of rest. The French call such an arbor a "Gloriette" and what name could be more fitting when it is canopied with Roses?

A Rose garden is not just a place to look at, but a place to live in. And roofed against the uninterrupted sunlight that the Rose so loves, this summer-house offers a needed spot to sit in peace and shade and enjoy the fruit of one's labors.

We may say "sit in peace," but what Rose-lover ever really views with a peaceful eye the landscape of his making? Given the slightest excuse

> *To grasp this sorry Scheme of Things entire*
> *Would not we shatter it to bits—and then*
> *Remould it nearer to the Heart's Desire?*

Color ... the Secret of Charm

BEAUTY THAT expresses or emphasizes a single dominant thought or feeling has been judged the height of garden art. It may be quiet or bold—unassuming or gay—florid or demure—in fact, the range is as wide as the complexity of emotional appeal suggests. With the season, its mood may be refreshingly varied, yet preserve intact its dominant characteristic—that which is indicative of its designer's personality. All the possibilities from the flamboyance of exuberance, through gayety, to quiet repose or the subtle suggestion of tranquil content, register an appeal to the senses through combinations, or shades, of color. *Power of Color*

In adapting that fact which the Orientals have long recognized—that is, that green is the color which engenders repose and relaxation from tension—wise Southwestern gardeners provide expanse of lawns and vine-covered arbors or trellises, as well as shade-trees and groupings of shrubs for boundary or foundation-planting. When one chooses a garden of predominant green, a certain graceful dignity is always present, which requires that width of paths, borders and central grass-plot which creates the illusion of, or is in actuality, spaciousness. *Green Engenders Repose and Relaxation*

Since far objects appear hazy, the smoky grey-green foliage of plants like *Leucophyllum* (Senisa) register distance; while, by placing subdued, tho deep, tones nearest the windows of the house, and strong virile ones at commanding intervals emphasis may be brought in relative force on near and far objects, and perspective lengthened. Rich dark-green-foliaged plants, especially those with stiff geometrical out- *How to Create Perspective* lines, when spaced within regular rows of planting that are edged by a precision of line, tend to create greater formality and at the same time constrict the apparent size of the garden, rather than enlarge it.

Altho shades must blend to create harmony, points of contrast are needed to excite interest, and lure one to unexpected beauty spots. Paths must blend in tone, groundcovers must be unobtrusive, and the general panorama, to be æsthetically pleasing, must offer both appeal and promise.

Gardens of One Dominant Color Limited in Variety

Many favorites must be rejected when a garden of one color only is chosen. There are some plants, such as Roses or Zinnias, that offer one range of color-choice that enables almost any desired shade to be selected, yet neither offers the blues or the blue-red combinations on the color-wheel, that is to say, the range from pale lavenders to deep purples. And the chief plants that offer these seldom include the yellows. In fact the white, yellow, red and blues, in their range of blends from one into the other are perhaps to be found only in the Iris or the Hardy Aster families. Of the Lilies, only those of the water-growing branches include the blues, reds, white *and* yellow. So a single-color garden is necessarily limited *in variety* and is restricted to those families of plants that offer what is desired.

Some Suggested Color Treatments in Tones of Yellow

Definite color treatments for a season or merely for a corner or portion of the garden, are not difficult to secure. If one wishes to have a yellow and green garden from Spring until frost, one may have Narcissus, (Daffodils), Jonquils, Tulips, Pansies, Dogtoothed Violets, Hyacinths, Forsythia and *Jasmine humile* (early), followed by sweet-scented Scotch Broom, California Poppies, Hemerocallis (Lemon and Orange Lilies), Wall-flowers, Gladioli, Cactus *Opuntia* (Prickly Pear), Daisies, Columbine, Lemon Phlox, Santolina, Iris, Cassia and Nasturtiums. Both Bush and Climbing Roses offer shades of yellow and most of the bush varieties bloom again in the fall. The Snapdragons, *Oenotheras* (Evening Primrose), Water-lilies, Trumpet Vines and Zinnias begin blooming early in the summer and continue until frost. Helianthemums, Helianthus and Helioposis begin to flower in the early fall and are followed by Lantana, Marigolds, Calendulas, Klondike Cosmos and many kinds and shades of yellow and orange Chrysanthemums.

BLOSSOMS FOR EACH OF THE TWENTY-FOUR HOURS

Should one wish a unique flower arrangement, a planting around a pool can be planned so that blossoms will come into flower each succeeding hour, beginning with the

Ragged Poppy .	. at 3 A.M.		Morning Glories	. at 7 A.M.
Swamp Rose .	. at 4 A.M.		Deanthus (Pinks)	. at 8 A.M.
Black Night Shade	at 5 A.M.		Marigolds .	. at 9 A.M.
Hemerocallis Lemon			Poppies .	. at 10 A.M.
Daylily .	. at 6 A.M.		Purslane .	. at 11 A.M.

Thistles . . .	at 12 Noon	Jimson Weed (Da-	
Dandelion and Potato	at 1 P. M.	tura) . . .	at 6 P. M.
Whiteday Waterlily .	at 2 P. M.	Night Blooming Ce-	
Iris . . .	at 3 P. M.	reus . . .	at 7 P. M.
Four o'Clocks .	at 4 P. M.	Honesty . .	at 8 P. M.
Evening Primrose		Night Blooming Jas-	
(Oenothera) .	at 5 P. M.	mine	at 9 P. M.

While the Pink, White and Yellow Tropical Waterlilies unfurl in succession from 10 P. M. until 3 A. M., and on moonlight nights the Yuccas open their pyramids of white bells, glistening under the moon's rays with unusually satiny sheen.

Tones of Blue

For a garden of blue, Scilla (Squill); Muscari (Grape), and other Hyacinths; Pansies and Bluebonnets (*Lupinus texensis*) come early. The dainty Blue-eyed Grass, Cornflowers, Iris and Larkspur begin blooming about the same time. The Clematis and the star-like Passion flowers first show among their curling tendrils. Picture a white frame house with snowy picket fence, amass with heavenly blue Cornflowers, the sole blossom during its season of bloom! Petunias and Verbenas, long spikes of Veronica, exquisite Tropical Waterlilies, several varieties of the graceful grey-foliaged Blue Salvias and Plumbago; the Vitex and Japanese Morning Glories begin blooming in the early summer, and to their ranks are joined, early in the fall, the fluffy-plumed Ageratum and the thorny Eryngium.

Lavender and Purple Blossoms

Shading toward red come the lavenders and purples. Earliest in the spring the lovely Wisteria droops its panicles of blue-lavender over Violets and many tones of Pansies and Hyacinths. Sweet Peas, Candytuft and pale lavender double Poppies, Penstemon *cobaea*, many tones of Iris and Columbine, Alyssum, Phlox and Gladioli—all pastel tones of delicate beauty—bloom throughout the spring, while *Physostegia virginiana* (False Dragonhead), with Trailing Lantana, Senisa and Verbenas carry these pastel shades throughout the fall months. Liatris (Blazing Star) is a deeper hue and is one of the glories of the fall gardens, together with the many shades that tie the blue purples into the reds found in the fall-blooming Hardy Asters (Michaelmas Daisies), and Chrysanthemums.

Brilliant red in the spring is the Standing Tree-Cypress, *Red Flowers* often called Texas Plume, gay and compelling, as outstanding as the fiery Cockscomb of the fall. Gaillardia (Indian Blanket or Firewheel) is as vividly red and yellow from spring until frost as is another native plant, the Poinciana, a graceful shrub with feathery foliage. Blooming late in the summer comes the unusual Spider or Guernsey Lily and the wine-cups of the Habranthus Lily and the native Primrose. The Cypress vine and the Scarlet Runner-bean carry the reds on the trellises while Portulaca (Flowering Moss) carpets the ground from early summer until late fall. Kochia and Poinsettia are brilliant foliage-plants, the former turning its gayest after frost, while the latter is fatally sensitive to a breath of cold air. Agarita (our native Barberry), with our native Holly and Yaupon are cherished all through the winter for their brilliant red berries, while Sumac *(Rhus)* flames when October nights bring frost.

Certain plants may be had both in the bright or dull reds *Rose and* and in the paler rose tones. Among these are the Tulips, Ama- *Pink* ryllis, Iris and Flowering Almond which bloom in the early *Shades* spring. Gladioli, Sweet peas, Phlox, Tropical Waterlilies, Pyrethrum (Painted Daisies) and climbing Roses bloom valiantly until the heat of summer descends. Bush Roses that blossom twice, together with Altheas (shrubs), Zinnias, Crape Myrtle, Touch-me-nots and Snapdragons are lovely throughout summer and fall.

In the rose tones only are the early blooming Bleeding-Heart and Flowering Peach. Weigeloa soon follows and the double rose Tulips, Poppies and Larkspur bloom together. The pink Crinums come in the late summer with the Speciosum Lily, and are followed closely by Cleome, the Sedums and that lovely vine known as Queen's Wreath.

White flowers for purity and moonlight! What could be *Rose* daintier than the early Spring Snowdrops (Galanthus), Rain- *Tones* lilies, Snowflakes (*Leucojum vernum*), or the trailing Star Jasmine! Pure white hyacinths perfume the air that is wafted over them. Spirea, or Bridal Wreath, trails long graceful sprays over low-growing Pansies. Delicate Baby's Breath (*Gypsophila*), single Poppy-cups, large and small, golden-centered Daisies, all are brought by Spring. The revered White Flag (Iris *Florentina*), beloved for ages by the Mohammedans, precedes Regale, Easter and Madonna Lilies. The tall Hollyhocks, Achillea, Mock Orange, Cosmos, Queen's Lace and Elders lift their lovely sprays of bloom above the lowly Candytuft and Phlox. Sweetpeas and Moonvines climb the walls and arbors, while Four o'Clocks, Snow-on-the-mountain, Magnolias, Alyssum, Snapdragons, Petunias, Verbenas, Abelias, Roses, Crinum, Yuccas—that open their bells in the moonlight—and Zinnias bloom in early summer and most of them continue through till late fall. Datura blossoms in late summer and is closely followed by the fragrant old-fashioned Tuberose and the Mexican Prickly Poppy. These, in turn, give way to the various members of the Chrysanthemum family. After every rain dainty Rain Lilies flower and Waterlilies float their wax-like cups in their beauty of perfection. Old-fashioned night-blooming Cereus and Jasmine lure one into the garden on warm nights, lest their exquisite loveliness be missed—they pass with the kiss of the sun.

A Wide Choice of White Blossoms

Fascinating as it is to experiment with blocks of color in one's own garden, what a thrill it is to plan a color-scheme for a neighborhood, a park, a town, or an entire State! In 1936—Texas Centennial Year—a planting-scheme general in scope, was outlined, which was a simple tho effective combination of those plants that flourish in the region—hardy, inexpensive, readily obtained, and needing little or no cultivation. It was heartily adopted, widely publicized, and beautifully carried out thruout the Southwest.

Keeping in mind that for celebrations blocks of a mass-color effect—not kaleidoscopic variations of many colors—produced by the extensive use of the same plant (selected because effects could be secured in the shortest time, with the least expenditure) shades of rose and gold were chosen to be emphasized, for yellows predominate among the flowers that thrive in the Southwest and rose as a contrasting shade is most effective, and more easily found in the hardy plants of the region. These were selected to be in dominance over the blues, lavenders, etc.; but not to exclude the use of those other colors, however.

Of the shrubs chosen Redbud, watermelon-pink Crepe Myrtle, and Abelia (low-growing, pink-and-white) carry the rose shade from spring to fall, produce a profusion of bloom, and blend in tone with the other flowering plants. These were supplemented by Roses—climbing, shrub, bush and Polyanthas.

Seeds that produce effective drifts of the chosen colors include Larkspur, Poppies, annual Phlox, Petunias (*Rosy Morn* and *Violicea*); Zinnias (including the *Salmon Rose Lilliput*), and Verbenas (in rose, pink, and purple, suggested for borders). The brilliant Tithonia (Mexican Sunflower), Helianthemums, and Cassia *floribunda* make valuable, tall-growing additions to the picture.

Orange, red, and russet Marigolds give fall brilliance, with Chrysanthemums and rose Lantanas.

Castor beans make a quick growth—a decorative hedge or screen—as do all Sumac (*Rhus*), with their gorgeous autumn foliage.

The orange, and the red Trumpet Vine are both brilliant and effective. Morning glories (especially the blue, and the rose flowers) combine charmingly with the fall bloom of the delicate rose of Queen's Wreath or the scarlet of Cypress, and the full splendor of the Moon-vine.

Charming as are single-color schemes, the fascination of color combinations intrigues most people to experiment with them rather than practice that rigid selectiveness which is invariably necessary to insure success with one shade or tone. Yet to obtain the most pleasing color combinations, particular attention to the relationship of the strong yellow light to flowers must be carefully considered. Certain shades are most difficult to place in harmony with the rest of the garden. Magenta tones are best in half shade. In fact, most of the reds are so insistent that, in general, it is wisest to use them sparingly. Against the tropical planting demanded by

Combinations of Colors Fascinating

the Spanish-type house, modified and adapted to the requirements of the Southwest, reds appear to best advantage. Deep rich red Poppies accented by a few spikes of blue Larkspur, Scarlet Lobelia *cardinalis* or *Gilia rubra,* "Texas Plume," rising from a haze of Plumbago *Capensis* are as effective as Scarlet Salvia amidst pure white Alyssum. A bed of rose and purple Petunias are as rich in tone as Bluebonnets with annual Scarlet Phlox. Cannas are best grouped alone. Dusty Miller, sheltering the delicate grace of the Spider, or Guernsey Lily, is an ideal combination.

The Fitness of Color Placing Emphasized

It has been long accepted that most flowers show best against neutral or light shades. Therefore, the pastel tones are most effective in combination with a colonial cottage because of the use of cream or white paint on the building. There is also a fitness in placing delicacy of coloring against lacy foliage, gaining variabilities through texture and heights rather than by the contrasts of rich, warm colors accented by, or accenting, paler tones.

Grey foliage plants tie the garden colors together with a more pleasing blend than where they are omitted. Of these the Artemesias have a misty quality—some taller than others—some even trailing. The *Verbascums'* foliage is silver-white—the *Eriophyllums* are yellowish; Mullein, Thyme, and Agrostemma have fat, downy leaves. Santolina, California poppies, Euphorbia *myrsinites,* Campanula *isophylla mayi* and Veronica *pectinata rosea* make excellent border plants. Senisa, Buckeye (*Aesculus octandra flava*) *Eleagnus angustifolia* are quite indispensable shrubs; while Cornflowers and Achillea *tormentosa's* uses are widely known.

GRAY FOLIAGE PLANTS

Achillea *tormentosa*	*Campanula isophylla mayi*	*Euphorbia myrsinites*
Agrostemma		
Aesculus *octandra flava* (Spanish Buckeye)	*Cerastium*	*Gypsophila*
Artemesias (in variety)	*Centaureas* (Cornflowers, etc.)	*Leucophyllum* (Senisa)
California Poppies	*Eleagnus angustifolia*	Mullein
	Eriophyllum	*Nepeta mussini*
		Salvias

Saxifrage	Stock	Verbascums
Sedum	Trailing Lantana	Veronicas
Sempervivum	Thyme	

COLOR WHEEL

Sometimes when a definite color scheme, or special treatment is desired for a corner, or portion of the garden, certain color-tones blended, or a single shade varied only by the texture and tone of leaf or height of plant, it is helpful to have a list of tested shrubs, vines and flowers arranged for quick, ready reference.

Warm Colors

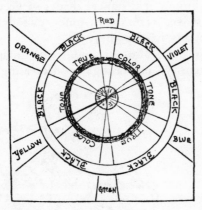

Cool Colors

Success in achieving pleasing effects handling flowers—whether cut blossoms or growing plants—depends on attention to a few essential color-facts.

Remember that . . .

White is the subtle, perfect blend of the three primary colors—red, blue and yellow.

Any color becomes "greyed" by the specific amount of white and black that is added to its "pure", "true" or "most vivid" state.

So-called Complementary, or Secondary colors, are formed where the perfect blend of the adjacent primary colors meet each other—i. e.,

red + blue = violet (complementary to yellow).
blue + yellow = green (complementary to red).
yellow + red = orange (complementary to blue).

True-color-zone (where colors are most vivid) is approximately half way between white and black, (which latter is an absence of light).

Intensity or purity of color varies with the degree, hue, and angle of light, plus background (dark to black backgrounds intensifying or brightening color; light to white backgrounds softening or blurring them).

To create illusion of distance: shades of grey (simulating haze) are employed (from dark tones towards pale, ranging outward from any fixed point).

Texture (of leaf, blossom, and stem) influences degree of color intensity, increasing or decreasing its relative

"purity" in direct ratio from *coarse* (large, thick, heavy, dark, etc.) to *fine* (delicate, lacy, airy, thin, etc.).

Red is termed the "warm" color; blue the "cool" color; yellow the "emotional variant". All warm shades, and tints impart light—cool ones appear to absorb it.

The "shade" is indicated by the amount of black in any color's "pure" or "true" spectrum state—its "tint" is determined by the degree of white.

Symbolically, colors have been used for untold generations to express emotions of almost infinite variety, range, and intensity. Judicious and skilled employment of color develops, or destroys, both men and animals.

FLOWERS LISTED FOR COLOR AND FOR SPECIAL PURPOSES

A Garden of White

Abelia
Alliums
Alyssum
Apache Plume
Astilbe
Baby's Breath (*Gypsophila*)
Candytuft
Chrysanthemum
Cosmos
Crinum
Daisies
Datura (Jimson Weed)
Dahlias
Four o'Clocks
Erythronium
Gladioli
Hardy Hydrangea
Hollyhocks
Hyacinths (Paper White, water, etc.)
Jasmine *Cestrum* (Night Blooming)
Larkspur
Lilac
Madonna Lily
Magnolia
Mock Orange
Moonvine
Mullein
Morning Glory
Pansies
Petunias
Phlox
Poppies, (including Prickly)
Portulaca
Queen's Lace
"Rain Lilies"
Regale Lily
Roses
Snapdragon
Snowballs (*Viburnum*)
Snowdrops (*Galanthus*)
Snow Flakes (*Leucojum vernum*)
"Snow-on-the-mountain"
Spirea
Star Jasmine
Stock
Sweet Peas
Touch-me-not
Tuberose
Tulips
Verbenas
Wisteria
Yarrow (*Achillea*)
Yucca
Zinnia

A Garden of Yellow or Orange

Achillea
Ascelepia Tuberosa
Cactus (*Opuntia*)
Calendula
Calliopsis
Cassia
Chrysanthemums (many kinds)
Columbine (very light)
Cornflower (Montana)
Cosmos (Klondike)
Daffodils
Dahlias
Daisies
Forsythia
Four o'Clocks
Gladioli
Honeysuckles

Helianthemum
Huisache
Helianthus
Heliopsis
Hemoracallis (Lemon Lily)
Hyacinths
Iris (several kinds)
Jasmine *humile*
Jasmine *Gelsemium sempervirens*
Jasmine Primrose
Jonquils
Linaria (grown extensively in El Paso)
Lantana
Marigold
Narcissus
Nasturtiums

Oenothera (Evening Primrose)
Orange Lilies
Pansies
Phlox (Light)
Poppies (California)
Roses (Bush and Climbing)
Rudbeckia-Coneflower
Santolina
Scotch Broom
Snapdragon
Tiger Lilies
Tulips
Trailing Mimosa
Umbalatum Lily
Wallflower
Waterlilies (three kinds)
Zinnia

A Garden of Blue

Ageratum
Agapanthus (Lily of the Nile)
Anchusa
Anchusa (*myosotidiflora*)
Bluebonnet
Clematis (Vine)
Cornflowers (Bachelor Buttons) (*Centaurea Cyanus*)

Cynoglossum (Chinese Forget-me-not)
Eryngium
Flax (*Linium*)
Hyacinths
Grape Hyacinths (*Muscari*)
Iris
Larkspur
Linaria (Toadflax)
Morning Glory (Jap.)

Pansies
Plumbago *Capensis*
Plumbago *Larpentae*
Salvia *farinacea*
Salvia *ballottaeflora*
Salvia (*Pitcheri*)
Squill (*Scilla*)
Tropical Water Lilies
Verbena
Veronica
Vitex
Violet

A Garden of Rose or Red

Red
Agarita (Berries)
Bottle brush
Cockscomb (*Celosia*)

Columbine (with yellow)
Cypress Vine
Gaillardia (with yellow)

Guernsey Lily
Holly (Berries)
Honeysuckle
Habranthus lily

Kochia *Scoparia* (foliage)
Linum rubrum (Scarlet Flax)
Lobelia *splendens*
Lobelia *cardinalis*
Monarda
Peppers
Perennial Pea Vine
Pomegranates
Poinsettia
Tree Cypress (*Gilia rubra*)
Salvia *splendens* (*coccinea*)
Salvia *Greggii*
Snapdragon
Sumac (*Rhus*)
Yaupon (Berries)
Yucca (*Hesperaloe*)

Rose

Anthony Waterer Spirea
Cleome
Coleus

Columbine
Cornflower (*Centaurea*) (Bachelor Button)
Crinum
Larkspur
Hyacinths
Mimosa *pudica* (trailing)
Peach (flowering)
Petunias
Primrose
Queen's Wreath Vine
Oxalis
"Rain Lily"
Sedums
Tamarix (salt cedar)
Yarrow (*Achillea*)

Both Tones

Almond
Altheas
Amaryllis
Cactus
Cosmos
Crape-Myrtle

Dahlia
Dianthus (Pinks)
Four o'Clocks
Geraniums
Gladioli
Hibiscus
Hollyhocks
Iris
Oleander
Peonies
Portulaca
Phlox *paniculata-Maculata*
Phlox *Drummondii*
Phlox *sublata*
Phlox *divaricata*
Poppies
Pyrethrum
Roses (Bush and Climbers)
Sweet Peas
Touch-me-not
Tulips
Verbenas
Waterlilies
Zinnias

A Garden of Lavender or Purple

Alyssum
Butterfly Bush
Candytuft
Centaurea americana (Star Thistle)
Chrysanthemum
Clarkia
Cleome
Clematis *Jackmani* (vine)
Columbine
Gladiola
Hyacinths
Iris

Larkspur
Lilac
Liriope
Liatris (*Gay feather-Blazing Star*)
Monarda (*purpurea*)
Pansies
Penstemon *Cobaea* (Beards Tongue)
Petunias
Phlox
Physostegia virginica

Poppies
Senisa (*Leucophyllum texanum*)
Statice (*annual*)
Sweet Lavender
Sweet peas
Stocks
Trailing Lantana
Verbena
Veronica
Violets
Vitex
Wisteria

A Garden for Fragrance

Alyssum
Bush Honeysuckle-early (*Lonicera fragrantissima*)
Broom (*Genista*)
Carolina Yellow Jasmine (*Gelsemium sempervivum*)
Cedars
Citrus fruits
Datura
Dianthus (Pinks)

Elder
Heliotrope
Honey Locust
Honeysuckles (*Lonicera*)
Jasmine (in variety)
Jonquils
Lavender
Lemon Verbena
Magnolias
Mimosa (all Acacias)
Mint

Petunias
Phlox
Prunus (in variety)
Roses (especially *Marechal Niel*)
Rose Geranium
Rosemary
Sweet Peas
Thyme
Tuberose
Viburnum
Violets

CHIEF DROUGHT-RESISTANT PLANTS

Need Minimum of Water

Achilleas (Yarrow)
Agarita
Ageratum
Altheas
Alyssum
Apache Plume
Arctores
Argemone
Artemesias
Ascelepias
Asters
Buddleia
Castor Bean
Celosia (Cockscomb)
Cornflowers
Coreopsis-Calliopsis
Crepe Myrtle
Daisies

Datura
Desert Willow
Euphorbias
Eryngium
Four o'clocks
Gaillardias
Greasewood
Helianthus family
Honeylocust
Lantana
Liatris
Mesquite
Mimosa
Monarda
Mullein
Myrtle (*Vinca*)

Oenotheras (Evening Primrose)
Parkinsonia
Petunias
Plumbago
Portulaca
Poinsettia

Redbud
Rudbeckia (Cone flowers)
Salvias
Senisa
Sophora
Solidago (Golden rod)

Tamarix
Texas Plume
Thunbergia
Trumpet vine
Verbena
Virginia Creeper
Zinnias

Feature Gardens

- 1932 -
Detaill from Frontispiece
by
Margaret Scruggs

PARADISI IN SOLE
Paradisus Terrestris.
or
A Garden of all sorts of pleasant flowers ···
··· Collected by John Parkinson ···
Apothecary of London
1635

Hillside Gardens

*Ideal
Hillside
Garden*

A MASS OF BLOOM on a slope or series of terraces is the ideal hillside garden, often mistakenly termed Rock Garden, for true Rock Gardens in the Orient, notably in China, feature the tumbled irregularity and fantastic shapes of the rocks themselves, with very little plant-growth among them.

*A Natural
Slope
Developed*

Where one has a natural slope, it may be built up without a great deal of labor, and transformed into a garden of delight by terracing it, and confining sufficient good, growing loam for various types of plants, through the skillful placing of large or medium-sized stones, here and there, with careful carelessness. Embed these deep into the hillside with very little surface exposed, in order that they may hold the moisture and keep the soil from slipping away from the plants. Pack the soil tightly around these rocks. Be sure no airpockets are left. The deep spaces between them will afford that amount of nourishment required by those plants that thrive on slopes. One of the greatest advantages in making a Rock Garden, artificially, is the possibility of having many pockets of different, friable soil mixtures (acid, neutral, etc.) whose basis is topsoil, in which one may experiment with rare, unusual plants.

*Kind of
Stones
Advised to
Be Used*

Select stones large enough that there may be sufficient space between them to prevent the soil in the various pockets from intermingling. Varying their size gives, also, a more artistic effect, just as avoiding the standing on end of many odd-shaped specimens, or the use of rounded, small-sized stones in profusion. The general strain of the stratification in which every type of rock is found in Nature's garden appears more realistic when followed in transporting them to other locations. Particularly on a hillside, the freshly broken surface of a stone should never be exposed. Where there is a choice of a weathered side, turn it uppermost, for it will blend much more naturally into the prevailing tone and general composition.

Remember, a rock *pile* is *not* a *Rock Garden*.

In designing the slope, certain artificiality may be avoided *Informality* by using curved walks that disappear around a clump of low shrubs, or winding paths that entice one to explore their length. Straight lines or geometrical shapes give that formality which is generally undesirable.

Winding paths and irregular outlines suggest hidden treas- *Dry* ures around their curves. One may come upon an unexpected *Walls* drywall, massed with bloom, the secret of the successful construction of which lies largely in tilting or tipping the stones, as they are laid in alternate layers of dry earth (composed of two-thirds sandy-loam to one-third peat) so tightly packed into the crevices that no air-pocket can remain, tilted a bit to let water drain into the soil rather than off the wall; and in taking care that the *thickness* of the *base* is at least one-third the finished, or *total height* of the wall. Such a wall is most useful and effective as a retaining wall for the different levels or terraces, especially useful when a pool is excavated from level ground. Planted, even overplanted for surer life of desired specimens, when in the process of construction, such a wall will be a continual joy.

Of utmost importance, though too often neglected, are *Path.* those little paths that thread the garden, particularly the hillside garden. When they are wide enough to insure easy motion, they lure one to explore them. When the surface of which they are made blends in color and texture with the general scheme of planting, and with the materials of which the buildings are constructed, they tone in as a component part of a perfect unit. There is great diversity both in the shades and in the materials, which offer one a wide range of choice, from the shiny jet-black of coal, through the duskiness of cinders, and certain crushed stones; the blue-greys or tones of red-browns in various kinds of stone; the tan of gravel, to the cream white of cement. Brick or tile also may be had in practically any color desired. Cement may be colored, or slate secured in dull tones. Yet, wherever possible, the soft, living-green of grasspaths is as lovely to walk on as to look at; although the runners of the Bermuda are difficult to keep clipped and within bounds.

Ground Covers

Living, non-flowering green ground-covers, other than grass, generally demand semi-shade, and will not admit of much walking-on. Where a light spring-green shade is desired for harmony "Creeping Charley" (*Nepeta hederacea*) or ground ivy (known by many other common names)—or the variety known as *variegata*, with its leaves speckled irregularly with white—gives a lovely carpet of tiny, rounded leaves. English Ivy's rich, shiny leaves make a distinctly unusual carpet, though it is slow of growth.

Steps

Terraces connected by low, never steep, steps—preferably made of large, flat stones—lure one by easy stages to the top of the slope. Most artistic are stones that are chosen with regard for their tone-blend with the predominant color of the soil of the locality in which they are to be used. Moss-grown, or practically covered with a trailing plant, these stone steps often are the means of exploiting the vividness and beauty of a plant, rather than being themselves too much in evidence.

Soil-Pockets

In the Southwest, where rocks are more or less foreign, to be in keeping with natural conditions the most artistic way to employ them is to sink them *so deep* into the hillside that they serve only as retainers of the soil and only very occasionally be allowed to be a feature. In planting around them remember proper *drainage* is *most* necessary. In some cases the soil-pockets should contain a layer of four to six inches of cinders, gravel or small pieces of stone or brick in the bottom of the hole. Where this is needed, the excavation should be at least two feet deep. Sometimes an inch or two of coal cinders in an eighteen-inch hole is sufficient. A layer of decayed vegetable-matter should be placed between the drainage stones and the growing-earth. This top layer should be at least twelve inches, of equal parts of sand, loam (rich dirt or topsoil), and leaf-mold. Bonemeal is said to be the best fertilizer to use *after* the plants are established, as well as when planting.

One may make a very effective Rock Garden on level ground (preferably with an eastern or northern exposure which afford most protection) by placing it in a corner with a vine-covered fence, or the greenery of massed shrubs as a background. The illusion of its being a portion of a true hillside may thus be cleverly simulated. Aesthetic beauty in gardens, as in every other phase of life, does not tolerate artificiality, therefore, frame and develop a little hillside with the greatest thought and care. *An Artificial Hillside*

In general, until one becomes what might be termed an experienced amateur, probably the greater number of gardeners will prefer to grow those tested groups of plants which will give the surer display of bloom. These may include dwarf bushes and those low or creeping plants that have been tested in our climate. It is seldom advisable to start Rock Garden plants from seed in the pockets. The idea that a Rock Garden or hillside should contain only Alpine (snow-level) plants which have developed immunity to all the extremes of weather conditions, is being superseded. Each locality is adapting the plan of planting slopes with those flowers acclimated and suited to its own peculiar requirements, emphasizing the lowliness of the plants and their diversity of color in foliage and blossom, rather than any specific group of varieties. Double or variegated flowers are not considered as artistic as large clumps of single tones. Simplicity is the keynote. And charm lies in the definite note of restraint—most essential in the smaller or miniature designs, in which one's ingenuity is taxed to the fullest. *Hillside Plants to Each Locality*

One's hillside may boast many of the smaller bulbs (see page 147) for early bloom—among the Alliums, Jonquils, and Dwarf Iris. Our native Bluebonnets—(*Lupinus texensis*), Primroses (*Oenotheras*), *Callirhoe* (Wine Cups), Pansies, Dogtoothed (*Erythronium*) and Wild Violets, and va- *Specific Hillside Plants Adapted to the Southwest* rieties of Astilbe are lovely. Perhaps the most satisfactory plants are the Sedums and Sempervivums. Low-growing Phlox, Thyme for fragrance, clumps of Pinks (*Dianthus*), white Alyssum, purple Teucrium, orange Wallflowers, the dusty foliage and fluffy golden balls of Santolina, Tulipas, dwarf blue Plumbago, Candytuft, Draba (wild Alyssum or Candytuft), Sweet William, Daisies, and certain of the Salvias may be varied with climbing and trailing Nasturtiums; California Poppies, Petunias, Verbenas, Lantanas, or Portulaca.

Unusual Effects

Polyantha Roses in some locations, or the native Texas Pixy-Rose (*Rosa foliolosa*), which is very hardy and quite low-growing, gives a decidedly different note. Certain of the Cacti, Aloes, Agaves and Yucca, also, may be used sparingly, for the chief attraction of a Rock Garden is the clever combination of ruggedness with rustic daintiness. Therefore, creeping plants, those of dwarf height and small, even tiny, blossoms should be used.

General Advice to Hillside Gardeners

Rock gardening is such a new phase in dry sections that it has not yet been tried sufficiently to offer more than these few general suggestions for trial. Since in the Southwest the question is "not what plants will survive the cold, but Summer's heat and drought, only experience with different genera over a period of several years can enable one to say just what will and will not prove satisfactory in this respect. Also, it must be constantly remembered that there are certain plants and shrubs for Rock Gardens that require a special soil—some acid, others acid of less degree, while the greater number revel in lime." Follow this wise counsel, it is urged, and plan to experiment judiciously, if one wishes a conventional rock garden in which only choice, small treasures may have especial culture and attention.

PLANTS FOR HILLSIDES

Agaves	Astilbe	Cacti
Aloes	Bluebonnets (*Lupinus texensis*)	Candytuft
Alyssum		Dwarf varieties of many plants
Alliums	Bulbs	

Erythronium (Dog-toothed violet)
Gilia rubra (Tree cypress) (Texas Plume)
Iris (low growing)
Ivy—English and *Nepeta hederacea*
Jonquils (Daffodils)
Lantana
Nasturtiums
  Climbing
  Bush
Portulaca
Penstemon
Petunias
Phlox
Plumbago
Poppies
Roses (low and trailing varieties)
Sedums
Sempervivums
Santolina
Salvias
Sweet William
Trailing Plants
Thyme
Tulips
Verbenas
Yucca

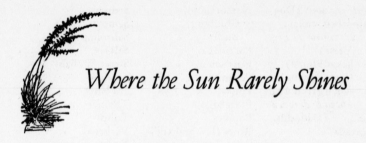

Where the Sun Rarely Shines

So OFTEN the question is asked, "What will grow in the shade?" that many gardeners *must* be keenly interested in the answer to this special query.

Semi-Shade Loving Plants

While there are comparatively few plants that will bloom in the deep shade, where the sun does not penetrate, yet there are a great many that will live *only* in partial shade. The semi-shade is a gold mine of delight for many a Southwestern gardener, especially that spot which receives approximately three hours, only, of sunlight in the morning, for there one may grow successfully certain rare flowers, and also many that have been declared unable to be grown in this section.

Particularly fortunate are those whose soil has been nourished by falling oak leaves, which add those necessary chemical qualities that a great group of plants require. All those cherished, longed-for flowers that have been marked "special care," will make this sheltered spot a delight—Columbine, Canterbury Bells, the various *Erythronium* (Dogtoothed) and Wild Violets, Perennial Phlox, Lobelia *cardinalis*, Foxglove (or *Digitalis*), Hypericum, those Iris of delicate shades, as well as Iris *cristata* and Iris *pseudacorus*, Gebera, Bleeding Heart and Dutchman's Breeches (the other variety of *Dicentra*), Scabiosa and the delicate Spring Beauty (*Claytonia virginiana*) . . . Even the lovely Windflower or Japanese Anemone, and the other Anemones, and the Hardy Hydrangeas have shown their appreciation of such an abiding place, so greatly to their liking.

Where there is a bit more of the morning sun at the edge of a woody place, Hemerocallis (or "Lemon Lilies") bloom well. Crinums; the Guernsey or Spider Lily; the *Lilium Speciosum, Rubrum* and *Melpomene,* and the Lilium *Henryi;* the red Habranthus; Calla Lilies; Funkias (*Hostia,* or Plantain Lilies) and Tulips are some others of the Bulb and Lily family that enjoy the semi-shade. Early flowering bulbs, too, will flourish when planted under deciduous trees and shrubs, for their blossom-period is gone before the leaves mature. *At the Edge of the Wooded Place*

Of the flowering shrubs, Abelias, the Viburnums, several of the Philadelphus, Eleagnus, Jasmines, Spirea, Forsythia, Weigela are some which will blossom well; while Mahonia goes more to leaf and the Nandina's berries are less brilliant than where there is more sun. Another interesting fact about those groups of plants, of which Nandina and Gaillardias are representative, is that contrary to the general belief that sometimes these plants, just as a matter of freakishness, develop deeper tones of red than at others, there seems to be no question that sandy, acid soil produces more gloriously-colored specimens, while clay soils that are highly alkaline give the green, with very faint tinges (if any at all) of red. *Flowering Shrubs That Will Grow in Semi-shade*

Coralberries, Hardy Asters, Sedums, Sweet William and *Physostegia virginiana* (False Dragonhead) are among the most dependable of the lower-growing plants. The *Ajuga,* or Bugle Weed, makes a lovely carpet, yet the Myrtle (*Vinca minor*) with its small blue flowers, and the striped-leaf variety (*Vinca minor variegata*), are perhaps the most dependable low plants. They are possibly the most universally grown. Phlox *subulata,* moss or mountain pink, blooms profusely; *P. divaricata* will thrive in neutral to semi-acid soil. Sweet Alyssum, with the Dogtoothed Violets and the Habranthus, are among the few which will flourish in heavy shade. Yet there is another ground cover that is much more delicate, known by many names, some of which are Ground Ivy, Creeping Charlie, etc. (*Nepeta hederacea*), which also spreads so rapidly that it takes watchful care to keep it within bounds. *Most Dependable Low Plants*

Mascarene ("Japanese") grass (*Zoysia tenuifolia;* or M.

densifolia, low and M. *Japonica spicata,* 15 inches) as a ground cover in shade has the unique quality of producing blue flower-spikes from late summer until frost.

Great Variety of Choice

In general one may say that practically all plants that are grown in other sections of the country will thrive in the semi-shade in the Southwest, *if* their required soil conditions are supplied. In fact, practically all of the plants, even some of the Roses, will give better results if shaded from the strong afternoon sun. Yet care must be taken to avoid planting under those shrubs and trees that have a network of roots near the surface, such as Ligustrums and Elms, for these consume the food in the soil, being gross feeders.

IN SEMI-SHADE

. . . at the edge of planting . . .

Shrubs

Abelia
Althea
Black Haw (*Viburnum*)
Blackberry
Broom (*genista*)
Buckeye (*aesculus octandra*)

Coralberry
Crataegus (Red Haw)
Dogwood (*Cornus*)
Eleagnus
Elder
Forsythia
Hardy Hydrangea
Ilex rotundifolia
Jasmines (in variety)
Mahonia *bealei*
Nandina
Pineapple *guava* (in the south)
Redbud (*Cercis*)
Rose mallow (*Pavonia*)
Viburnums (in variety)

Weigela
Wild Plum (Malus)

Plants

Ageratum
Ajuga (Bugleweed) Green . . . *variegata*)
Anemone (Windflower)
Asters (Michaelmas daisies)
Balsam
Bleeding Heart
Bush Clover
Calla Lilies
Callirhoe (Wine Cup)
Canterbury Bells
Claytonia (Spring Beauty)
Columbine (Aquilegia)
Crinum
Datura
Dutchman's Breeches

Erigeron
Erythronium
Ferns
Funkia (*Hostia, Plantain*)
Foxglove (*digitalis*)
Gaillardias
Gerbera
Godetia

Habranthus
Guernsey Lily
Hemerocallis
Iris
Lilies
Lobelia
Myrtle (*Vinca*)
Oxalis

Phlox (annual and perennial)
Plumbago
Sedums
Sweet Alyssum
Snapdragons
Tradescantia
Tulips

Pools for Delight

*Universal
Appeal
of Water*

ONG AGO the Orientals realized that the green garden that so rested their eyes and senses was immeasurably enhanced in beauty by the inclusion of water in some manner. Dwellers in all semi-arid countries know this deep longing for limpid pools and strive to obtain them. Following a subtle secret learned by clever imitators of Nature's handiwork in creating the illusion of cool comfort, the successful garden in semi-arid regions retains a bit of the austerity of the desert in its expanse of open green lawn and in the strong emphasis placed on formalized design, geometric line and pattern, and in concentration of masses—yet it features that which is quite foreign to the general landscape, streams and pools of water, which because of scarcity become a luxury keenly desired.

So the young civilization in the Southwest, having wrested a home from the prairie, is following in the footsteps of past ages in beginning to seek methods to secure for themselves this cherished possession, and the attempt to overcome and utilize those limitations set by Nature offers a most fascinating challenge to them.

*Charm of
a Garden
Enhanced
by Water*

The lure of ever so tiny a bit of water, for reflection if nothing more, is always powerful. Everyone loves water, and wherever there is a pool, large or small, or a babbling stream, are attracted at once to its banks. Even the tiniest, shallow, irregular-shaped bird bath that may look like a huge curled waterlily leaf, giving a duplicate image of a nodding, scarlet Poppy or a single perfect Rose, brings joy to the soul of the beholder. Therefore, to say that one's garden will be infinitely more attractive by the skillful inclusion of a pool is true, yet the possibility or probability of being *able* to do so may be questioned.

Anyone may have a pool. This is a broad statement, yet on most people's property there is a spot where a tub may be sunk, or a small excavation be made and lined, waterproof. On a city lot, averaging 50×150 feet, if one assigns no more than 15×20 feet to the garden spot, a corner, an end or the center of this may be dug for a pool. Even the ice-box drip may be converted into an economical pool! On this limited, perhaps the smallest, space one may assign to a comprehensive garden, there are almost unlimited possibilities for a great variety of plants, and a succession of bloom over which to rejoice.

Plan for a Pool

Sometimes there is too shady a spot, under trees, along a wall or beside the house, to grow grass or most plants. Dig this spot out, it is suggested, with irregular outlines. Vary the slope of the sides of it toward a three-feet depth. Then prepare cement and sand, and pour in a layer of two to three inches thick. Mould it to the lines or contours desired, and lay in a piece of wire-netting (or some other reinforcing, tying material), and pour on two to three inches more of concrete; in which one may embed, while soft, boulders or field-stones, the better to simulate nature in preparing an informal pool.

Details of Construction

Let this "set" for three or four days. Then fill with water, and allow it to remain for several days. After this, drain off *all* the water (because there is generally something in fresh cement chemically bad for both fish and plants which the first filling and stand of water carries off). It may then be safely filled for use.

Special Treatment of Fish or Plants Used

Planting—If one wishes to grow aquatic plants, soil must be prepared. If the plants are to be grown directly in the pool (not in pots or tubs), put in six inches of manure at the bottom, then a layer of ten inches of topsoil. Plant the tubers directly in this and cover with four to six inches of sand, or fine gravel, to keep that transparency in the water necessary to enable one to see the darting fish, which are so essential aside from their beauty, for they feed on mosquito larvae.

Soil Preparation for Aquatic Plants

Suggestions for Drainage

In preparing the pool, if one has a tiny one, it may be refilled and drained with the garden hose. But, if it is somewhat larger, it is wisest to provide a drain-pipe within the concrete bed, by which the water may escape. This method of drainage may be of the simplest—by allowing it to enter the sewerage directly; or it may be converted by pipes to be utilized in watering certain other parts of the garden. Or, what may be most elaborate, a series of overflowing, shallow pools may be arranged, terraced one a bit above the other with the lowest spilling over to create a marsh, or bog. This is especially adapted to some grounds, though in growing aquatic plants, it is usually best to avoid running water.

Place Where Least Evaporation

Generally speaking, however, water is too precious to admit of this extravagant use. With hot summer skies, one is wise to place a pool where it will suffer least from evaporation.

Shady Pools Are Mirrors

In a shaded or semi-shaded spot Waterlilies, however, usually will not flourish, though Water-Hyacinths may, or Cat-tails and other non-flowering aquatics. Be content, generally, to have a very shady pool merely be a mirror, with darting gold fish for color; and, if you are not going to grow aquatic plants in it, put only a layer of gravel on the bed of it. This will make it seem more like Nature's handiwork than man's.

Semi-shade Planting

There are many blooming plants that do well in shade, or semi-shade (see page 238), which, if placed to overhang, or at a point where their image may be reflected, at once become an integral part of an exquisite composition. Pools that mirror green things, only, are restful, yet those that reflect other colors, too, in pastel or in vivid shades, have an irresistible charm.

Keep to Scale in General Scheme

In designing that feast for one's senses, the pool, it is of greatest importance to *keep it to scale* with the property and buildings. Do not forgot how essential is proportion. It, too, should conform to the general plan and follow the broad scheme of planting in relation to the architecture of the buildings. It too should emphasize formality or informality of design by its shape, size, and setting.

Where informality is desired, always place the pool where it is screened and secluded, never in the center of the garden. Its most effective combination is at the foot of a slope, a hillside, or beneath an overhanging ledge. When one has level ground to deal with, artificial slopes and ledges, even a miniature rugged hillside (see page 232) may be effected by adding a few stones and a little more earth to that surplus dirt taken from the excavation of the pool. Irregularity of outline, both in the contour of the pool and in the borders of shrubs and flowers, demonstrate that level ground and straight lines never make as interesting an informal garden as undulating irregularity.

For Informality

A natural, or man-made rocky ledge, or barren slope, is the ideal spot on which to use one's imagination in an effort to capture that holiday spirit of Nature—alluring informality. Trailing vines overhanging a pool are always enchanting. Blue or rose Morning Glories, or Golden *Oenotheras* (Evening Primrose) grown from the ledge above, droop in panicles of green, studded with color.

Over-hanging Ledges

As has often been observed invariably a pool draws one to its *very edge* in the hopes of being able to peep over and down into the limpid depths. So, where the reflection is loveliest, what fun it is to be able to step out over the water on a large, flat stone! From this natural vantage point, one can enjoy to the fullest the beauty of the scene. How clever is that artist-gardener who, with skillful artifice, reproduces all those chief attractions that one finds in Nature's scenic loveliness!

Naturalistic Effects

What is more graceful than a weeping willow dipping into a sheltered pool! Or what exotic beauty more appealing than the waxen perfection of a Water Lily!

Water Lilies

Yet Water Lilies must have an abundance of sunlight . . . at least four or five hours of the direct rays upon them, preferably in the middle of the day. Of these there are two kinds, the hardy and the tropical. The hardy kinds do not have to be disturbed after the original planting except to insure large blossoms, thin out their too luxuriant root-growth, provided care is taken that their roots do not freeze in severe weather.

Care in Winter

A covering of eight or ten inches of water above the surface of the soil, generally gives them sufficient protection. Although in extreme conditions, a topcovering of boughs and leaves, held down with wire netting, may be loosely put over planks that have been put across the pool, taking care that the oxygen of the circulating air is not cut off.

Remove Oak Leaves

As oak leaves often contain an acid and tannin bad for aquatic plants, it is best never to cover with these. Also see that none of these are ever allowed to remain in the water.

Tropical Water Lilies

Tropical Lilies are natives of the hot countries—Africa, South America and Australia—where they grow in profusion. They are generally too delicate to survive even the mildest winters, and not being expensive, are too much trouble to attempt to keep, unless one has a very large indoor pool. Even then, it is usually more satisfactory to purchase new young plants rather than try to handle the mature old ones. Their spread is slightly greater than the hardy varieties (which require a radius of at least three feet of space for each plant). They are so lovely, standing many inches above the water on their stiff stalks, it would be a decided deprivation not to plan to include at least one in every watergarden. Their range of colors are exquisite—blues, pinks, white, reds and yellows, of wider choice than the hardy varieties, although these latter include all colors except blue.

The Two Chief Varieties

Where the temperature is about 80 degrees Fahrenheit and there is full sunshine, the day-blooming tropical Water Lilies remain open between seven in the morning and five or six in the afternoon, while the rarer night-bloomers open about eight in the evening, remaining lovely until the middle of the following morning. When it is cloudy, or cooler and grey, often these two varieties reverse their usual habits. It is intensely interesting to note that both the temperature and the amount of sunlight have such definite, material effects on these more tender Lilies.

How to Plant Water Lilies

The initial planting of all Water Lilies may be made directly into the pool, when one has placed on the floor of it the layers of earth to receive them, leaving at least twelve to fourteen inches of water above the soil, which in turn should have a depth of at least sixteen to eighteen inches. Or they may be put in large earthen pots or wooden tubs, usually two to three feet in diameter, *planted under water* (not outside and submerged afterward).

This latter process enables one to transplant or divide them, especially when the pool is large, easier than when not thus restricted. In dividing roots, there are two types of growth; one, like bulbs, forms into multiple "crowns" (which can be pulled apart); the other sends out runners or creeping root-stalks, which should be severed by a slanting, clean cut. If the Lilies seem to produce fewer flowers than expected, often the reason is they are planted too deep, or there is too much nitrogen in the soil. They should be planted with the "crowns" just below the surface of the soil.

Other Types of Aquatic Plants

If one wishes to grow several types of aquatics in and around the pool, the habits of each of these plants should be carefully considered, for some like full sun, some require semi-shade, and each likes a particular depth of water above its roots. In fashioning the pool, this latter requirement may be provided for by the contour of the slope of the sides being formed into steps. Sometimes a large, flat-topped stone makes an ideal, natural step, on which to place the wooden container in which the plant is to grow (for the use of metal, particularly copper, is never advised in a pool, because of the chemical reactions). Smaller stones encircling the container give a further appearance of naturalness.

Contour and Design of Pools

Informal pools admit of an infinite number of varying methods of treatment. In direct contrast, garden pools adjacent to certain architectural styles of buildings are required to have geometrical, formal outlines. Rectangular, elliptic oval, round, triangular, in fact any precise, mathematically correct shape should be used in connection with such special types of dwellings as a Spanish patio, an Italian villa, a French château or an English manor house. A suggested proportion for a rectangular pool is one whose width is two-thirds its length. This placed on the lowest level of the grounds (always the ideal place for water) may have a "Primrose path" leading down to it, or it may be near the end of a shrub-bordered expanse of lawn, broken by the regular lines of a few, effectively featured, specimen plants.

The most artistic selection possible for the pool is in a semi-secluded green spot, giving one a thrill of delight on the unexpected discovery of it. The gleam of the white, birch-like bark of the sycamore and some of the cottonwoods against the deep green of cedars lures one toward the spot where their mirrored image shows doubly beautiful in the waters of a pool. Reflections of green rather than the harsher lines of buildings are always much more pleasing. Variabilities of texture, height and shape of shrubs and trees, relieved by contrasts of well-placed color-tones, give one continual joy. This—the appropriate setting for a pool—enables it to fulfill its greatest possibilities.

TO REMOVE SCUM FROM POOLS
(*not injurious to fish*)

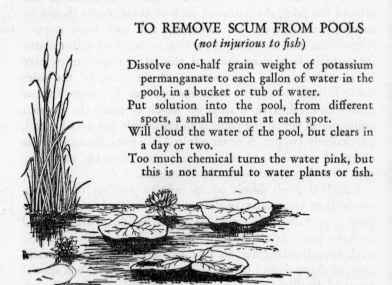

Dissolve one-half grain weight of potassium permanganate to each gallon of water in the pool, in a bucket or tub of water.

Put solution into the pool, from different spots, a small amount at each spot.

Will cloud the water of the pool, but clears in a day or two.

Too much chemical turns the water pink, but this is not harmful to water plants or fish.

The Semi-Dry Garden

O MAKE a garden fair there must be water—plenty of water. So everyone has always thought. Greedily thirsty are most of the members of the plant world, yet, bend low and hear an amazing discovery! An almost dry summer garden, with a surprising wealth of blossoms, may be yours for the making! It matters little whether one has a rocky hillside or a bit of level ground, whether the soil is rich, poor, or neutral. Even the intensity of the sun has been braved by an incredible number of gay, sturdy garden denizens, some of which are old favorites, while others can be said to have scarcely shed the imprints of the wilds.

During the great drought of 1930 gardens everywhere suffered. It was truly a survival of the fittest among the flowers. Yet an astonishing number seemed not to have noticed either the heat, or the curtailing of moisture. They continued to blossom, despite all adverse conditions. It is true, however, that their Spring root-growth was well established by plenty of water some weeks before they were called upon to meet the severe test of the Summer. Yet it is equally true that the amount of water they received during the severe heat of three to four months' duration was, comparatively, *very* little in most cases, and none at all in a few.

The fern-like foliage and delicate-tinted pinky-orchid flowers of the Desert Willow were as unaffected as the Crape Myrtle, Althea, *Genista* (Spanish Broom), Buddleia and Vitex, all of which grow quite as tall. Poinciana, Parkinsonia, Honey Locust, Senisa, Greasewood (called also Creosote-Bush), Tamarix (salt cedar), the Mexican Elder, and the

Sumacs (Rhus) have the additional qualification of being, with the Desert and Reed Willows, indigenous to the Southwest. Of the good drought-resistant shrubs of medium height and excellent foliage, but which blossom almost as early in the Spring as the Red Bud, are the Forsythia, the Spireas, the Syringas, Pomegranates, and Mulberries. Those of our natives which may be used for early-flowering hedges are the many Wild Plums and the Spanish Buckeye. The Agarita is our own native Barberry, whose foliage and berries make it pleasing used as a specimen plant or grouped as a clump or for a hedge (though, as with many others of the native shrubs, it is not hardy where severe, freezing weather must be endured during Winter).

The Salvias (Sage) carry the scarlet and shades of blue throughout the season. Salvia *Greggii* is the perennial sage brush. Salvia *splendens* is scarlet, while *farinacea* and *Pitcheri* are, respectively, the light and the dark blue varieties.

Fall Shrubs

Artemesia (Dusty Miller) is invaluable as a blending and binding color-tone for the gay garden. Its grey-green, silvery foliage and stems may be dried for winter bouquets, being as valuable in this office as is Statice though of much more density. It is beautiful with the prickly Eryngium ("Blue Thistle"), or with the tall lavender plumes of the Liatris (Blazing Star) both of which, when dried, retain their color for many months.

Shrub-like Annuals and Perennials

Of shrub-height, though grown each year from seed, or by division, are the tall Cleome, the Coreopsis, the Lantana, Four o'Clock, Eryngium, Castor Bean, various Achilleas and Fall Asters, all of which, except Four o'Clocks, are native and bloom until Fall.

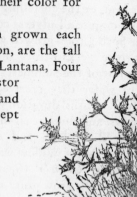

Four Native Shrubs From Seed

At least four of our native shrubs which develop into small trees may be grown readily and quickly from seed. And as it happens, these same four very nearly blossom in succession. They are Red Bud, Sophora, Mimosa, and Mesquite (*Acacia Julibrissin*). By planting the seed as soon as they are matured (in sand deep enough to coax the new little roots downward through it into the layer of well-rotted manure and rich earth mixture, that should lie beneath the deep layer of sand), the little plants, kept

moist and well-shaped, will reach the height of eight to ten inches the first season and may be transplanted. By the third year they will be nearly four feet high and are usually grace-ful, Japanese-like little shrubs, producing flowers and ap-pearing as fine an ornamental plant as anyone could wish. The foliage of each is practically pest-free and differs widely, making a charming contrast in color and texture.

Laburnum and Kolkwitzia (Beauty Bush), which are not native to the region, grow well, though probably are not as drought-resistant, may also be propagated in the same manner.

Should one wish to keep these plants of shrub height, their habit of growth from the beginning should be encouraged to widen, rather than prune for upward tendencies. The Sophora, especially, sends several shoots from the original seed. None of these need be pinched off, for all will become stout branches. Like the Pussy-Willow and *Pyrus japonica* (Burning Bush), the Red Bud can be forced to bloom in-doors. So the removal of the superfluous branches on the shrubs should be made as soon as the buds begin to swell. Place in water and the heat of the house will cause the flowers to open much sooner than those out in the open.

Semi-Arid Plants

With this wide choice of shrubs for screens and hedges, a varied background is amply provided. Against this, the blue Plumbago *capensis*, the dainty Sea-lavender (*Statice latifolia*) with the deep blue Platycodon bells, combine delightfully with Coreopsis, "Apache Plume," "Snow-on-the-Mountain," Monarda, several varieties of the Datura (Jimson-weed), and the large white prickly poppy (Mexican *Argemone alba*), this latter forming an unusually attractive low hedge with its spiny leaves and large white flowers.

All these thrive lustily, for they are natives. The fluffy tufts of blue Ageratum, the blue spikes of Veronica, the light violet-blue flowers of Nigella and the hardy Fall Asters, many of which are native, carry the blue-lavender tones into the late Fall, blending with the lovely pinky tones of the bush Morning Glories.

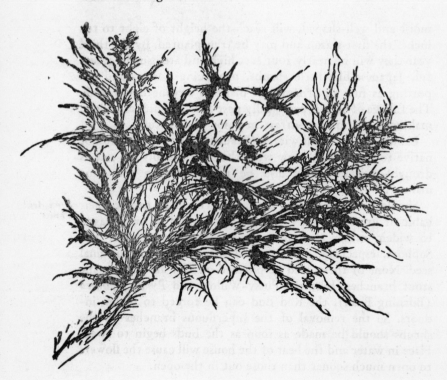

Gaillardias (Indian Blanket), and Rudbeckias (native, with daisy-like flowers), Thunbergia (Black-eyed Susan), Helenium, Arctotis (African Daisy), Anthemis (Marguerites), and both the English and the Shasta daisies, give one white and orange representatives of this family for diversification in the semi-dry garden. These are friendly with the taller-growing yellow *Helianthemums* (Sun Rose), the *Helianthus maximiliani* (and other native Sunflowers), and the orange *Heliopsis*. The Marigolds, and Lantana (native) have also the same intense orange-red tones.

It seems all the fire-tones (that is, those hues of orange and red, varying to the blue-purples of flame) thrive in the heat of the sun. The range of colors of those flowering plants that seem unaffected by scorching weather are similar, too, to those that come with the fall season. The pastel-tones, particularly the shades of rose and pink, pale greens, blues, yellows and lavenders, are rare compared with the stronger, more vivid tones. *The Fire Tones*

Zinnias, both short and tall, the *Achilleas* (Yarrow), and the several varieties of Goldenrod (*Solidago*) contrast in degree, yet are most friendly with the more intense orange of the Wall flowers and the native *Ascelepias tuberosa* (Butterfly Milkweed). The brilliant red of *Celosia* (Cockscomb) must be placed carefully, though as an accent it is most valuable; while for variation the wide-leafed Mulleins may be used, or *Baptisia* (False Indigo). *Orange*

The exclamation points, one might say, are the Gladioli, which bloom well (though are not as tall without water); the tall spikes of the native purple Liatris (Blazing Star), Texas Plume (*Gilia rubra*) and the plumy Pampas Grass.

The low White Alyssum and the vari-colored Portulaca are untiring in flowering. Its short bloom-stalks and tendency to develop compactly make the Alyssum an admirable border or rockery plant, demanding very little water after the root-growth has become well established in the spring. Portulaca is of more sprawly growth and has the advantage of not being restricted to all white flowers. It is very gay and makes a charming ground-cover, on a hillside or where grass is diffi- *Low-Growing Drought-Resistant Plants* cult to grow in any spot that is in full sun. It is flatter than the ground Myrtle (*Vinca Minor*) which, however, prefers the semi-shade, Mimosa (or creeping Sensitive-plant) with its fluffy, rosy-pink balls or the variety with golden yellow balls, and the Passion-flower's (*Passiflora caerulea*) heavenly-blue stars are contrasting climbers. They will ramble down a hillside or up the stems of leggy plants. The *Oenotheras* (particularly the large yellow *Missouriensis* or Evening Primrose) are lovely among rocks or clambering over a ledge. Their habitat is limestone bluffs of poor soil and their pure gold cups are a delight to the eye. The lovely pink variety has been overshadowed by the more showy, taller-growing white one.

Creepers

Petunias, with a choice of gay colors, when their runners are not kept cut back, like to climb over obstacles, just as Verbenas do. The gay yellow and orange Thunbergia, that insists on growing *up* a hillside *instead* of down, and trailing Lantana of such hardy, vigorous growth will bloom profusely if the seedpods are kept cut to postpone maturing until late fall.

The Honeysuckles (*Loniceras*), the desert gourd and the coarser-textured Woodbines (orange and scarlet, and yellow Trumpet-Creepers) give one further choice of more adventurous climbers, which may be trained over a trellis to form a shady nook.

The five-fingered Virginia Creeper, like Woodbine, grows unruly and rank, so requires space or constant care.

Conservation of Moisture Methods Suggested

The problem of conservation of moisture for the semi-dry garden may be met in several ways, foremost of which is obviously the selection of those plants which have been proved best qualified for drought and heat resistance. Mulching, or cultivating these will give the highest degree of satisfaction. In many cases, a thorough, slow drenching of the plant once a month, or once in every two or three weeks (dependent on the range of the temperature), will be quite sufficient. This moisture may be said to be blanketed-in, with a layer of straw-mulching, or grass-clippings (taking care that the grass has not gone to seed when cut) or possibly mulched with half-rotted leaf-mold, where this is available and of the correct chemical combination for the soil over which it will be placed.

If one chooses the other method, cultivating, remember it *must* be frequent. Cultivating has its advantages, for *only* by this method is free circulation of air given the plant-roots; and, where this is a requisite, one must cultivate, water, or face the loss of the plant.

Another item of vital importance to insure success in a *Soil* semi-dry garden is—the soil must not be of heavy texture. *Texture Important* This may be secured by the addition of at least fifty per cent (preferably greater) humus (in the form of well-rotted vegetation, leaves, cottonseed hulls, straw, or commercial peat-moss, which is sold baled), (remembering that peat-moss *must* be *thoroughly saturated* with water *before* using, or it will have the opposite effect from that which is desired, that is, will be moisture-consuming rather than moisture-holding for the plant). Also, if the flower bed is dug out at *least* to a depth of eighteen inches, and the top soil mixed 40 per cent (preferably 60 per cent) with humus *before planting,* and a slow soaking given the plant after placing it, little or no cultivation (only occasional) need be given. Generally these enumerated plants for a dry garden will bloom profusely, but the bushes are more stunted, and the blossoms are smaller than where more water is supplied.

Prepare for the plants as for a cherished, welcome guest. They will respond generously, especially if they have been used to the climatic conditions and are immune to their intensities. Give them nearly the same growing conditions as they had in their habitat, with just a *little more* richness of food, and the reward will far exceed expectations.

Desert Plants

Range of Choice

WHEREVER one may wish to adopt one of the desert Yuccas, Sotols, Agaves or Opuntias into the general scheme of planting, one finds a surprising list of variations from which to choose in what is usually thought to be a strictly limited class of plants. Be sure, however, that this type of plant fits into the plan and that they are truly desired and admired, for very few bear transplanting easily. Cactus, especially, seldom survive the second or third season. Many gorgeous specimens have been dug, most of which have died, for contrary to the popular belief, many are fully as slow in growth as forest trees, and as difficult to move with permanent success. They have as many pests and diseases and possibly more, than any other family of flowers. Greenhouse varieties often become covered with plant lice and scale, which may be controlled by a special spray containing denatured alcohol (the formula published by *Desert Magazine*), while out-of-doors, even the sturdiest, the Opuntias, often become infested with many kinds of bugs and lice. The large bugs that so deface and injure them may be controlled by a five per cent solution of kerosene emulsion. Yet when Opuntias do live, their blossoms are as lovely as any tropical water lily. Of these there are many varieties that propagate easily from cuttings and other methods, some of which are most strange.

Propagation

The Opuntia seed pods, even, when stuck into sand while green, will sprout; and often small particles of the plant will become detached, taking root where they drop. Sometimes these are carried considerable distances from the parent plant by their lightness and the buoying effect of the wind against the long spines.

Probably the most universally grown of all the large Cactus family are the modernistic-looking Opuntias, whose eco-
nomic habit of growth has dispensed with both stem and
stalk, retaining only the large fleshy, thorned leaves, usually
the size and thickness of a man's hand. Even the exquisite
flowers have no stem, but emerge from the thin edge of an
upright leaf. These golden blossoms remind one of a Water
Lily by some strange chance poised lightly in an extremely
uncongenial environment. However, the Opuntias are not
stingy in the numbers of their blossoms or in their response
in rapid growth to good soil conditions when given them.
The fact that they do not demand rich soil or much moisture
(except in Spring), does not deny their liking for it when it
is provided. They are most adaptable to circumstances, and
are very resourceful.

Opuntia Cacti

The general impression of Cactus is that it grows best in
alkaline soil and in very dry places; though, in reality, scientists tell us they were originally bog plants which have re-
sourcefully adapted themselves to the most adverse conditions. They have been found flourishing in rich, decomposed
plant matter (or leaf mould) that has lodged against trees or
rocks. These latter obstructions have answered a twofold
purpose in supplying a soil that Cactus delight in having, and
in keeping their roots cool by helping to hold what moisture
there is in the ground. Therefore, in preparing a Cactus bed,
it is wise to recognize all these facts. In general, Cactus will
relish a soil composed of one part good, dark earth, to one
part leaf-mould, to which is added one part large grained
sand.

*Soil Con-
ditions
Cacti Like*

Of strange, unusual growth is the *Ocotillo*, the "Mani-
cured Fingers of the Desert,"—so called because the scarlet
bloom-cluster is at the tip of and is in reality a continuation
of the long, narrow "fingers," which seldom appear singly—
several generally sprawling irregularly, being of as many
varying lengths as are the fingers on a human hand. The stiff
stalks are heavily spined, and studded with tiny, rounded,
fleshy-soft, green leaves, for a season, that scarcely protrude
beyond the spines and cover the cane from the ground to its
extreme length—or to the "bloom." The plant is very odd,

decorative, and lends a distinct atmosphere to Spanish grounds.

Others of the Cacti

Others of the Cacti that may be employed for their decidedly individual contributions to a garden are those of the Opuntia, known as Tree Cactus, of which the Opuntia *Arborescens* possibly has the loveliest blossoms; the Rat-tail Cactus (*Opuntia leptocaulis*), an erect bushy plant composed of greyish green stems, usually considerably smaller than a pencil and bristling with spines; or the various *Echinocactus*, great rounded heads with fairly long spiky thorns radiating from geometrically placed centers, the most common being the "Hedgehog," the "Pin Cushion," the "Nipple," and the "Barrel" or "Water" Cactus. Of the *Echinocereus* family, probably the "Strawberry" or "Banana" Cactus, or Classen's Cactus are the most ornamental, both producing shell-pink to deep rose-colored flowers in profusion.

White Yucca

Loveliest of the White Yuccas are the *filamentosa* (Adam's Needles) whose bloom stalk grows very tall, having a pyramid of white bells drooping from wide-spreading arms. Those which differ only by their lower bloom stalks are the Yucca *elata*, or *glauca*, and the Yucca *arkansana*. This group are also locally known as "Bear Grass". The Spanish Dagger (*Don Quixote's Lance* or Yucca *Treculeana*) whose bloom stalks are considerably shorter, has wider, more sharply-pointed leaves and their habit of growth, instead of remaining grass-like near the earth, radiate in a crown from a single or branched, palm-like trunk.

The Red Yucca

The "Red Yucca" (*Hesperaloe parviflora*, or *H. Engelmanni*) sends up and outward, gracefully curved, arching, bloom stalks whose stem in addition to the pendant blossom-bells with golden clappers, is scarlet. Its rush-like rosette of drooping leaves, quite characteristic of Yuccas, have those curling white threads along their sword-like sides found on many of the varieties of this family of plants.

Sotol

The Sotol, or *Dasylirion texanum,* grows in a very large rosette of long, very slender saw-toothed leaves from which an extremely tall, sand-colored flower stalk emerges, ending in a slightly enlarged spike-head of inconspicuous, creamy-white, tiny flowers which attract bees from great distances.

This plant is very odd, making a striking addition to the planting scheme, particularly adaptable to the Spanish-type house. It is peculiarly decorative when used judiciously. After the bloom stalk dies, the plant sends up several new shoots and the parent plant dies.

This habit of reproduction is true of many of the desert *Agaves* plants. The Agaves, or Century plants (*Lecheguilla* and *americana*) which have much more fleshy, more upright standing, thicker spiny leaves and tall (sometimes twenty feet high) branching flower stalks, from which bell-shaped, upward-turned small flower clusters that grow out at right angles like opened fans, from the main stem, give all their life to the production of this stalk. Its flowers, too, are very fragrant and delightful to the bees, yet in the northern portion of the Southwest, generally speaking, Agaves or Aloes are not hardy—hence they are seldom attempted. Since it usually takes from fifteen to twenty years for an Agave to produce a flower stalk, the possible reward for nursing a plant through inclement weather periods is thought too hazardous.

On the whole, decidedly the most satisfactory of all the desert plants are those that can be secured from reputable commercial merchants.

On a hillside, in a corner, grouped or alone, any and each of these desert plants are effective and picturesque.

To lend a tropical effect, use . . .
Agave and Aloe
Cacti
Ocotillo
Yucca
Bambusa *vulgaris*
Canna, and Caladium
Washington *filifera* (Palm)

Additional lists are
on page 107

Combating Plant Enemies

I. INSECTS AND PESTS

OUR GARDEN's ultimate success does not depend entirely on the selection of the plant material best suited to the locality, nor even the preparation of the soil, but largely on the ability to recognize the danger when plants first show signs of being "sick", to be familiar with the symptoms and to be ready to apply first aid with the necessary remedies.

There are several distinct causes for the drooping of the leaves or for their slow turning from the living green to the sere yellow which foretells ultimate destruction of the plant, such as the dreaded mildew and other fungus diseases. Yet, often the real trouble is caused by some type of insect. When one has learned to recognize that effect which is caused by those insects that suck the very life from the leaves and stems, and the one caused by that group that chew the foliage to destroy it, and has become familiar with the remedies to be applied for each distinct kind of trouble, the battle is half won.

Then there are also a number of large bugs and worms that must be dealt with in a different manner. Some can only be killed with poisoned bait, while more often cut-worms must be located and dug from the ground where they have hidden after a night of feasting.

Leaves skeletonized, punctured or partly destroyed show attack by insects of the devouring or chewing kind.

Chewing insects can only be killed by covering the plants with poison, for it is swallowed as they eat the foliage. Caterpillars and bugs are the greatest offenders of this class. The mixtures that contain *arsenate* of *lead* and *Paris Green* are most commonly used.

POISON SPRAY

A good stomach poison spray is made as follows:

       3 level tablespoonfuls *arsenate of lead*
       6 level tablespoonfuls hydrated lime
       3 gallons water.

Make the arsenate of lead and lime into a paste in separate containers, then mix them with the remainder of the water.

BAGWORMS OR TUSSOCK
MOTHS

(a) Spray with
      2 tablespoonfuls *arsenate of lead*
      1 gallon water
(b) 1 ounce powdered *arsenate of lead*
      2 gallons water
      2 ounces laundry or resin fish oil soap, or 8 tsp. sprayoil.

Leaves curled backward, drying up or showing brown at the edges indicate the presence of insects of the sucking class.

Sucking insects cannot be reached by stomach poisons, yet there are a number of materials that kill by direct contact. *Nicotine* (tobacco) is the one most generally used. When it covers the soft-bodied insects, like plant lice (Aphis), it is absorbed and causes death almost immediately. The simplest method is to use nicotine sprays, diluted, or combined with other materials.

One cannot use this until the pests appear, yet an early application *after they have been discovered* gains control of the situation. (Often as early as February.)

When the bodies of the insects are not soft and the *Nicotine* cannot penetrate, then an oil spray or soap and oil must be used to completely smother them, for they breathe through pores. Direct contact with each insect is required to entirely destroy them, therefore, it is safer to spray once a week for several weeks, beginning when foliage is at *height of maturity*.

Sucking insects, such as aphids or plant lice, can be controlled *only* by some material that will kill them when it comes *in contact* with them. DDT requires expert information and *greatest* caution. Protect birds and pets!

REMEDIES

A good contact spray is:

$1\frac{1}{2}$ tsps. 40% *nicotine sulphate*

$\frac{1}{4}$ lb. white laundry soap

3   gals. water

Dissolve the soap in a small quantity of the water, then mix all of the ingredients together.

Aphids (Thrips—Aphids or Plant Lice)
(*Green, Red, White or Black*)

On Chrysanthemums, Salvia, Larkspurs, Phlox, Roses, Iris, Nasturtiums, Snapdragons, etc.

(1)   1 heaping tbs. of soap

1 gal. water

$\frac{1}{3}$ ounce *Nicotine*

Dissolve the soap in the water after it reaches the boiling point, then add the nicotine, stirring vigorously. Spray plants after the mixture becomes cold; or dip the affected parts into the mixture if very thickly covered.

(2) . . . Spray with *quassia-chip* water or with

1 wineglassful paraffin

$\frac{1}{2}$ lb. soft soap

2 gals. warm water

(well mixed)

Or use *tobacco powder,* blown on dry for red, green or black Aphids.

(3) . . . (Especially Roses)

> 1 tbs. Fish Oil soap in little hot water
> 2 tbs. *Black Leaf 40*
> 3 gals. water

May be doubled if insects are bad.

(4) . . . (Especially Iris or Roses)

> Spray with *Tri-ogen*

(5)   A . . . (on Gladioli)

> 1 tsp. *Paris Green*
> 2 lbs. brown sugar
> 3 gals. water

Apply when leaves are 6 inches high every day for ten days or until buds appear.

> B. (Dahlias, Gladiolus, etc.)
> Spray with *Pyrethrum* or *Nicotine Spray*

Red Spider and Mealy Bug

Spray with *Nicotine* and soap solutions, *if* the *strong spray* from the hose does not destroy them. They particularly dislike water and moist conditions.

> *Dusting Sulphur* is also advised.

(1) "Glue solution"—spray

> ½ lb. cheap ground glue dissolved
> in a little hot water and add
> 5 gals. hot water

Spray: and dust with *Sulphur* while wet.

(2) "Dry *lime of sulphur*"—spray

> 2 tsps. to 1 gal. water

(3) . . . On Phlox

> Dust with *sulphur* or *Copper-lime*.

Root (or Blue) Aphids, Etc.

(1) Use strong solution of tobacco water. As a preventive, mix wood ashes into soil in which asters and zinnias especially are to be planted.

(2) . . . (Especially on Asters)

Work *tobacco dust* into soil at base of plants or apply solution (once a month).

> 2 tbs. *nitrate soda* in
> 2 gals. water

Kerosene Emulsion

Kerosene emulsion has been found most effective in ridding "Opuntia" of stinkbug. It can be used for other large bugs that have gathered on trees, or among trash, or to kill scale. This is advised during the dormant season. It will prove dangerous for delicate foliage. It can be used to control all sucking insects.

> ½ lb. whale oil (preferably soap)
> 1 gallon water
> 2 gallons kerosene
> *Smaller Quantities*
> 1 ounce soap
> 1 pint water
> 2 pints *kerosene*

Cut the soap into chips or shavings and dissolve in the water, while it is boiling. Remove the hot solution from the fire! . . . add the *kerosene* very slowly, stirring constantly. It is important to have the solution hot, as well as to agitate it thoroughly, while adding the *kerosene*. After all the *kerosene* has been added, pump the emulsion through the nozzle for several minutes back into a suitable container. This will make a creamy emulsion that may be kept tightly bottled until ready to use.

On trees or plants that are dormant, dilute this with five or seven parts of water, forming a spray containing eight to eleven per cent of oil. On trees or plants that are in leaf, one should dilute the stock solution with ten to fifteen parts of water. *Soft-bodied insects* are usually killed with a *five per cent* solution . . . 12½ parts of water to one part of emulsion—this is the strength to use on Cacti.

Kerosene emulsion should be applied on bright, sunny days when the wind is not blowing, since a considerable quantity will evaporate quickly and the danger to the plants will be reduced.

For Stink-Bugs on Cacti

Use *Kerosene Emulsion*.

Mites

Spray with
> 1 tsp. *Black Leaf 40*
> 1 gal. water

Greenhouse Disinfectant

Spray with
> 1 tbs. oil spray to
> 3 qts. water

SCALE INSECTS

These should be attacked when plants are dormant.

"*Arsenate of lead* is superior to *Paris Green*, as it does not settle so quickly in the spray-tank, is much more adhesive to the foliage, and does not burn the plants."—(By permission of the Texas Agricultural Experiment Station, Bulletin No. 187.)

On Magnolias, and other shrubs
  Spray freely with
    2 tbs. *Lime Sulphur* in
    1 gal. water
On Euonymus
  "West India" or
  "White Peach Scale"
  Spray with
    (1) *Sunoco* in solution
          or
    (2) 1 lb. Fish Oil Soap in
       4½ gals. water
    (3) As preventive spray
       . . . in fall to kill larvae
       1 part *Sunoco* to
       33 parts water
       Dilute half in mid-summer.

Spray with strong solution of *lime Sulphur* when plant is dormant.

Scale on Cacti

"The customary instructions to wash scales from plants cannot apply to spiny cactus-plants; therefore other methods must be used. Spray with:

    1 pint of *denatured alcohol*
    ½ pint of water
    10 drops of *Black Leaf 40* (or 40% Nicotine Sulphate)

"A cheap atomizer is very handy for spraying the plants. After one or two applications of this mixture have been made, a few days apart, use a forceful, fine spray of clear water to wash off the dead scales."—(Courtesy of *Desert Magazine;* recommended by E. E. Davis.)

ANTS
In Flower Beds

Water in which potato skins have been boiled (let stand twenty-four hours), poured *in and over* ant hills will destroy ants. Also, *with extreme care,* kerosene emulsion poured down the nest, *or* one heaping tablespoonful of *disulphide carbon* put into the hole (and closed in quickly at once by pressing earth into the opening with the foot) is effective. Thin rings of *asphaltum* paint surrounding the hill will catch and destroy all ants going in or out.

Caution

Remember all poisons—especially vapours—are *extremely dangerous.*

Beware of *Paris Green* and *Carbon Bisulphide. Take utmost care.*

Nesting in the Ground

Punch hole 4 to 6 inches deep near nest. Pour in tablespoonful *carbon bisulphide*. Close hole with earth to keep fumes in; or

Solution sodium cyanide, 1 oz. to 6 gals. water. Sprinkle ground and water in thoroughly afterward.—U. S. Bureau Entomology.

(1) Pour a quart of gasoline down the hole and plug it shut with dirt. The vapors arising will reach every part.

The Argentine Ant

The Argentine ant can only be eradicated by killing the queen, who lays great numbers of eggs each day. To reach her, poison bait (such as *Antrol*) must be carried to her by the worker-ants.

Where large quantities of poison are needed, directions for preparing may be secured from Government Bulletins.

(2)   1 ounce *Paris Green* mixed in the dry form
       1 lb. brown sugar not granulated

The ants will collect the small poisoned particles of sugar and carry them back to their nest where young and old will be poisoned by eating it.

For small amounts:

½ tsp. of *Paris Green* mixed with
8 tsp. brown sugar

Where ants are discovered on plants it generally indicates the presence of lice, or mealy bug. These insects cannot be entirely destroyed until the ants are controlled.

Ants and Sow-Bugs

Mix well and scatter

2 parts insect-powder
1 part powdered *Borax*

POISON BAIT
For Pill-bugs, Sow-bugs and Cut Worms

1. A crumbly sweetened poison
   5 lbs. bran
   1 pint of heavy molasses, mixed with
   1 quart of water
   4 ounces of *Paris Green*

This mixture should be moistened thoroughly with the molasses and water, but not be dough-like. It should fall apart when pressed in the hands. Some authorities add the juice and grated rind of a lemon to the above. Others claim that orange-juice attracts some types of bugs particularly.

This mixture should stand for several hours until the bran absorbs the poison. As it is more effective if slightly damp, it should be put out after the yard has been watered, or after a rain, in the late afternoon. Place it *under* low foliage, or under pieces of wood, or under flower pots.

Great care should be taken to *cover* the mixture so that the birds and animals cannot get it. It should be carefully collected, and buried deep in the ground after it has gotten hard.

Another warning . . . Remember that when arsenical poisoning is used, if it reaches many of the tender young plants their roots will take up the poison and be harmed.

2. Pill-bugs, Sow bugs and Cut-worms
>   9 parts sugar
>   1 part *Calcium Arsenate*

Use as No. 1, and always place *under* some object, where birds and animals will not be able to get at it. It is effective spread on potato peelings.

3. Pill-bugs, Sow-bugs, Cutworms and Snails.

A half rind of orange or grapefruit, inverted, often serves as an effective trap for pill-bugs, sow bugs, cutworms and snails, which may then be gathered up and destroyed by dropping them into a bucket of boiling water, or water with *kerosene* in it.

4.   1 lb. *Paris Green*
>   25 lbs. bran
>   Mixed with common molasses

5.   5 parts meal or graham flour
>   1 part *Paris Green*

Just enough molasses to roll in fingers in small balls. Place around plants after watering.

6. Crushed moth balls (or *naphthalene* flakes) placed near plants and lightly covered with soil is said to drive away pests.

7. *Anarol* and *Bait-M*

Both useful, should be put out in the evening after thorough watering. Best to spread at least twice, two weeks apart.

8. *Sulphide of Iron*

Placed in soil around plants drives away some insects.

9. Several firms are offering an efficacious deadly poison for slug —among them *Kil-Slug*.

Slugs

Slugs can usually be detected by the slimy trail they leave behind them as they move about the garden. They often cause much of the trouble attributed to sow-bugs. Happily the same poison-mash can be used for both.

Wireworms and Grubs

Crush all you see—and spray with *nicotine-sulphate* solution to kill out.

BORERS
Shrub or Tree Borers

Inject *carbon bisulphide* in burrows with medicine dropper an´ plug opening; or remove branch affected.

Iris Borers

Spray with

> 1 oz. *Arsenate of lead*
> 1 oz. *Casein*
> 1 gal. water

Use as *fine mist* once a week—must adhere to leaves.

Keep the Iris leaves covered with a *sulphur* dust containing *lead arsenate* from early spring until late in the summer. The sulphur will control the leaf spot while the poison will kill the little Iris borer larvae when they hatch from the over-wintering eggs.

Iris borers rarely appear in the Southwest.

Rose Borers

To prevent borers from entering stems of rose bushes keep soil well-packed on the roots, especially in the extremely dry weather, and when winds are high.

To eradicate, cut back punctured stem—on an angle—past opening—burn removed portion.

Apply earth (clay, grafting wax) on stem after pruning affected part.

BURROWERS
Gophers, Moles, Mice, Etc.

Bisulphide of iron (protect birds and animals by throwing loose earth over where it has been applied), will kill burrowing animals.

It is an old legend that the Castor Bean plants drive them away —will not remain in same vicinity.

II. DISEASES

Leaves dropping from the plants entirely usually show disease—or root trouble.

CHLOROSIS

Chlorosis (loss of green color)—when a diseased condition, rarely can be cured. Pull up and burn all affected plants. Spray unaffected plants with a copper solution (such as *Bordeaux*) as disease is transmitted, usually by an insect known as the "Six-spotted Leafhopper." Yellowed, or sickly-green to pale yellow-green foliage sometimes is an indication of lack of sufficient *nitrogen* in the soil (see chapter on Soil), or a deficiency in balance in the required constituents for nourishment. *Gypsum,* or *Sulphur,* is effective when this is the case.

MILDEW

Mildew and other fungus diseases seem to be caused largely by climatic conditions. It is very much better to use preventive measures than to wait until the plants become affected where one has reason to believe the disease will occur.

This type of trouble reaches the plant from outside contact by means of bacteria and spores. They quickly spread over the entire plant after reaching some part of it. To combat this, the entire surface of the leaves and stems must be covered with some material that destroys the disease. *Sulphur,* in some form, is considered the most effective remedy, in solution or as a dusting powder. *Massey Dust,* which can be prepared at home, is extensively used. *Bordeaux Mixture* is often advised, but it has the objectionable quality of discoloring the foliage.

Experts differ as to the most effective way of applying remedies, as a dust, or as a liquid spray. Under either method, *not only* the top of the leaves must be covered, but the *under part and the stems* also.

Peat moss tends to combat lime-loving fungus matter.

MILDEW OR RUST

Massey Dust . . . *dust dry!*

        9 parts dusting *sulphur*
        1 part *arsenate of lead*

Pomo green is *Massey dust* colored green that it may not disfigure the foliage.

Funtrogen—A highly concentrated fungicide. Should be sprayed on Roses and other plants affected with mildew. Will control Blackspot; prevents rot; and eliminates Rust, on Hollyhocks especially.

"August Mildew"—On Crape Myrtle, and other plants; use *Potassium Sulphide* freely as a spray.

Mildew on Crape Myrtle

        1 pint Oil Mulch Spray
        5 gals. water
        ½ pint *Formaldehyde*

On Phlox, Columbine, Snapdragon, etc.: Dust with superfine dusting sulphur . . . or spray with

> 1 oz. *Potassium Sulphide*
> 2 gals. of water

To prevent Mildew: Avoid water on foliage. Water in mornings, never after sundown because of dew.

Crown Gall

On shrubs or roses *no cure*. Burn to save unaffected plants, and *disinfect soil* where sick plants were with a solution of

> 2 lbs. *Copper Sulphate* (or *Blue Stone*) dissolved in
> 50 gallons water.

Soak ground to depth of at least 2 ft.

Crown Rot

On Columbine, etc., pour on plant-crown and roots a solution of 1 tablet *corrosive sublimate* in 1 quart water.

2. . . . Bulbs

As a preventive solution before planting, and to kill rot, or scab organisms—

Soak bulbs 12 hours in solution of—

> 1 oz. *Corrosive Sublimate* (*Bichloride of Mercury*)
> 8 gallons water

in glass or earthen, never metal, vessel. Dry thoroughly—then plant.

Treat all bulbs for "Blue Mold" before planting (with *Formaldehyde*).

Formaldehyde . . . solution, to sterilize. 1 pint to 10 gallons of water.

Root Rot

1. Iris root-rot
   - (a) This is the one dreaded disease of Iris—dig up, remove soft parts, and wash with a solution of *Potassium Permanganate* (see Mr. Wm. Dykes' book on Iris).
   - (b) If discovered in early stages, without digging up cut away soft parts, expose to sun, spray both Iris and ground with one tablet *corrosive sublimate* in one pint of water; allow to become *very dry*.
   - (c) Two handfuls of *gypsum* to one plant, worked into soil . . .
        or
   - (d) Drench ground with solution of one tablet of *Corrosive Sublimate* in 1 quart water (in severe cases 1 pint instead of 1 quart water) or 1 pint of *Formaldehyde* to 10 gallons of water.

Root Knot

No cure—destroy affected plants and disinfect soil with boiling water. If case bad, add Chloropicrin.

BLIGHT

1. Lily Blight Control (especially *Candidum*, *Auratum* and *Tigrinum* Lilies)
Spray with—

    1 oz. *Sulphide of Potassium*
    3 gallons of water

in which a little soft soap is mixed to make the poison adhere to the foliage.

2. Bulb Blight Control
Dip all bulbs that have been exposed to blight, especially Gladioli, in *Formaldehyde* before planting, and place a few pieces of peat in the hole underneath them, taking care to *surround* the bulb with about an inch layer of sand.

3. Dahlia Blight Control
Spray with *Nicotine* when the leaves begin to curl (in July) every ten days to two weeks until the blooms appear.

Slime-molds

The lowest group of parasites on plants—may be controlled by application of *lime* to raise the soil above neutral—or if case is bad fertilize liberally with *ammonium sulphate*, and in extreme cases add *sulphur* to the soil.

ROSE DISEASES AND PESTS

The more you work among Roses and try first this remedy and that for any trouble, once it has started, the more you are apt to recall, "To cure disease is not easy; to prevent it, is much more feasible."

MILDEW AND BLACK SPOTS

The medicinal treatment of mildew and black-spot is the same, for both are fungus troubles, though widely different in character. The cause of mildew is a disputed question. It is as inherent in some plants as the shape of their leaves and the color of their blossoms. One environment will develop it and another won't.

Mildew being a fungus trouble, a fungicide is the thing to correct it. Most fungicides are excellent when used as dormant sprays, but discolor foliage too seriously to be much used after a plant has put out leaves. There are a few sulphur compounds that are good to use then as some do not burn. Beware of burning tender, new foliage!

Dusts that contain sulphur are widely used for mildew. But they are better for beds of Roses than for Climbers, whose height and size make them more easily sprayed.

For those who believe mildew comes from the ground, there are several good things to do to the soil to help build up in your plant a resistance to the disease. Potash, which develops hard wood, is good. Many successful growers put a liberal quantity of hardwood ashes, which contain potash, around their Rose plants, especially their Climbers, every August and again often in early Spring. Treating the soil as well as the plants with any good fungicide is a good preventive measure. Plain powdered sulphur dug into the ground around a plant will help.

For black-spot, just plain commercial *sulphur* shaken from a flour sifter over some Rose plants once every week or two has been known to keep them covered all Summer with luxuriant foliage, free from black-spot. Wet foliage to make dust adhere.

All the remedies recommended for mildew are effective in control of black-spot on most varieties. But, as in the case of the Ramblers and mildew, the Pernetianas, which breed black-spot, are better segregated in beds to themselves.

The chief precaution which may be taken is to *keep* the surface of the ground in a Rose bed *perfectly clean*. Never allow old leaves or flowers or trash of any kind to accumulate around the plant, and keep all infected leaves picked off and burned.

Some excellent suggestions are:

a. Withhold all barnyard fertilizer and use a chemical instead until trouble clears up.

b. Renew the top three inches of soil each year with fresh uninfected earth.

c. In May, before the disease usually presents itself, spray thoroughly both the plants and the ground with a non-burning fungicide and then put on an inch or more layer of commercial sheep manure. This will give a fresh surface to the bed, provide a dust-mulch and furnish some valuable nourishment. Add a half cup of bonemeal, scratched in first around each bush, to carry Roses safely through the hot weather.

ROSE ENEMIES

As for the control of insects, if you add to your fungicide sprays in May, December and February some good nicotine compound for the sucking insects and arsenate of lead for the chewing kind, you will go a long way toward freeing your garden of an unreasonable amount of pests.

The sucking insects, such as the Aphis, come in a variety of colors—red, green, white and black. But the one that most often troubles Roses is green and is widely known as "Green Bug." It saps the vitality of the leaves and ruins the buds. It is particularly virulent in the wet, cool weather of early Spring and tends to disappear of itself when the dry heat of Summer sets in.

Spray with a good nicotine solution every day until the insects depart. To this spray may be added a soap solution composed of one tablespoonful of fish-oil soap dissolved in boiling water and cooled before mixing. The soap acts as a "spreader" and makes the spray more effective. (Another formula is 2 tablespoonfuls *Black Leaf 40*, 1 tablespoonful soap, to 3 gallons water.) But the main idea is to wet *all* the insects thoroughly, since they are destroyed by smothering, not by poisoning. One caution to observe in the addition of soap is not to use it too strong in the heat of the day, as it will burn tender foliage and do as much harm as the insects themselves.

Never add soap to a *combination spray!*

The chewing insects, caterpillars, cut-worms and the like have to be poisoned. *Arsenate of lead*, either in a spray or dust, is effective. But in a spray it discolors and often burns. A better suggestion for the growing season is to use a poison-food-compound around the base of the plant.

Thrip (small, white, villainous creatures) start on the inside of a bud their sapping process, so that it is most difficult to reach them with sprays. The Rose turns brown around the edges and usually withers without opening. Thrip resemble lice and breed in open Roses, under blossoms left lying on the ground, and in very heavy Roses, which, due to their own nature or atmospheric conditions, do not open fast enough. The best way to prevent Thrip is to keep full-blown flowers cut off your plant, never allow old blossoms to fall on the ground, and to discard all those Rose varieties which are known to "ball" consistently.

To conserve time and energy, kill two bugs (the sucking and chewing) with one spray and steer clear of fungus diseases as well by using a good all-around Plant Spray *before* any trouble starts, while it is going on, and after it is apparently over to safely speed the parting guest.

III. COMBINATION REMEDIES

Much labor may be saved by combining sprays for insects and diseases.

For general pest-control: mixtures that will combine:

A—

Lime Sulphate—Milk of Lime
  (fungicide)
Nicotine Sulphate
  (contact-spray)
Lead Arsenate
  (stomach poison)

B—

Bordeaux Mixture
  (fungicide)
Nicotine Sulphate
  (contact-spray)
Lead Arsenate
  (stomach poison)

It is possible also to combine—though not so effective:

C—

Bordeaux Mixture
Nicotine Sulphate
Paris Green or *Calcium Arsenate*

D—

Lime Sulphate
Nicotine Sulphate
Calcium Arsenate

These combinations are all that are recommended to mix well —be effective—and avoid undesirable chemical reactions, which might result from indiscriminate combinations.

Unless large quantities are to be used—advise purchase of commercially prepared combination sprays.

IV. THE WELL-STOCKED GARDEN MEDICINE CHEST
includes:

As a spray for disease; either
Chemical *hydrated lime*
or
Powdered *Copper Sulphate*
Dosage for each:
4 ozs. of each in
3 gallons water
To prevent leaf and plant destruction—etherized combination sprays:
Lead arsenate, to kill *chewing* insects, spray freely.
Nicotine
Bordeaux Mixture
Paris Green
Corrosive Sublimate
Sulphur—Lead Arsenate (or **stainless** variety) to control

rust, use *when the air is quiet* and *little moisture is on the foliage;* ratio 85–15 or 90–10; and *temperature* is *low,* or will burn.

Gypsum (for yellow leaves)
Pyrethrum

Black Leaf 40 (or preparations containing at least 40% Nicotine Sulphate)

Sunoco (or any proprietary material in the form of an oil emulsion)

Vigoro (or selected fertilizer manufactured and sold by the large companies)

Kerosene Emulsion

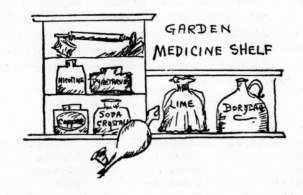

GARDEN MEDICINE SHELF

TABLE OF COMPARATIVE WEIGHTS AND MEASURES

Liquid Measures	*Dry Weights*
16 oz. equals 1 pint	28.4 gm. equals 1 oz.
2 pints equal 1 quart	16 oz. equals 1 lb.
1 pint equals 473.11 cc.	1 lb. equals 1 pint
1 oz. equals 30.0 cc.	
1 tsp. equals 4.0 cc.	

For valuable information on the control of pests, and remedies for plants, trees, etc., secure Texas Agricultural Bulletin No. 187, and U. S. Farmers Bulletin No. 1495, remembering that the exact amount of money (stamps not accepted) MUST accompany all requests for bulletins where a sum is charged.

V. BIRDS

The great value of attracting the birds other than for their beauty of song and flashing colors, cannot be over-estimated —their invaluable destruction of worms and other pests on trees, shrubs and other plants.

The three essentials to attract them are to provide adequate water, safety from cats and small boys' guns, and food. This latter is secured largely by planting berry-bearing bushes—Mulberries are considered by them most delectable —and the weeping tree is not as wide in its root-spread as the other varieties. The Virginia Creeper and the Blue Cedar berries are equally relished, while the Haws, both black and red, vie with them in popularity. The fruit of the Hedgehog Cactus, one of the Echinocactus family, is greatly enjoyed by them also.

Some Plants That Attract Birds

Arbor Vitae	Cedar	Crataegus
Asters (Michaelmas daisy)	Chickweed (*Stellaris media*)	(Hawthorn)
Astilbe	Chinaberry	Dandelion
Barberries	Chokeberry	Elderberry
Blueberry	Clover	Geum
Buttercups	Coralberry	Grape
		Haws

Helianthemums
Honeysuckle
Ligustrum
Meadow rue
Mulberry
Oaks
Oxalis

Privet
Rubus (Brambles)
Salix (Willow)
Saxifrage
Sheepsorrel
  (Rumex)
Sumac (Rhus)

Veronica
Vetch
Viburnum
Virginia Creeper
Wild Cherry
Wild Plum

Especially Attractive to Humming Birds

Columbine
Larkspur

Thistle (*Cirsium austrinum*)
Foxglove (*Digitalis*)

Sweet William
Hollyhock
Regale Lilies

Bibliography

Bibliography

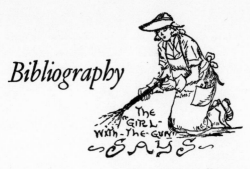

We are indebted and give thanks to the authors of the following books that have been used to verify much of the material that has been presented—

Gray's Botany.

Westcourt "Beautifying the Home Grounds." Bulletin 126 C. I. A. (Texas.)

Bailey's Standard Cyclopedia of Horticulture.

Curtis' Botanical Magazine.

Schulz "Texas Wild Flowers".

Fletcher, "Soil".

United States and States' Department of Agriculture, Bulletins and other publications.

Garden Dictionary by Norman Taylor.

Garden Magic by Roy E. Biles. (Cincinnati, Ohio.)

As several most valuable books have been written, giving detailed information on certain types of plants, used for special localities, no effort has been made to duplicate the information they contain, especially—

Bessie Buxton—*The Window Garden* (Orange Judd) and *Begonias* (Hale, Cushman & Flint).

Sarah Coombs—*South African Plants* (Stokes).

Ellen D. Schulz's *Cactus Culture* (Orange Judd, New York) and *Texas Wildflowers* (Laidlaw). Also, *The Garden Book for Houston*, all of which present adequate, specific data about Texas plants.

Detailed information regarding Garden Clubs, their organization, by-laws, subjects for programs, flower shows and various items of interest can be secured from—

Judging Amateur Flower Shows by Combs, Crocker and Carrath (Natl. Council of State Garden Clubs, Inc., 500 Fifth Ave. New York 18, N. Y.).

Flower Shows and How to Stage Them by Adele S. Fisher (120 E. 39th St., New York, N. Y.).

A Garden Handbook, by Fae Huttenlocker (Meredith, Des Moines, Iowa).

Index

Index